CORAL
REEFS

A grey angelfish (Pomacanthus arcuatus) *in the Caribbean Sea.*

CORAL REEFS

A global view by diver and aquarist Les Holliday
Consultant: Dr Elizabeth Wood

a Salamander book

Published by Salamander Books Limited
LONDON • NEW YORK

A Salamander Book

All correspondence concerning the content of this volume should be addressed to Salamander Books Ltd.

Credits

Editor: Geoff Rogers
Designer: Stuart Watkinson
Layout: Stuart Watkinson and Stonecastle Graphics Ltd.
Colour Reproductions: Scantrans Pte. Ltd.
Filmset: SX Composing Ltd.
Printed in Belgium by Proost International Book Production.

Author

Les Holliday was first introduced to the world of coral reefs as an eleven year old when he became enthralled while reading the book *Under the Red Sea,* which recorded the exploits of the famous diver and author Hans Hass. This passion for the coral world remained into his teens, when he trained and qualified as an advanced SCUBA diver. His skills as a diver and an underwater photographer developed and he participated in marine expeditions around the world, serving as diver, marine biologist and underwater photographer. He has personally led a number of expeditions to the Red Sea and Caribbean and has twice acted as expedition leader for Operation Raleigh, the around-the-world expedition founded by HRH Prince Charles. Accomplishments in this field include a national award for his film *Coral Reef Creatures* and the Duke of Edinburgh Award for contributions to marine science for his marine research work on the reefs of St. Lucia in the Caribbean. Since 1984, Les Holliday has been actively engaged in the introduction of marine parks, in both the Indian Ocean and Caribbean, and has taken a personal interest in work towards the designation of marine parks in the Turks and Caicos Islands. His interest in fishkeeping has spanned over forty years, first becoming involved in the marine hobby in the late 1950s, when his interest was aroused in native marine fishkeeping. His SCUBA expertise, and his interests in coral reef biology and underwater photography have combined with a wide experience of marine fishkeeping to give him a firsthand insight into the coral reef world. He is a leading contributor of articles and photographs to UK and international marine hobby and diving magazines.

Consultant

Elizabeth Wood BSc., PhD., is a marine biologist whose work as a consultant and lecturer has involved her with a wide range of projects in the UK and overseas. She has twenty-five years experience of SCUBA diving, and spent three of these in Malaysia, working mainly on the coral reefs around the island of Borneo, but also visiting other countries in Southeast Asia. This period gave her the opportunity to write a book on the biology and identification of corals, and also instilled an abiding interest in the ecology and conservation of coral reefs and their inhabitants. Subsequent work has taken her to many other reef areas, especially on projects concerned with the development of protected areas and the conservation of reef resources.

Previous page: *An Indo-Pacific coral reef thronging with golden jewelfish.*

This page: *Fossilized hard corals left high and dry in the Gulf of Aqaba.*

CONTENTS

Grotesque but beautiful, the lionfish never fails to fascinate.

INTRODUCTION

Part One: The Coral Reef Environment

When describing describing coral reefs, writers often lapse into colourful prose celebrating the delights of exotic tropical locations. Small islands with brilliant white sandy beaches and waving palm trees become the starting points for undersea odysseys to explore beautiful coral gardens alive with strange and colourful creatures. Excitement is usually provided by lurid tales of encounters with large and dangerous denizens of the deep. There is no doubt that within the pages of this book you may recognize similar accounts to these. I make no excuses for any such lapses because I, like the many others who have experienced the pleasure of visiting and exploring many coral reefs around the world, cannot fail to be impressed. The purpose of this book is not simply to recount a series of tales of exploits in the tropical oceans, however. It is primarily an introduction to the fascinating and complex ecosystem we call a coral reef. And by way of a journey around the world exploring some of the most magnificent examples, I also hope to illustrate the many and varied facets of this, the last natural environment largely untouched by man.

The first impressions of any coral reef are of the large numbers and wide diversity of unfamiliar creatures that live there. If these animals are largely unfamiliar today, consider the situation just over a century ago, when there was almost total ignorance. This resulted mainly from the lack of opportunity to further knowledge due to the isolation of such areas. Pioneer scientists such as Charles Darwin were the first people to discover and record the marine life of the coral reef and to provide the first theories about the origin and nature of reefs. The voyage of HMS *Beagle* in 1836 provided Darwin with the opportunity to study coral formations at close quarters. This voyage was quickly followed by others, culminating in the famous voyage of the *Challenger*, which spent three years exploring the oceans of the world undertaking scientific research in the early 1870s. Such work meant that marine animals were properly classified for the first time, and in the wake of these pioneers followed scientists from all over Europe and the USA.

Today, the level of our knowledge of coral reefs is very much broader than in Darwin's time. Even so, many of his theories are still recognized. What we have learned since Darwin's time is that coral reefs are very complex and diverse ecosystems that still pose many mysteries. To attempt to cover the whole spectrum of this subject within the covers of one book would be futile and, similarly, to attempt to be comprehensive would be beyond the space available. Therefore, our approach has been to provide simple answers to the basic questions of why coral reefs have formed, how the coral reef and the animals making up the reef ecosystem live and function, and where the best examples of coral reefs are to be found.

Coral reefs mean different things to different people. To the student biologist, reefs are laboratories in which a tremendous amount of scientific study is still awaiting to be undertaken. To the SCUBA diver and underwater explorer, they are the last frontier, an unspoilt natural world waiting to be investigated. To the marine aquarist, coral reefs represent a vibrant source of fascinating subjects for the aquarium. With the advent of SCUBA diving and long-distance tourism, the world of the coral reef is also becoming accessible to a wider range of informed travellers eager to experience the wonders of the coral reef at first hand. Hopefully, there will be items of interest here for members of all these groups plus, for the armchair traveller and wildlife enthusiast, a voyage of discovery into another dimension.

Finally, the theme running throughout this book is of the extremely fragile nature of the coral reef ecosystem and the ease with which it can be destroyed. Coral reefs originated 500 million years ago and were allowed to develop unscathed by man until relatively recently. As industrial and urban development proceeds, waste materials and refuse of all kinds are produced in large quantities and inevitably finally end up polluting our seas. Coral seas have not escaped such pollution and this, together with turbity and siltation caused by massive deforestation schemes, the effects of overfishing, and inept coastal development and damage, could mark the demise of these natural wonders. The message must be that continuing to abuse natural resources in this manner could inevitably jeopardize the very existence of our own species. Our only hope is that drawing attention to such abuse and its possible consequences will stimulate combined action to avert the total destruction of our natural environment.

Les Holliday

Above: *Coral reefs still pose many mysteries. This Caribbean barrel sponge* (Xestospongia muta) *is a common species, but little is known about a large number of other sponges which have not yet been scientifically classified.*

Right: *The coral reef ecosytem is fragile and fishes such as this French angel* (Pomacanthus paru) *could easily be added to the list of endangered species of the future. Spearfishing and pollution have driven it away from many Caribbean reefs.*

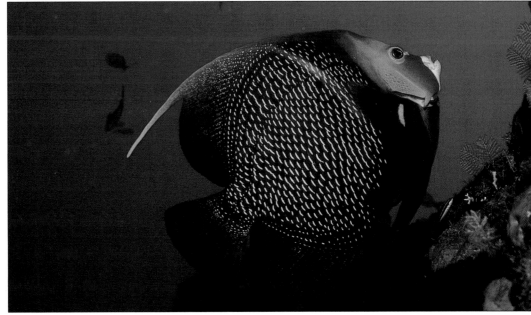

What is a Coral?

Any mention of corals is likely to conjure up visions of warm, clear, azure-blue seas and beautiful coral 'gardens' teeming with life. The exquisite patterns and colours of stony corals found on tropical reefs readily prompt the comparison with a flower garden, and in the early 1900s some amateur biologists did consider classifying reef corals as plants. It is easy to understand why these fascinating marine animals could be regarded as such, because they do not conform to our normal understanding of how an animal should look or behave. They *do* look like plants, however, need sunlight to function and are found growing in a fixed position forming treelike branching structures or shapes similar in appearance to plants. So what exactly are corals?

The biology of corals

Corals are basically very simple animals that belong to a large group of organisms called coelenterates. This group also includes jellyfishes, sea anemones and sea fans. All these organisms have a number of characteristics in common, the most fundamental one being that they share a simple radial body plan in which one opening serves both for the passage of materials into the body and the means of expelling wastes. In keeping with the coelenterate plan, the soft parts of corals are composed of animals called polyps that are essentially cylindrical in shape with a central opening surrounded by tentacles.

A major feature of corals and other coelenterates is their remarkable defence and prey-catching structures called nematocysts. These tiny capsules contain within them coiled, sharp, often barbed threads which can be triggered, by a combination of mechanical contact and the chemical 'taste' of the predator or prey, to shoot out and inject a venomous and paralyzing fluid. Some of the larger jellyfishes, such as the Portuguese man-of-war (*Physalia physalis*), are capable of inflicting painful stings. These have been known to be fatal to small children and even to adults who are particularly sensitive. The nematocysts are housed in large numbers in long

filamentous tentacles which, in the Portuguese man-of-war, can trail for up to 10m(33ft) from the animal and be very difficult to see underwater because they are rendered almost invisible.

Types of coral

The name 'coral' can be associated with a large number of animals but the two basic kinds are best defined as hard and soft corals.

Hard coral polyps are formed in three layers, the middle layer forming a jelly mass sandwiched between the 'walls' of the outer and inner layers. The outer layer secretes skeletal limestone that forms a hard, intricately patterned casing around the animal. Hard corals generally live not as single animals but as part of a colony. This means that the individual members live together in a permanent association that enables each to survive by their combined responses to the environment. In a sense, like the individual residents of an apartment block pooling their efforts for the common good.

Soft corals also have a similar body plan and form colonies, but they do not have a solid limestone skeleton. The feathery tentacled alcyonarian corals (Order Alcyonacea), which are

Above: *Large numbers of hard coral species predominate on the upper reef slope, as shown here in the Red Sea. These sunlit slopes support huge, tightly packed communities of corals containing up to 20 species in a small space.*

Left: *If the amateur biologists of the 1900s had been able to take excursions into the coral world using modern SCUBA gear, there is little doubt that they would still have been tempted to classify reef corals as plants and such scenes as gardens, here complete with flitting 'butterflies'.*

Right: *Soft corals are a beautiful feature of many Indo-Pacific reefs. This large* Dendronephthya *sp. is often aptly referred to as a soft tree coral.*

a common feature of Indo-Pacific reefs, have tiny limestone crystal structures, or sclerites, in their tissues but the animals themselves are essentially soft and flexible in composition. The gorgonians, which include sea fans and sea whips, are a further type of soft coral which may have sclerites in their tissues, but they also have a second skeletal framework of central axial rods made up of a flexible material called gorgonin.

A vital animal-plant partnership

All reef-building corals and a large number of anemones and various other coelenterates contain within their tissues millions of single-celled plants known as zooxanthellae. These plants, safely protected inside the tissues of the polyp, are able to photosynthesize, using the energy of the sun to convert carbon dioxide and water into carbohydrates and oxygen. The zooxanthellae benefit the coral by providing a supply of oxygen in its tissues for respiration. There is also evidence to suggest that a high percentage of the carbohydrates produced through photosynthesis 'leak' out of the algal cells and are used by the corals as food. This enables the coral polyps to deposit their limestone skeletons more rapidly.

It is a sobering thought that this association between a microscopic plant and a simple form of animal has produced the magnificent coral reefs we see today, which include the largest structures on earth built by a life form. The Great Barrier Reef of Australia, for example, is so immense that it is visible from far out in space and overshadows any similar accomplishments by man.

Below: *The calm sheltered waters of the Gulf of Aqaba in the Red Sea encourage masses of delicate gardenlike coral growths and produce huge reef formations, very popular with divers.*

Right: *The largest and most developed reef system on earth is the Great Barrier Reef, off Australia. Here, a floating hotel on John Brewer Reef is dwarfed by the huge sweep of corals.*

A closer look at hard corals

Taking a closer look at an individual hard coral polyp reveals an anemonelike creature, the polyp. The structure of each polyp is simple. The cylindrical body is surmounted by tentacles, which can vary in number with species, and these surround the opening leading to the body cavity. The body cavity is partitioned by sheets of tissue called mesenteries.

Each polyp is encased in a stony skeletal cup, the upper surface of which is fashioned with vertical folds that produce the intricate symmetrical patterns we associate with the different types of stony corals. The stony cups that form the colony can be arranged in a wide variety of configurations, including in a flowerlike fashion on stalks or in a star-shaped arrangement forming a mound. (See page 29 for illustrations of these.)

Right: *Each hard coral polyp consists of a cylindrical structure with one opening surmounted by tentacles armed with* *stinging nematocysts. The inside is formed into a large stomach cavity lined with folds of soft tissue called mesenteries.*

The structure of a hard coral polyp

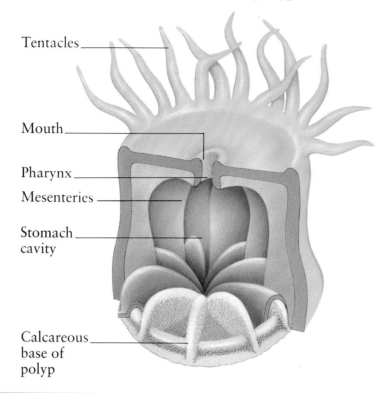

Tentacles

Mouth

Pharynx

Mesenteries

Stomach cavity

Calcareous base of polyp

Above: *The intricate patterns of hard corals are produced by the combination of the polyp shape and the calcareous skeleton it secretes. This 'skeleton' of a brain coral clearly shows the pattern of each 'cup' and how they are linked.*

Left: *The polyps of the Caribbean Flower coral* (Eusmilia fastigiata) *are individually large and appear to be growing on stalks. At night, the transparent tentacles extend to feed, as is just happening here, eventually smothering the calcareous 'foundations'.*

Above: *The branching hard corals typified by this staghorn coral* (Acropora sp.), *are in many ways ideally shaped for their way of life. The matrix of branches allows a large number of polyps to be exposed to water currents carrying food.*

Right: *Some of the polyps of this tree coral* (Tubastrea micrantha) *are withdrawn into their cups, revealing the stony skeleton of the coral. This particular species lacks zooxanthellae in its tissues and is therefore not dependent on strong sunlight to thrive.*

Above: *The shapes of hard corals are infinitely variable. Indo-Pacific reefs are often dotted with these mounds of* Porites *coral, here alive with golden jewelfish (*Anthias squamipinnis), *one of the most common reef fishes.*

Left: *The Caribbean pillar coral (*Dendrogyra cylindricus) *is one of the most spectacular of stony corals, its columns often reaching more than 3m(10ft) in height.*

Right: *The convoluted patterns of brain corals are produced by asexual subdivision of the coral polyps without the formation of dividing walls, leaving the polyps attached together in these convolutions. This brain coral,* Leptoria phrygia, *set in a bed of* Acropora *coral, is a classic example.*

Above: *The variable configurations of this Indo-Pacific hard coral* Turbinaria mesenterina *allow its zooxanthellae to take full advantage of available sunlight, thus enabling the coral to* succeed where others *would fail. In shallow water, where the sunlight is intense, the coral takes on a convoluted shape; in the dim light conditions of deep water, platelike forms develop.*

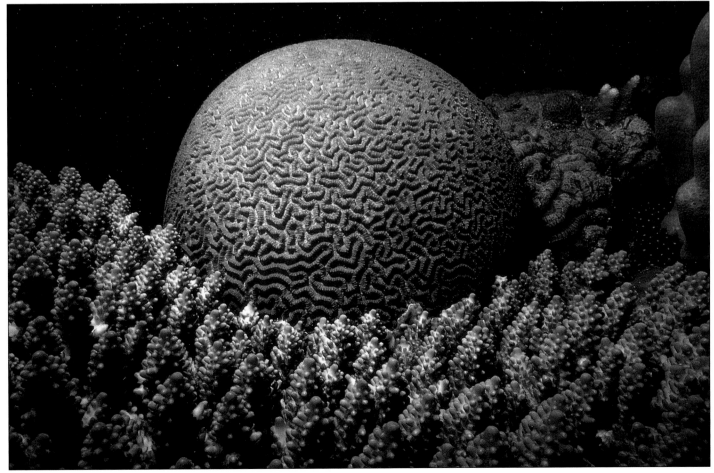

Soft coral polyps

The structure of the soft coral polyp is similar to that of the hard coral but without a solid limestone skeleton. Many species are classified as octocorals because they have eight fringed tentacles whereas the hard corals usually have smooth tentacles formed in rings of six or multiples of six. The soft coral polyps are arranged on the outer surface of the main tissue mass of the colony and are supported by tiny limestone crystals, or sclerites.

A number of species, typified by the feathery alcyonarian corals (such as *Dendronephthya* spp.), do not play host to zooxanthellae and may be brilliantly coloured in shades of orange, pink or purple. This colour may be furnished by the polyps or by the sclerites visible through the translucent tissues. Other species are not as spectacular and may, like the leather corals (*Sinularia* and *Sarcophyton* spp.), be drab.

Below: *The translucent tissues of the soft coral* Dendronephthya rubeola *clearly reveal the sclerites that act as an internal skeleton for the colony.*

Right: *Typical soft coral polyps, with a simplified cross section to show the internal structure. In this octocoral, each polyp has eight tentacles.*

The structure of soft coral polyps

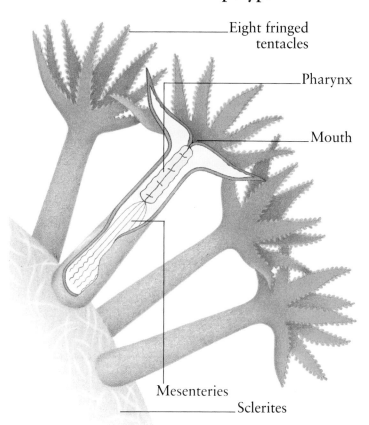

Eight fringed tentacles

Pharynx

Mouth

Mesenteries

Sclerites

Above: *The soft leather coral* Sarcophyton trocheliophorum *is a daytime feeder, here extending its polyps to ensnare zooplankton.*

Right: *The same leather coral as above shown on a reef at Heron Island, Australia. Note how the appearance changes where the polyps are withdrawn.*

Below: *A close view of a few soft coral polyps, clearly showing the mesenteries within the internal cavities.*

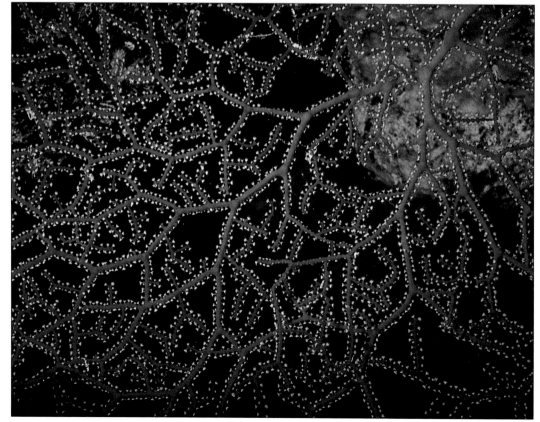

Above: *Soft corals are often represented by branching forms. This common Caribbean* Plexaura homomalla *is a bushy gorgonian, with horny flattened growths.*

Left: *This portion of a deepwater Red Sea gorgonian coral shows the typical growth pattern in one plane to form a fan shape. This allows a large matrix of polyps to filter zooplankton from the passing currents.*

Right: *The fan-shaped growths of deepwater gorgonians usually grow at right angles to the prevailing water current and may reach impressive proportions – up to about 3m(10ft) across.*

How corals feed

All corals are carnivorous and the polyps are capable of shooting out nematocysts, their microscopic venomous darts, from extended tentacles to paralyze and disable their prey. Zooplankton forms the basis of their diet and, once trapped, this is passed by the tentacles into the mouth opening and down into the stomach, where the food is rapidly digested by secretions from the mesenteries. Zooplankton is most plentiful at night in shallow waters, as the vast range of creatures that make up the plankton rise from the depths to feed. Most hard corals live in shallow waters and are, therefore, nocturnal feeders, while soft corals, which generally occur in deeper water, feed during the day. The reef is a competitive environment, however, and there are many exceptions to this generalization. And, as we have seen, the zooxanthellae in the tissues of many corals also help to provide vital nutrition.

Coral polyps can vary considerably in size, from microscopic proportions to the large single polyps of the mushroom corals (*Fungia* spp.), which can measure up to 15cm(6in) in diameter. Naturally, prey taken by corals also varies in size, from the microscopic to a variety of small shrimps and other invertebrates, and also juvenile reef fishes.

How a nematocyst works

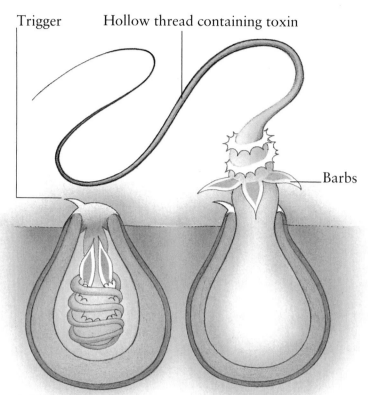

Trigger   Hollow thread containing toxin

Barbs

1. Nematocyst capsule with thread coiled within cell and trigger poised

2. Triggering causes thread to turn inside-out by hydrostatic pressure

Above: *The nematocysts are activated by chemical signals or touch. Once triggered, the barbed threads whip out to lash at predator or prey. The venom is irritating to humans, but can disable small marine life.*

Left: *The polyps of the mushroom coral (Fungia) are huge by coral polyp standards, measuring up to 15cm(6in) across. Here, two mushroom corals are positioned side by side, the tentacles of one withdrawn while the other polyp is open and in feeding mode.*

Right: *A cup coral* (Dendrophyllia) *feeding at night on a small marine animal that has ventured too close. The hapless creature is being drawn down into the stomach cavity to be digested.*

How corals reproduce

In most corals, as the polyps grow they divide, or bud, asexually to form daughter polyps, each original polyp becoming two. Later in the process, the older polyp is cut off from its offspring by the formation of a limestone partition between the two and thus a chambered mass of limestone – the colony – is built up. Where growth develops by asexual subdivision of the polyps without the formation of dividing walls, the colony may eventually become convoluted, as in the brain corals (such as *Leptoria* spp.).

A great deal of research has taken place to record the growth of hard corals. Their rate of growth, contrary to earlier thinking, has been found to be quite rapid in some cases. Staghorn corals (*Acropora* spp.), for example, can cover several square metres of reef floor in two or three seasons, and some boulder corals and brain coral colonies may double in size over a 20-year period.

Corals also reproduce by a sexual process. Sex cells located on the mesenteries produce eggs and sperm. In some corals, the eggs are released into the water through the central mouth and fertilized externally by spermatozoa also discharged into the water. In many corals, the ripe eggs remain attached to the mesenteries inside the stomach cavity of the polyp and are fertilized by sperm carried in water currents from other polyps.

After a short period of development, the fertilized eggs are released in the form of tiny, pear-shaped animals with rapidly beating hairs, or cilia, which allow them a limited ability to swim in their new environment among the zooplankton (the vast floating population of tiny animals that drift and migrate in the sea). These free-swimming larval stages, or planulae, survive for days or possibly weeks until they finally reach a suitable hard surface on which to attach and colonize. Once established, the upper surface of each planula becomes indented to form an opening, tentacles grow out from the rim and the outer skin quickly begins to form a stony skeleton. During the free-swimming period, the planulae have the opportunity to drift in the plankton for considerable distances and this accounts for the wide distribution of many species.

Below: *Staghorn corals* (Acropora *sp.) reproduce by means of tiny egg-sperm bundles that consist of eight microscopic eggs surrounded by sperms. They spawn at full moon.*

Right: *Coral polyps often reproduce asexually, each one splitting into two offspring. Look closely at these polyps and you will see some elongating before they divide.*

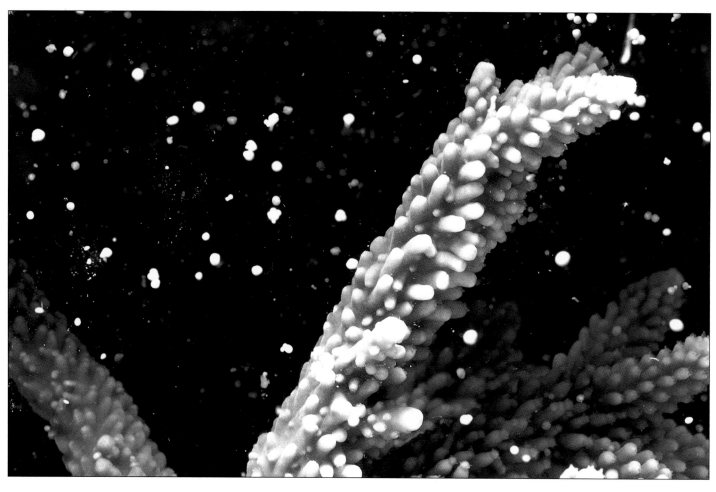

How coral colonies grow

All coral colonies arise from a single polyp. Here we show two classic growth patterns. The mound-forming corals *build up in layers, while the branching species develop in a longitudinal fashion to form more fragile twiglike growths.*

Branching coral

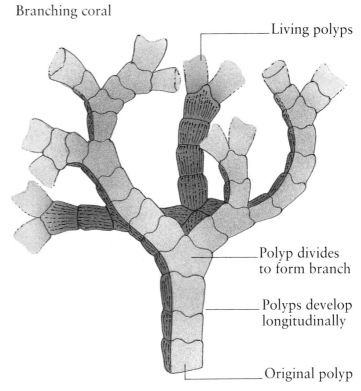

Living polyps

Polyp divides to form branch

Polyps develop longitudinally

Original polyp

Mound coral

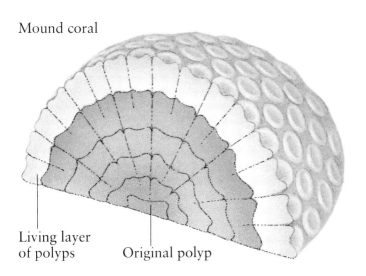

Living layer of polyps

Original polyp

Silent battles

As mentioned earlier, nematocysts can be used in defence as well as for disabling the coral's prey, and they are equally effective against other corals. The reef is far from being the serene, calm and peaceful place it appears. Silent battles are constantly waging as coral colonies fight each other for available space. By turning their batteries of stinging cells towards neighbouring colonies, the more invasive species of coral can deter advances in growth by less aggressive species. The stinging cells of some corals are capable of actually killing the polyps of others, thus allowing one colony to completely overgrow another. The outcome of such encounters is often for one species to become dominant in that part of the reef while others succumb. The characteristic zoning of species within the reef complex is not determined simply by these processes, however. As we shall see later, zoning of corals is primarily due to their responses to environmental factors, such as light and water currents.

Healthy reef growth

The main factors that encourage healthy reef coral growth are warm, clean sea water with strong sunlight. Sea water temperatures need to lie within the range of 16-36°C(61-97°F), and most active reef growth only takes place within a much narrower range, perhaps 23-25°C(73-77°F). Salinity of the sea water is also very critical and needs to be at an optimum concentration of 35 parts per thousand (35gm/litre). A range between 25 and 40 parts per thousand can be tolerated but the extremes of this range are harmful to many corals as well as other reef plants and animals.

Clean water is necessary to allow sunlight to penetrate to where corals live for the benefit of their associated zooxanthellae. Corals are also unable to withstand large amounts of sediment, particularly fine silt, because it clogs the mouth and tentacles, preventing feeding and breathing. Since they are carnivorous animals, however, they cannot live in entirely sterile conditions, but require a constant supply of small floating or swimming creatures on which to feed. Finally, since corals are unable to move, they must be exposed to currents that will provide food.

Thus, the picture emerging is one that shows reef corals as animals that require a stable environment and particular conditions in order to thrive. Living in such conditions, they have limited resistance to outside influences such as pollution. To illustrate this point, it has been found that nitrates, which are produced by nitrifying bacteria as they break down organic pollution, are fatal to most coral species in concentrations as low as 20 parts per million (written as 20ppm and also equivalent to 20mg/litre). As a comparison, many fish can withstand nitrate concentrations as high as 50-100ppm, or even higher.

In order to understand the water quality requirements of these creatures, it is necessary to look more closely at their natural environment and discover just what conditions are found there. Anyone visiting a coral reef for the first time is enthralled by the clear water and spectacular living matrix of intricately shaped corals so transparently and dramatically revealed. Every hard surface seems to be covered with life and a closer look confirms this, for in among the corals a wide range of other sessile (attached) animals abound. All these life forms are competing for planktonic food and thus form an enormous, super-efficient filtration system that ensures that the pristine conditions continue. A series of tests of the water at any tropical reef location shows that the chemical composition remains remarkably stable. The pH value of the water (reflecting its acid/alkaline balance) is consistent within the narrow alkaline range of 8.0-8.3, thanks to the buffering effect of large amounts of calcium carbonate in the reef structure slowly dissolving into the ocean. Above all, the water chemistry is stabilized by the relative lack of any outside influences and by the sheer volume of water involved.

It is not surprising that in such clean and stable conditions the many animals inhabiting coral reefs are not tolerant to changes in their environment. Corals are no exception and show signs of distress in the wild if some outside interference, such as manmade pollution, is allowed to affect the reef. This is a theme we will be exploring later in the book, particularly on pages 58-67.

Right: *Here, two Red Sea hard corals are locked in silent combat for the available space and resources on the reef. It appears that the white brainlike configurations of the* Platygyra *colony are overtaking the weaker colony of* Turbinaria mesenterina. *Many battles such as this wage across the reef; each coral employing batteries of tiny stinging cells as very effective weapons.*

Architects of the Shallows

As we have seen, the accumulation of the stony 'skeletons' of coral animals has enabled huge reefs to form. The continuing growth of these immense structures is the responsibility of a thin veneer of living coral polyps that flourish on the limestone remains of their ancestors. The exact form and shape of these reefs can vary considerably and were first defined by Charles Darwin as long ago as 1842 into three types:

Fringing reefs he described as forming elongate ridges typically extending 50-500m(164-1640ft) offshore and running parallel with the coastline.

Barrier reefs were described as forming elongated structures, again running parallel with the coastline, but further out to sea, perhaps 1-5km(0.6-3.1 miles) out and generally enclosing moderately deep water between the reef and the shoreline.

Atolls, the third type defined by Darwin, are reefs that arise from deep water and that when viewed from above are typically circular in structure.

Darwin's definitions still hold true today and are used by marine scientists all over the world. Before we look in more detail at these three classic types, we should perhaps add the following terms to describe particular reef forms:

Patch reef is a term widely used to describe a small, separate hill-like reef developed in relatively shallow water – usually less than 20m(66ft) deep. Good examples of patch reefs often occur in sandy lagoons in very shallow water (such as on the Great Barrier Reef); these are relatively small, measuring less than 200m (656ft) in diameter.

Platform reef is a term used to describe separate hill-like reefs more than 300m(984ft) wide.

Coral knoll is used for small reef outcrops of less than 50m(164ft) in diameter – often called 'bommies' in Australian waters.

The development of fringing reefs

Fringing reefs begin to develop in relatively shallow water as a thin strip of living coral parallel to the shore. Under suitable conditions, this strip broadens into a platform of part dead and partly living coral extending horizontally from the shore. In fact, fringing reefs can extend almost unbroken for many kilometres along the coastline, often forming a calm lagoon between reef and shore.

The living and actively growing part of the reef is on the seaward face. This is because conditions are more favourable in this direction; on the shoreward side, high temperature and high salinity levels occur and increased amounts of deposited sediment offer a less conducive environment for coral growth. Further development into deeper water depends on coral broken by storms falling to the base of the slope and building up to a level that will allow growth to continue and/or on the presence of a suitably solid base for attachment.

The dependence of reef corals on their symbiotic association with tiny zooxanthellae only allows vigorous growth where strong sunlight penetrates. Sunlight is very quickly absorbed by sea water and luxuriant growths are seldom found deeper than 30m(100ft). Below 50m(164ft), the light-loving stony corals are substituted by those that do not contain zooxanthellae and by sponges and soft corals, which are also not dependent on sunlight.

As the reef extends outwards, the top of the reef also extends outwards, cutting off the supply of clean water to the corals trapped behind. Although some corals can thrive in this back reef area, over a period of time, the natural progression is for this trapped part of the reef to die and the coral rock remaining to be reduced to sand, thus forming a sandy lagoon. Fringing reefs exist in many parts of the world, with good examples occurring along the shores of the Red Sea, the east coast of Africa and in parts of the Caribbean.

The development of barrier reefs

The development of barrier reefs is more difficult to explain because there is not total agreement among scientists today as to how some examples

Left: *Patch reefs are hill-like reefs that often occur in sandy lagoon areas or on the upper reef slope of gently inclined fringing reefs. Large numbers may occur in favourable conditions, each a separate ecosystem of thriving reef life of fishes and invertebrates.*

Below: *The fringing reef develops by successive stages, the living coral growing as a thin strip parallel to the shore. Development continues along the coastline, often forming a calm lagoon between the reef and the shore. Further development into deeper water depends on coral breaking from the reef to form a base shallow enough for coral growth.*

How a fringing reef develops

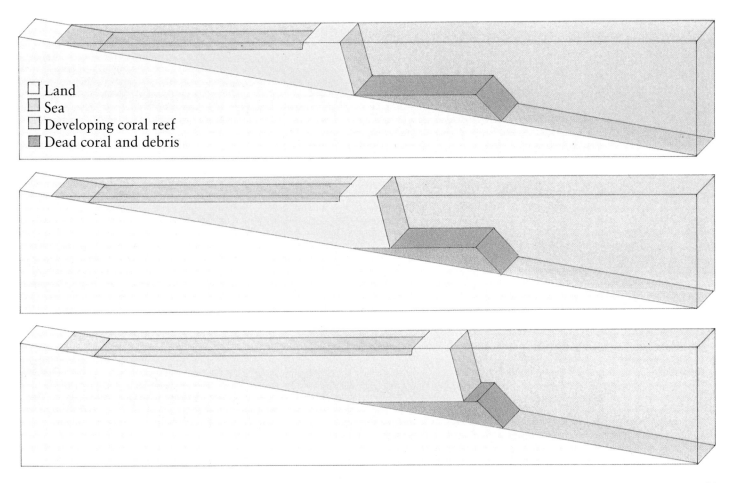

☐ Land
☐ Sea
☐ Developing coral reef
■ Dead coral and debris

of these types of reef were formed. The Darwinian theory depends on changes in sea level – either by the water level rising or the land moving – to explain the development of reefs rising from the great depths. There is certainly considerable evidence to show that the global level of the sea has altered significantly over geological time due to the fluctuation in the size of the ice caps during the ice ages. The theory is that these reefs were formed at times when the earth's sea levels were as much as 70m(230ft) lower than at present, and as the level slowly increased the corals grew, keeping pace with this gradual change.

On the other hand, there is ample evidence of the reverse situation in various parts of the world, especially so in the Gulf of Aqaba leading into the Red Sea, where small cliffs of fossilized coral reefs can be found well above present-day sea levels and hundreds of metres inland. The Darwinian theory did not consider changes in the sea level in isolation, however, but suggested that if the land bordering the sea was to gradually sink or rise a similar or reverse effect could occur.

Large barrier reefs occur mainly on the eastern side of large landmasses. This is due to global ocean current systems, which in the northern hemisphere tend to travel north to south down the western seaboards, carrying cold water with them, while those to the east carry warm water south to north. This clockwise circulation in the northern hemisphere, and the reverse movement in the southern hemisphere, is due to the earth's rotation. A typical result is the large barrier formations on the Queensland coast of Australia and similar developments in the Caribbean, all located on the eastern side of their respective landmasses. On the other hand, the Galapagos islands, located on the equator but on the western seaboard of the Americas, does not have luxuriant coral reefs because of cold currents sweeping from the south.

While scientists still use these theories to explain why barrier reefs were formed, modern technology has allowed a much more detailed study of these phenomena to take place, leading to the proposal of alternative theories for reef formation.

Barrier reefs, for example, have been found to occur in areas where originally the seabed was uniformly shallow for many kilometres from the land. Currents sweeping along the shoreline appear to have encouraged parallel reef

How a barrier reef develops

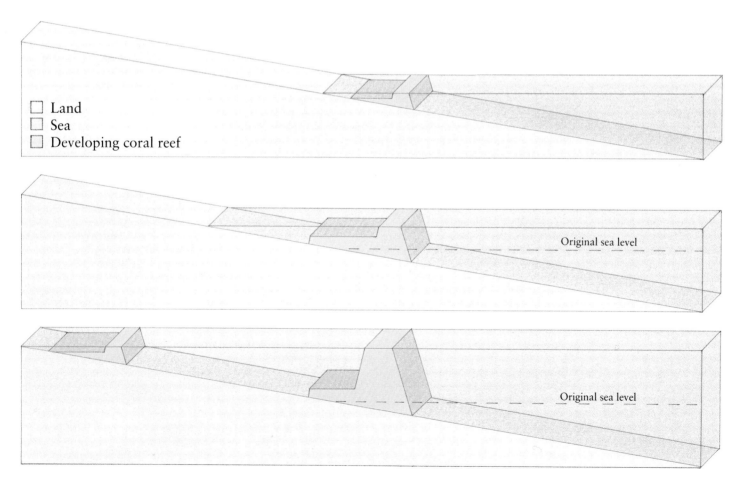

☐ Land
☐ Sea
☐ Developing coral reef

Original sea level

Original sea level

development, sometimes a considerable distance from the land. The formation of such a reef will naturally channel currents to its shoreward side, etching deep channels between the land and the reef, producing a different form of barrier reef.

The development of atolls

The formation of atolls is easily understood using Darwin's theory of land and sea level changes. Imagine a small round volcanic island with a fringing reef around it. If the reefs were formed at a time when the sea level was lower than at present, it is feasible that a barrier reef would encircle the island as the level began to rise. If

combined with subsidence of the seabed and the island itself, the result could be the familiar doughnut-shaped island or circle of islets we associate with atoll formations.

One alternative theory for the formation of atolls is based on a patch reef becoming progressively larger. The most active coral growth occurs around the outside rim of the reef and sandy patches often tend to appear in the centre, where circulation of water is restricted by the presence of the outer reef. Eventually, the corals in the centre of the patch die, leaving a sandy lagoon.

Atoll formations are most abundant in the central Indian Ocean and Pacific. The Maldives are an excellent example, consisting of atolls built up on a huge ridge of long-dead volcanoes that stretch from the equator northwards to the west of Sri Lanka. Charles Darwin learned of this area (but did not visit it) in 1836 during his epic journey of discovery aboard HMS Beagle and developed his theories of atoll development on the basis of careful studies of these islands. The English word atoll was derived from the Maldivian 'atholhu', the Maldivian atolls being classic examples of this type of coral formation.

Below left: *These sections reflect Darwin's theories on barrier reef formation. First, a fringing reef develops. Then the land slowly subsides, extending the distance between the reef and shore. The offshore reef becomes a barrier and a fringing reef forms close inshore.*

Below: *Darwin considered that atolls developed in a similar way to barrier reefs, but based on an island rather than on a long shoreline. Sea level changes combined with land subsidence can result in atoll formations hundreds of metres thick.*

How a coral atoll develops

Side view

Top view

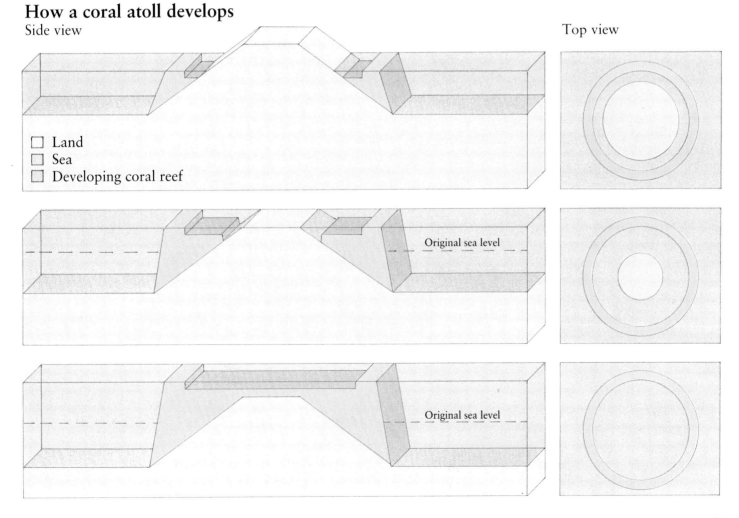

- ☐ Land
- ☐ Sea
- ☐ Developing coral reef

Original sea level

Original sea level

Zonation of fringing reefs

Each reef type has its own sequence of zones. Here, we look more closely at the zones of a fringing reef, using the classic type of fringing reefs found along most coastlines of the Red Sea as our example. In reality, the demarcation between different zones may not be entirely clear; they may merge into one another and may not follow this exact pattern in other parts of the world. However, it is helpful to highlight the following zones, starting from the shoreline:

The **lagoon,** the first zone from the shoreline, is a sandy area where growths of brown and green algae or sea grasses flourish in the shallows. In the deeper parts towards the reef, in depths which may average only one metre or so, the general vista is of sand with an occasional coral mound, featuring types such as brain corals (*Platygyra*) and boulder coral (*Porites*).

The **back reef** area is usually defined by a distinct step up of about half a metre to a metre in height and normally features a greater variety of corals. The diversity of life in the main part of the lagoon is inhibited by the high temperatures, high salinity and lack of current, whereas the back reef is influenced by open ocean water breaking over the reef and is thus richer in life. This part of the reef offers hard surfaces for corals to colonize and, although parallel to the shore, is dissected by surge channels and breaks to the open sea.

The **reef flat** is a shallow area immediately adjoining the back reef, which may be inhospitable because of wave action. Where it is not crisscrossed by channels, it is a level and often smooth platform that in exposed situations is populated by small-shelled molluscs and coated

Above: *Spur-and-groove formations may feature on the upper reef slope, where the reef front is exposed to winds. The profile of the reef is intersected by many channels running out to the open ocean between spurs of living coral.*

Left: *This Red Sea view shows the wide diversity of hard corals that can appear in a reef edge community. At least ten species are visible, such as* Acropora, Favia, Pocillopora, Goniastrea, *and* Montastrea.

Top right: *A classic form of fringing reef, as found in the Red Sea. Here, the continental shelf slopes steeply and is admirably suitable for coral zonation, each zone being clearly defined and very close to the next.*

Zonation of a fringing reef

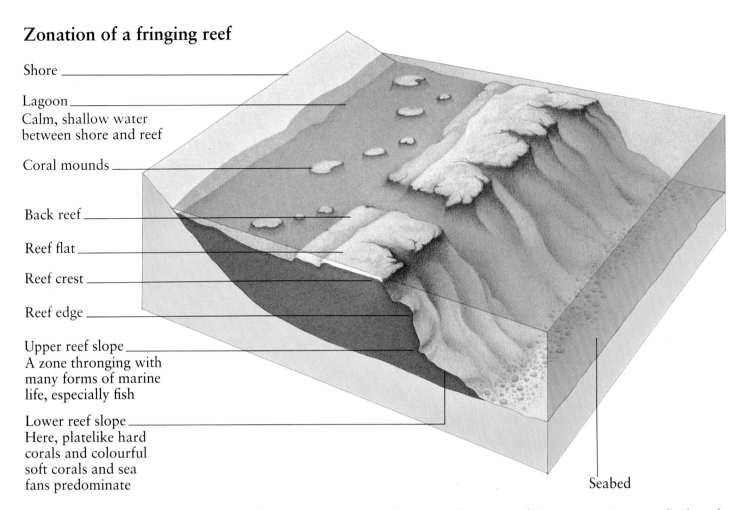

Shore

Lagoon
Calm, shallow water
between shore and reef

Coral mounds

Back reef

Reef flat

Reef crest

Reef edge

Upper reef slope
A zone thronging with
many forms of marine
life, especially fish

Lower reef slope
Here, platelike hard
corals and colourful
soft corals and sea
fans predominate

Seabed

with encrusting calcareous algae. (These encrusting forms of calcareous algae are distinct from the higher, plantlike coralline forms mentioned below. Both types precipitate calcium carbonate from the water and help to 'bind' the reef structure.) Sheltered parts of the reef flat are often quite well colonized by small, sturdy corals.

The **reef crest** is the highest point of the reef and is subject to high-energy wave action. It is composed of a serrated and stepped, seaward-facing surface covered with coralline algae and short turflike green algae. In deeper sections, organpipe coral (*Tubipora musica*) thrives.

The **reef edge** (often known as the reef front) is the next zone. It is usually stepped down a metre or so from the crest and is often home to wave-resistant corals such as fire coral (*Millepora platyphylla*) interspersed with *Favites* and branching colonies of *Pocillopora* and *Porites*.

The **upper reef slope** is the most productive area of the reef and can vary in shape from a gentle slope to a sheer vertical drop. The corals on this outer slope are often spectacular, with a wide diversity of species that includes staghorn coral (*Acropora*),

Porites and star coral (*Goniastrea*). Fine algal turf and bright pink coralline algae fill in the niches between the living corals and colonize dead coral rock. Here, fish life is most varied and abundant.

The **lower reef slope**, the final zone, is beyond the depths which many shallow-water corals can tolerate and is populated by platelike colonies of *Montipora*, *Podabacia* and *Oxypora*. Caves and overhangs are often a feature of this zone and these areas are rich in *Dendronephthya* soft corals and gorgonian sea fans.

The same basic reef profile often varies in different parts of the world. In the Caribbean, and in some other areas, the profile may be intersected by channels running out to the open ocean, known as 'spur-and-groove' formations. These develop on the windward margin of the reef front and extend down to about the 20m(66ft) depth level. On Red Sea reefs with more gently sloping areas of reef face or where the slope is terraced, large coral knolls can form, reaching up to the surface. A variety of corals can develop on these knolls due to the wide range of conditions offered for colonization, from deep to shallow habitats, sheltered and exposed, facing the land or the sea.

Zonation of barrier reefs

The barrier reef, as typified by locations on the Great Barrier Reef of Australia to the north east of the town of Cairns, are fringing reefs in the 'grand manner', offering separate and quite different coral communities to the leeward side of the reef from those on the outward, exposed reef face. Zonation of a barrier reef can be divided into five zones: the leeside face, reef flat, reef crest, the upper reef slope and the lower reef slope.

The **leeside face**, towards the land, fronts onto relatively open ocean conditions rather than a lagoon and is an area of prolific coral growth. *Acropora* corals dominate this zone, growing in water so shallow that at certain times of the year they are left exposed for periods by the low tide. (They secrete a thick mucus to help retain moisture and can survive for several hours before the tide turns.)The leeside reef face can be a gentle slope consisting of a mixed habitat of sandy areas and branching coral outcrops, or there may be deeper sections with caverns, canyons and gullies leading to a sandy slope. Here, in favourable conditions, patch reefs and coral knolls (or 'bommies', as they are known in Australia) form in depths down to 20m(66ft) before giving way to a sandy seabed.

The **reef flat** is usually much wider than on a typical Red Sea fringing reef, creating a spacious platform, perhaps up to a kilometre or more across. The outermost part of this flat, shallow zone – immediately backing onto the reef crest – is colonized by coralline algae. Small coral growths are found in the calmer areas behind this, and these progressively increase in diversity and cover towards the leeside face.

The **reef crest** (and **reef edge**) are not important zone definitions, because this area is very exposed and subject to high-energy wave action, restricting coral growth to the outward-facing reef slope.

The **upper reef slope** is usually fairly steep, sometimes vertical or terraced. Spur-and-groove formations can be a feature of the more exposed reef faces, accompanied by dense coral cover.

The **lower reef slope** may vary in gradient from gradual slope to a vertical cliff, depending on its proximity to the edge of the continental shelf. This area is populated by colonies of *Dendronepthya* soft corals, *Gorgonia* sea whips and fans, and *Antipathes*, the jeweller's black coral, so-called because it is used for making jewellery.

Zonation of a barrier reef

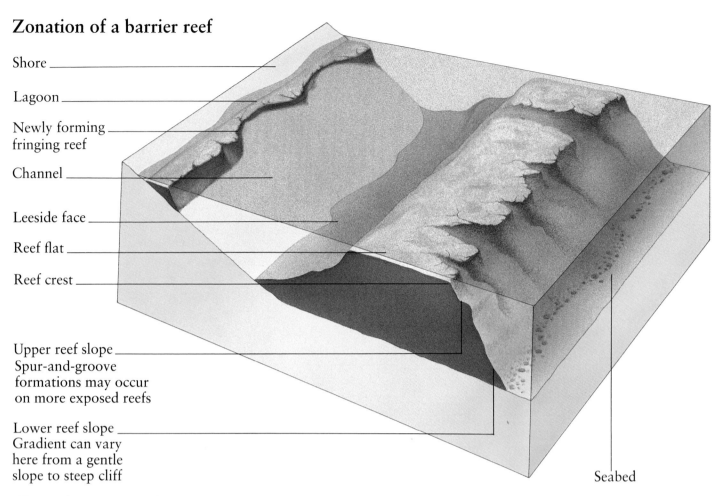

Shore

Lagoon

Newly forming fringing reef

Channel

Leeside face

Reef flat

Reef crest

Upper reef slope
Spur-and-groove
formations may occur
on more exposed reefs

Lower reef slope
Gradient can vary
here from a gentle
slope to steep cliff

Seabed

Above: *A cutaway section of a typical barrier reef. Note the gently sloping leeside face, which is an area rich in coral growth and other marine life.*

Left: *The coral community in a 'pond' in the Great Barrier Reef. Often located long distances from the mainland, the leeside of the reef supports quite different corals and other marine life compared with the exposed reef face.*

Right: *Coral knolls such as this are known as 'bommies' in Australia. These coral communities are fascinating examples of coral zonation in miniature, and one small bommie may harbour ten or more hard coral species, all reaching up towards the sunlit surface.*

Zonation of atolls

In many ways, atolls are the most interesting reef formations. The reefs surrounding an atoll are very similar to those of the barrier reef or fringing reef, except that they are circular or, more accurately, tear drop in shape.

The **central lagoon**, inside the encircling reef, is a calm area of shallow water seldom more than 20m(66ft) deep. It takes a variety of forms, depending on the degree of open ocean water flushing into it. Where water circulates freely, favourable conditions are provided for lagoonal patch reefs and large coral knoll formations, but generally this area is not very productive in terms of hard corals. One atoll formation in the Aldabra group of islands in the Indian Ocean (north of Madagascar), provides a shallow lagoon furnished with large areas of submerged sea grasses. Huge land tortoises, which have difficulty in existing on the sparse terrestrial plant growths on the islands, have taken to the waters of the lagoon to feed upon these lush sea meadows.

The **outer lagoon**, on the leeward side of the reef, is lined with encircling sand banks that produce small islets or, in its classic form, the familiar doughnut-shaped island with occasional breaks from the open sea to the lagoon. Typical forms of this type of reef formation abound in the Maldives and the Cocos-Keeling Atoll (both in the Indian Ocean) and Nukulaelae Atoll in the Tuvalu group of islands (due north of Fiji).

The **reef faces** are steeply sloping and can plummet into very deep water. These are a major feature of many atoll formations, isolated as they are from mainland areas. Reef faces are affected by different degrees of exposure, however, depending on their relationship to prevailing winds and currents; a snorkel excursion around one of these reef formations can often reveal steep slopes to the windward side of the atoll but sheltered, gently sloping areas of prolific coral growth to the lee.

Bottom left: *This view of a small islet, part of a Maldivian atoll, shows the classic zones from central lagoon at bottom left to open sea at top right.*

Bottom right: *Bolt Reef off Australia shows a typical atoll shape.*

Right: *The typical form of an atoll is a tear drop-shaped island or circle of islets, as here. Because they often develop thousands of miles from other landmasses in deep water, such formations often have steeply sloping reefs on exposed faces.*

Zonation of an atoll

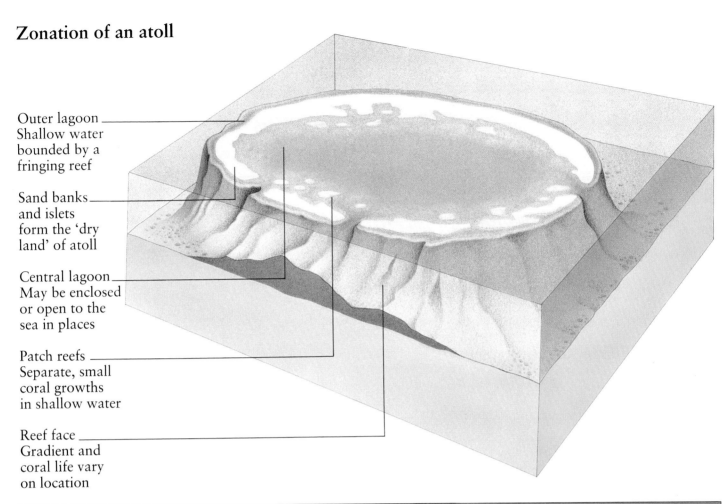

Outer lagoon
Shallow water
bounded by a
fringing reef

Sand banks
and islets
form the 'dry
land' of atoll

Central lagoon
May be enclosed
or open to the
sea in places

Patch reefs
Separate, small
coral growths
in shallow water

Reef face
Gradient and
coral life vary
on location

The Coral World of Fishes

The first and overwhelming impression of any coral reef is the sheer brilliance, abundance and diversity of the reef fishes. Brightly coloured, gaudily patterned fish of every conceivable body shape dart among the corals or hang in huge shoals in midwater. It is not unusual to find 20 or more species living closely together on just one small coral outcrop, and large reef areas, such as the Great Barrier Reef of Australia, can be home to a remarkable 2000 species.

In such a crowded environment, the competition for food and space is ever present. In order to survive and to get the most from their surroundings, reef fishes have adapted in shape and behaviour to live in various parts of the reef and become dependent on different food sources. Feeders on coral polyps and the tiny worms and crustaceans that live in cracks and holes in the reef have needlelike snouts and highly compressed body shapes to allow them easy access to deep crevices that other fishes cannot reach. Teeth may be fused together to form a parrotlike beak for scraping off algae covering the coral or combined with powerful jaws to feed on the coral itself. The main food source for the majority of reef fishes, however, is other fish, and 'eat or be eaten' is the general rule for survival.

Below: *The plaid markings and vivid red coloration of the tiny hawkfish* (Oxycirrhites typus) *blend with the tracery of a branching gorgonian as it lurks motionless, ready to dart out and snap up passing small fish or crustaceans.*

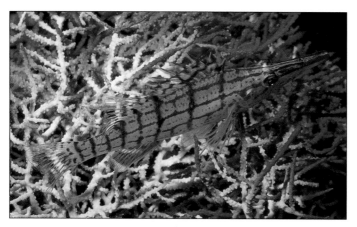

Offence and defence on the reef

To overcome the immense difficulties of surviving in such a competitive situation, reef fishes have developed an armoury of weapons and defence strategies and these are used by predator and prey alike. Here, we look briefly at a number of these strategies for survival.

Cryptic camouflage

Camouflage is a universal strategy on the coral reef. Predators use it to conceal themselves as they lie in wait to surprise any unsuspecting prey coming within their reach and many less aggressive species hide behind the cloak of camouflage as a means of evading predation. A good example of the former is the Indo-Pacific giant moray eel (*Gymnothorax javanicus*), which reaches over 2m(6.6ft) in length and hides within crevices and holes in the reef, perfectly camouflaged to mimic the surrounding coral. This formidable fish feeds on a wide variety of reef fishes and its gargantuan proportions indicate just how successful its hunting technique can be. A good example of defensive camouflage is seen in the yellow-spotted stingray (*Urolophus jamaicensis*). This small, placid ray from shallow sandy Caribbean waters hunts by excavating depressions in the sand to expose the small shellfish and various other invertebrates on which it feeds. To elude its predators, the body of the ray is covered in yellow spots that blend with the seabed and it has a chameleonlike ability to change colour, shade and pattern to match its surroundings. If all else fails, a further weapon is provided by a sharp venomous spine at the base of the tail, which is known to deter the ray's most ardent predators, including large lemon and hammerhead sharks.

Behavioural camouflage

Behavioural camouflage is seen in the tropical Atlantic trumpetfish (*Aulostomus maculatus*), a common reef fish that often hovers vertically, nose down, among gorgonians and sea whips, cleverly hiding in wait for passing small fishes and shrimps.

Left: *The Atlantic trumpetfish is a clever hunter. Blending in with the surrounding sea whips, it adopts a nose-down position and hovers realistically, moving gently to and fro with the current, ready to engulf any small fish or shrimp that ventures too close.*

Below: *Animals that use camouflage as a defence often have the amazing ability to rapidly change colour and markings to match their surroundings. The yellow-spotted stingray is one of these creatures and is almost undetectable at times.*

Closely related to seahorses and pipefishes, this bizarre creature has an elongated body with a head extended into a long, trumpet-shaped snout. It can often be observed adopting a further subterfuge, using other, non-aggressive fishes such as herbivorous surgeonfishes as cover to sneak up on its prey. Almost invisible within a shoal of slow-moving surgeonfishes, the trumpetfish will suddenly dart out and pounce on a small fish or shrimp, sucking the unsuspecting prey into its tube-shaped mouth.

The power of advertising

Camouflage coloration is one method to deceive a predator or gain a meal, but by far the largest number of coral reef fishes are gaudy and colourful. Bright colours and patterns can serve purposes other than simply to adorn. It often pays to advertise, and if you are a fish that evades predation by having poisonous or distasteful flesh it is important that predators know this before deciding to sample you for themselves. Bright yellow, especially combined with black spots or bars, is a universally recognized indication of a poisonous species, and is used by terrestrial as well as aquatic animals. The juvenile phase of the Indo-Pacific cube boxfish (*Ostracion cubicus*) is an excellent example, using this type of livery to advertise the poisonous mucus covering its body.

The art of deception

Butterflyfishes (family Chaetodontidae) are among the most attractive reef fishes and have a 'state of the art' ability to use colour and pattern to aid their survival. They have a disclike, highly compressed body and often display bold patterns that disguise the fish by breaking up its body outline or masking conspicuous features such as the eyes. Such disruptive coloration serves as an effective means of evading capture, and many eye-

masked species take the illusion one stage further by employing conspicuous false eyes on the base of the tail or on the dorsal fin. This confuses predators into attacking the 'wrong end', while the fish dashes off in the opposite direction.

Drastic measures

Not all reef fishes employ disguise or deception to survive; many have evolved other strategies to protect themselves. This is shown to perfection by members of the porcupinefish family (Diodontidae). Porcupinefishes are easily recognized by the prominent spines that cover the head and body. These erect spines are a major deterrent and are made even more emphatic by the fishes' extraordinary ability to inflate themselves with water into spiky balls at least double their original size, effectively preventing attacking predators from swallowing them whole. In addition to this impressive defence mechanism, the horny skin and poisonous flesh act as a further discouragement, and the parrotlike beak is capable of delivering a nasty bite.

Unfortunately, porcupinefishes have not evolved a defence mechanism effective against their worst enemy – man! The very ability that protects porcupinefishes in the wild has resulted in their downfall. Inflated specimens are popular as souvenirs and many are collected for the curio trade, dried, varnished and offered for sale as mantleshelf ornaments or lampshades. The bridal burrfish (*Chilomycterus antennatus*), one of four porcupinefish species represented in the Caribbean, is rapidly becoming threatened due to the large numbers taken for sale, and there is an urgent need to protect this particular species.

Below: *When combined with black spots, the bright yellow body of the cube boxfish provides an* *effective way of warning would-be predators of the poisonous mucus covering its inviting flesh.*

Left: *The bridal burrfish has an impressive armoury of weapons. Its sharp spines, horny skin and beaklike mouth deter most predators.*

Right: *More ardent predators would soon discover the burrfish's second line of defence, an ability to inflate to double its size or more.*

Below: *Fully inflated, the once tiny burrfish becomes a spiky ball, preventing predators from swallowing it whole.*

Living in harmony

Not all living interactions on the reef are based on aggressive predator/prey relationships. Within the teeming diversity of plants and animals that live together on a coral reef, there are many examples of widely differing life forms involved in intricate and interdependent liaisons. After all, the very existence of a coral reef depends upon a symbiotic relationship between the stony coral polyps and the microscopic zooxanthellae algae that live within their tissues.

One of the most interesting of the mutually beneficial associations is that between clownfishes and their host anemones. These brightly coloured fish are found singly or, more often, as a pair or small group hovering above their host anemone and seek a safe haven within its venomous tentacles at the first hint of danger. The immunity enjoyed by clownfishes has only recently become properly understood. The clownfish acquires its immunity from the otherwise deadly stinging cells of the anemone by the dual strategy of manufacturing a sugar-based mucus to disguise its natural protein body composition and by slowly covering itself with a layer of mucus from the anemone. (In fact, young 'unprotected' clownfishes have been observed 'dashing' through the tentacles of an anemone to pick up some of the mucus.) The main trigger mechanism that activates the anemone's nematocysts, or stinging cells, is the protein-based mucus covering most fishes. As the anemone is naturally equipped to avoid stinging itself by recognizing its own mucus, it is deceived by the clownfish's 'cloak of disguise' into assuming that the fish is part of itself.

The clownfish obviously benefits from the safe protection offered by the anemone's tentacles but any advantage to the anemone is less clear. One theory is that the bright coloration of the clownfishes acts as a warning to would-be predators of the deadly consequences of approaching too closely to the tentacles. Of course, this also keeps potential prey fish at bay,

Below: *The association between the clownfish and its host anemone is well known. The dependence the clown attaches to its host is such that the numbers of anemones available on a reef can directly effect the size of the clown population.*

but it seems that anemones only feed on fish 'by chance', with juvenile 'inexperienced' fish being the most common victims. The bulk of the anemone's food source is composed of other invertebrates and zooplankton.

A life of service

Cleaning symbiosis is a further type of mutually beneficial arrangement, which is common on land as well as underwater. Coral reefs have many examples of this fascinating practice; over 50 coral reef species of fish and quite a number of invertebrates have given up the conventional means of hunting for food and live by cleaning parasites, small pieces of dead tissue and fungus from the fish living on or visiting the reef.

Cleaner species often set up business at particular locations on the reef, known as 'cleaning stations'. The large numbers of fish they attract often form into orderly queues as they patiently wait their turn to be groomed. The cleaners provide an essential service in relieving their 'clients' of parasites and minor infections, while earning themselves a meal at the same time. The tactile experience resulting from the cleaning process often seems to be enjoyed, some clients living in close association with, and becoming very protective towards, their cleaners. The relationship between client and cleaner usually works to a defined set of rules. The cleaner is allowed to perform its duties all over the body, even inside the mouth and in the gill cavities, and in turn can trust its host not to make a meal of its defenceless companion in the process.

Cleaning symbiosis has evolved to become a very specialized arrangement. There are full-time cleaners, those that mix normal feeding patterns with part-time cleaning, and the juveniles of certain species which act as cleaners only when young. The list of juvenile cleaners includes many species, of which young angelfishes and butterflyfishes are perhaps the most familiar examples. It is not uncommon to find the juveniles of a number of different species working in combination to service a cleaning station or joining forces with a full-time cleaner.

Cleaning gobies (*Gobiosoma* spp.) and cleaner wrasses (*Labroides* spp.) are the two main groups of full-time cleaner fishes, the gobies performing the service in the tropical West Atlantic and the labrids filling the same niche in the Indo-Pacific. There are six species of the cleaner goby, of which the neon goby (*Gobiosoma oceanops*), which employs a dazzling, electric blue lateral stripe to advertise its cleaning service, is perhaps the best

known. The cleaner wrasse (*Labroides dimidiatus*) sports a similar blue lateral stripe, a trademark of many full-time cleaners, and is one of a number of cleaner wrasse species distributed widely over the whole of the Indo-Pacific.

Cleaner shrimps head the list of invertebrate cleaners and are represented by the Caribbean red-backed, or painted lady, shrimp (*Lysmata grabhami*), the Indo-Pacific *L. amboinensis* and the circumtropical banded coral shrimp (*Stenopus hispidus*). The cleaning methods used by cleaner shrimps are very similar to those adopted by cleaner fish. They also establish cleaning stations and attract clients by sporting conspicuous patterns and coloration and by waving their white, threadlike antennae back and forth.

Above: *A cleaner wrasse* (Labroides dimidiatus) *performs its cleaning duties on a large tusk wrasse which has visited its cleaning station.*

Below: *This cube boxfish appears to be enjoying the tactile experience of being thoroughly cleaned by a red-backed cleaner shrimp* (Lysmata grabhami).

Daytime on the reef

During the daytime, the coral reef is often a crowded place. From the early grey of morning to the bright, sunlit hours of midday, there is a progressive increase in the numbers of fish and other animals venturing into activity until, finally, the water and the surface of the reef are filled with movement. Hundreds of colourful fishes hang in shoals or busily forage for food. Small damselfishes hover just above outcrops of staghorn corals, never straying far away and always ready to dash to safety at the first sign of danger. Suddenly, a large predator in the form of a grouper or barracuda moves in for the kill, the distressed victim relaying a warning message across the reef and causing momentary panic as fish dive for cover in all directions.

These daytime predators arrive at dawn to feed, and are succeeded by huge populations of fish that graze and browse. These grazers fully exploit the many food sources provided by the reef. The herbivores feed on the algal turf growing in the niches between the living coral or use their chisel-like teeth to scrape off the thin film of algae adhering to coral surfaces. Parrotfishes are the most common of these algal grazers and can form large shoals, systematically grazing large areas of submerged reef flat. Surgeonfishes also form aggregations and are the true farmers of the reef, reserving large areas of reef flat for the shoal and

protecting their fields of algae from other herbivores. The tiny herbivorous damselfish *Stagastes nigricans*, found in the Red Sea and Indo-Pacific, follows a similar practice, tending and cleaning its square metre or so of algal turf and, despite its diminutive size, pugnaciously defending its adopted territory from other much larger herbivores that try to take over.

The coral polyp grazers are represented by members of the butterflyfish family, with their long, forcep-shaped snouts perfectly designed for reaching into crevices in the coral and their laterally compressed bodies allowing access through the narrowest of gaps. Well named, these colourful marine 'butterflies' flit among the coral heads like their airborne counterparts fluttering from flower to flower. The angelfishes, closely related to the butterflyfishes, form a further group of grazers that devote the daylight hours to browsing on sponges and algae. In the Caribbean and tropical West Atlantic, where sponges feature as one of the largest constituents of the reefs, angelfishes are often prolific, flourishing on the rich pastures available to them.

The major remaining group of animals of the daytime can also be distinguished by their feeding patterns. These are the midwater feeders searching for food in the currents laden with zooplankton that often sweep along the reef edge. Indo-Pacific communities of these fishes would include various damselfishes and the golden jewelfish (*Anthias*

Below: *The daytime-active parrotfish were once thought to be carnivores, grinding up corals with their beaklike jaws, but they are herbivores that feed on algae covering dead coral.*

Left: *The tropical sunlit shallows are often ablaze with colour. Here, Red Sea masked butterflyfish gather in shoals to feed, using their long snouts to probe crevices for polyps and invertebrates.*

Below: *The red-throated sweetlips (*Lethrinus chrysostomus*) from the southwest Pacific feeds mainly on small fishes. Primarily a night feeder, it does not miss the chance to stalk its prey during the hours of daylight, too.*

squamipinnis), which hang in clouds close to the reef. The pennant butterflyfish (*Heniochus diphreutes*), a species quite unusual for members of the butterflyfish family, also patrols along the reef in aggregations of many hundreds to feed in this manner. The Caribbean counterparts of this group would include the creole wrasse (*Clepticus pharrai*) and the sergeant major damselfish (*Abudefduf saxatilis*).

Carnivorous corals, with tentacles withdrawn, rest and await the richer pickings of the night, when the zooplankton will rise from the depths to feed and in turn provide a meal for the millions of hungry coral polyps. Bathed in sunlight, the corals by day are transformed into tiny greenhouses, their symbiotic microscopic algae harnessing the energy of the sun to benefit their coral hosts. Many other reef animals have entered into a

similar partnership with these tiny zooxanthellae, including anemones, sponges and clams. The huge giant clam (*Tridacna gigas*) of the Indo-Pacific is an excellent example, which can reach more than 1m(3.3ft) across and weigh 254kg(560lb). Living in shallow, brightly lit water, the clam exposes its colourful fleshy mantle that houses large numbers of zooxanthellae. By maintaining just the right levels of algae in its tissues, the clam is often able to rely upon them for nutrition. It controls the algae population by consuming only sufficient of their numbers to maintain optimum levels.

By mid-afternoon, the search for food has subsided and the reef becomes a more relaxed place. The major predators have returned to deeper water and, as the light wanes, the animals of the daytime prepare for darkness, scurrying to safety in the recesses of the reef.

Left: *Fusilier fish (Casio sp.) are prominent Indo-Pacific midwater feeders on zooplankton. These sleek, streamlined fishes form large schools and rely upon speed and amazing manoeuvrability to evade their predators. A flash of blue bodies is often all that is seen of these elusive creatures. During the day they do not stay close to the reef.*

Above: The Tridacna clams are all hosts to tiny zooxanthellae that thrive in the mantle. This small Tridacna crocea is a close relative of the impressive giant Indo-Pacific clam.

Right: *These blue-green chromis seek refuge in the branches of an Acropora coral. Here, they will spend the night safe from prowling predators.*

The reef at night

The pressures on food sources and space are such that activity continues throughout the 24-hour period, and the reef at night is a lively place. Before the night's proceedings can take place, however, the members of the daytime community must withdraw to safe retreats.

The midwater feeders are the first to leave, realizing how vulnerable they are to attack from dusk predators, such as large mackerel or jacks, in the fading light. They are followed quickly by the herbivores. Disc-shaped surgeonfishes disperse from their shoals and wriggle into incredibly small clefts in the reef flat. Large solitary parrotfish become very defensive at this time and may either nervously take flight if approached or hold their ground, making mock aggressive displays. Presently, some species of parrotfish will select a hole in the reef and settle inside it for the night, enveloping themselves in a cocoon of mucus. This mucus shroud deceives predators, both by disguising the fish's outline and also by masking its taste to confuse those that hunt by using this sense. (A highly developed sense of taste can assist underwater predators in much the same way as a keen sense of smell serves terrestrial predators.)

Many reef fish change colour at night, predators as well as their potential victims. They may take on more muted shades or, surprisingly, use bright red coloration as effective camouflage in the nightly battle for survival. Soldierfishes and squirrelfishes have large eyes and a pink or red coloration – a good indication that these fishes are

Below: *Nestling beneath a ledge, this parrotfish (Scarus sp.) is enveloped in a mucous shroud. This protective cocoon appears to discourage any likely predators by masking the fish's shape and taste.*

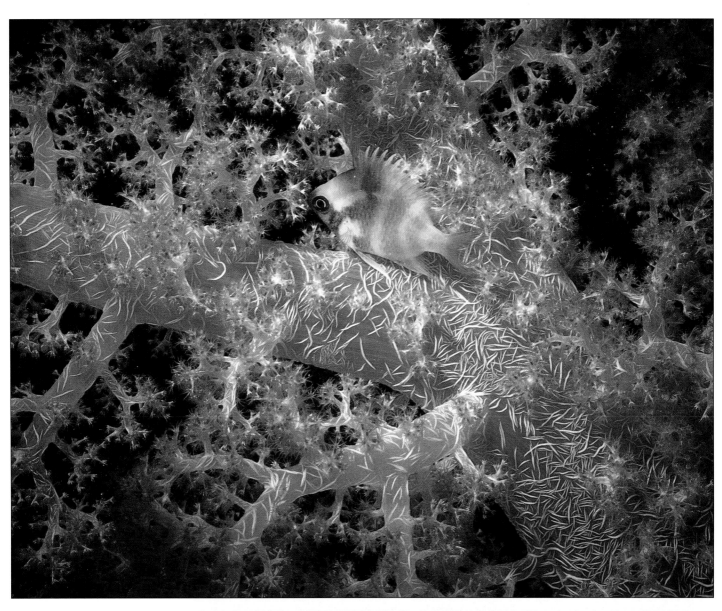

Above: *Revealed in the glare of a flashgun, a dainty damselfish* (Amblyglyphidodon *sp.*) *rests in the branches of a soft coral during a long Red Sea night.*

Right: *As darkness falls, a big-eye* (Priacanthus hamrur) *leaves its refuge in the reef to begin the night's hunt. The damsel shown above has every reason to seek shelter because it may well be a target for this prowling Indo-Pacific species that feeds mainly on small fish as well as taking crustaceans from the rising zooplankton.*

nocturnal predators. Their squirrel-like eyes are an adaptation to their nocturnal mode of life and the gaudy pink or red livery really does act as low-light-level camouflage. This is because water quickly filters out red wavelengths of light, making pink and red appear grey or black in the gloom.

One nocturnal reef fish, the aptly named flashlight fish (*Photoblepharon palpebratus*), confounds all recognized theories of night-time coloration. This tiny, sombre grey fish, common in the Red Sea and Indo-Pacific, sports a pair of elliptical 'flashlights', one beneath each eye. These luminescent organs are filled with bacteria that can generate light by a series of biochemical reactions. The light produced not only helps the fish to hunt but also actively attracts the zooplankton on which it feeds. It is easy to assume that these points of light act as beacons to attract would-be predators, but in reality the reverse is true. Flashlight fishes hunt in shoals, using their glowing lights as an important means of communication, and this tends to confuse predators rather than entice them. Amazingly, these extraordinary fishes can turn their lights on and off at will by manipulating muscles beneath the eye.

As darkness falls, fish are not the only predators in action. The reef itself springs into life, as corals spread their delicate tentacles to trap passing zooplankton with batteries of lethal stinging cells. Crinoids, feathery-armed relatives of the starfishes, make for the highest points on the reef and spread their arms to take a share of the plankton soup.

Herbivorous feeders are generally associated with the daytime reef community, but *Diadema* sea urchins, slow-moving, open-reef animals that defend themselves with long, needle-sharp spines, are an exception. Each night, they migrate from the reef slope up onto the reef flat pastures, now vacated by their daytime occupants, and feed undisturbed on the algae. Brightly coloured sea slugs appear from beneath the coral rubble at the base of the reef edge and join the sea urchins, some species grazing on algae while the carnivorous ones – the nudibranchs – feed on sponges and coral polyps, seemingly immune to the stinging nematocysts.

The nightly saga of the reef unfolds and continues until dawn, while the daytime feeders rest, hopefully to live and feed another day.

Below: *The flashlight fish is one of the most unusual of nocturnal creatures. The large elliptical organs beneath the eyes are sacs filled with bacteria that create biochemical light. The fish can turn these on and off, using them both as a torch and lure.*

Left: *Nudibranchs are mostly nocturnal feeders that spend the daylight hours hiding beneath coral rubble at the base of the reef. This dorid has been photographed during its nightly patrol on the Great Barrier Reef. Most dorid nudibranchs are specialist feeders on sponges and sea squirts.*

Below: *These tropical Atlantic zoanthid anemones withdraw their tentacles during the day.*

Above: *Feathery-armed crinoids unfurl their delicate fronds to capture another night's meal of zooplankton in the Red Sea. These crinoids often form small groups and return to a favoured position every night, clinging by means of tenacious gripping appendages called cirri.*

Below: *As darkness falls, their tentacles reach out to trap the rich clouds of rising plankton.*

The coral web of life

The coral reef and adjacent areas of mangrove swamp and lagoon seem able to support an endless diversity of life. Living organisms claim two essential requirements from their environment: a habitat and a food supply, both available in abundance on the reef and in nearby waters. The fundamental interaction between the members of the huge complex community of animals, plants and bacteria that make up the reef ecosystem is based on the food chain. In fact, this chain is so complex that it is more appropriate to think of it as a food web. The two main ingredients that fuel this system are the energy of the sun and the supply of nutrients in the form of decomposing organic matter. Since these nutrients are a product of the organisms living within the ecosystem, they form the bond that makes the food chain a never-ending process.

The first level of feeders are the plants, the so-called primary producers that use the energy of the sun to convert the nutrients into living matter by the process of photosynthesis. (Just to complicate matters, there are some fishes and invertebrates, called benthic feeders, that feed directly on detritus before it is broken down into nutrients and processed by the plants.) The many herbivorous fishes and other reef animals occupy the next level since they take advantage of the food source represented by the plants. Such herbivores include browsers and grazers that feed on algae and on plant material growing on the reef itself.

The connection between plant life and the next group of feeders is by way of the zooplankton, simple, tiny animal life forms that float in the water and feed on microscopic plants known as the phytoplankton. The zooplankton thus form the basis of a wide range of different feeding strategies. For example, animals such as corals feed directly on the zooplankton (but also rely heavily on their symbiotic relationship with the zooxanthellae in their tissues). Other carnivorous creatures feed on small fishes and invertebrates that have in turn fed upon the zooplankton. At the top of the 'feeding tree' are the large carnivores that feed on a wide range of animals in the other levels of the coral web of life.

This very simple classification does not reflect the true complexity of the reef feeding pattern. There are omnivorous fishes and other animals, for example, that feed on both animal and plant material. Also, feeding patterns and food preferences often change during the life cycle of some members of the reef community; zooplankton-feeding juveniles may become

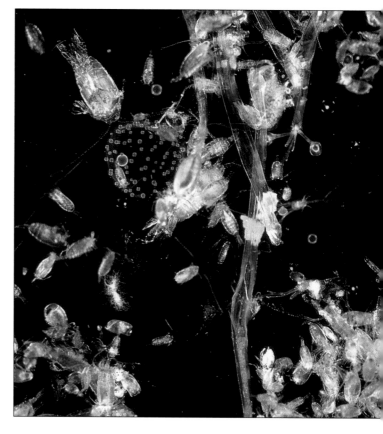

herbivores or carnivores as adults and some species may move from shallow waters to feed in deeper waters at a later stage in their lives.

Reef fishes can be classified into five groups by their adult feeding pattern:

Feeders on algae, such as parrotfishes, surgeonfishes, some damselfishes, and blennies.

Feeders on zooplankton, such as cardinalfishes, fusiliers, some damselfishes, jewelfishes, manta rays and whale sharks.

Feeders on sessile invertebrates, which include the coral and sponge feeders and are represented by butterflyfishes and angelfishes.

Feeders on large invertebrates (e.g. molluscs, crustaceans and echinoderms), such as snappers, stingrays, puffers, boxfishes, triggers, some wrasses and emperors.

Feeders primarily on fish, such as many sharks, barracudas, groupers, moray eels, cornetfishes, needlefishes and hawkfishes.

A number of fish families, such as the triggerfishes, damselfishes, wrasses, puffers and boxfishes, are omnivorous and where these are included above, the category shows their main feeding preference.

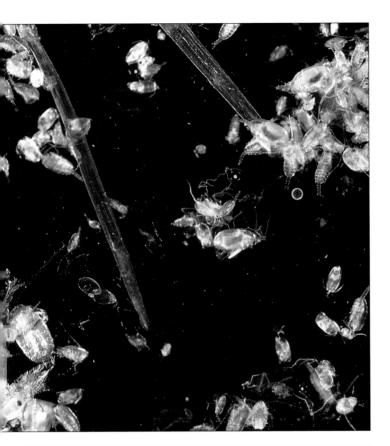

Left: *Plankton, the nourishing soup of the sea. Phytoplankton, the tiny plants in the soup, are consumed by equally tiny animals known as zooplankton, which in turn provide nourishment for many forms of life.*

Below: *The brilliant coloured polyps of this coral extend to feed each night upon the rich horde of zooplankton rising from the depths. Many corals species take advantage of the richer pickings of the night.*

Above: *The emperor angelfish* (Pomacanthus imperator) *is a good example of a specialist feeder on sessile invertebrates. Much of its diet consists of sponges, despite their seemingly unpalatable nature.*

Right: *At the top of the food chain are the sharks, many species of which feed primarily on other fish. Their position cannot be contested in any part of the world's oceans as, once adult, they have no predators – except man.*

Conservation

As we have discovered, coral reefs are very stable environments in which the complex relationship between animals, plants and bacteria can easily be disturbed or destroyed by outside influences, particularly by man. The growth of the marine fishkeeping hobby has presented just such a threat to coral reefs all over the world.

Collecting for the marine aquarium

Almost all the marine fishes sold over the counter are wild caught and are not reared on fish farms or commercially bred in aquariums. Consequently, the export of marine tropical fish for the aquarium trade has become a lucrative business and a major part of the economy of a number of third world tropical countries.

In the past, fish mortality from this trade has been the subject of some concern, largely because of the collecting methods involved, which have included cyanide-based drugs and needlelike harpoons. Justifiably, these methods have received universal condemnation. The alarming and disturbing reports of unscrupulous fish collectors and exporters eventually caused importers to respond in some cases by imposing voluntary bans on imports from the areas concerned.

Delicate cargoes

Marine fishes and invertebrates are very delicate and are not able to cope easily with the varying conditions that occur when they are taken from the wild, transferred to a holding facility and transported halfway across the world to the dealers' tanks. Not surprisingly, attention has become focused not only on the methods used to catch marine creatures but also on the exporters' holding facilities and the conditions the animals must endure in transit. Amid this concern, some exporters' holding facilities have been described as little more than rows of small plastic bowls crowded with fish, unprotected from heat and with little attention being paid to the well-being of the creatures and to the water quality in which they are expected to survive. Despatching fish by air has also come under attack, with concern being shown over delayed and abandoned shipments and the inevitable fatalities involved.

These problems have now largely been addressed, with major importers in Europe and the United States providing capital investment to improve exporters' holding facilities and to overcome transit difficulties. In a number of third world countries, importers have their own representatives on the spot, taking part in the management of the collection and holding facility to ensure that exported fish have the very best chance of surviving and continuing in good health.

The Maldives experience

To gain an insight into how marine fish and invertebrates are collected, held and transported, let us look at the work of a typical collecting and holding facility in the Maldive Islands in the Indian Ocean. This account is based on a real example and reflects true cooperation between a native Maldivian and a European importer of marine tropical fishes.

The modern holding facility in the Maldives reflects a 'high-tech' approach, with close attention being paid to maintaining optimal water quality. The installation consists of 200 large tanks served by a closed, centrally filtered system based on a 27,000-litre(6000 Imp. gallon/7200 US gallon) reservoir. Huge, 4m(13ft)-high wet and dry trickle-fed towers efficiently filter the water using natural nitrifying and denitrifying bacteria and banks of ultraviolet filters combined with a jumbo-sized protein skimmer complete the cleansing process.

Fish and invertebrates are provided for separately so that medications can be applied to the fish side of the system that could prove harmful to the invertebrates. A watchful eye is continually maintained on all the aquariums, not only to monitor the water chemistry, but also to locate any damaged or unhealthy animals among those newly collected. This allows combined quarantine and treatment arrangements to be initiated at the earliest stage. The aim is to have all stocks of fish and invertebrates healthy before shipment. A number of further acclimatization

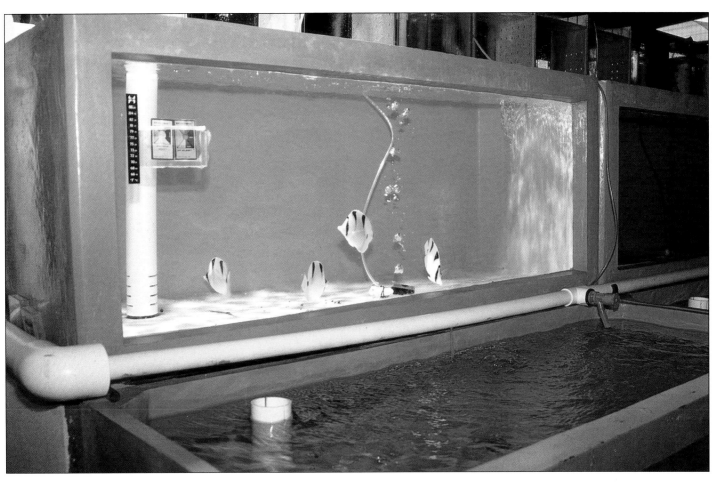

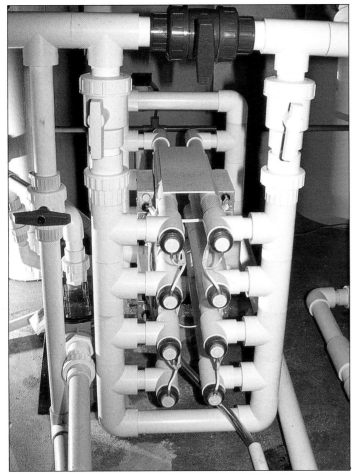

Left: *This modern holding facility is a mass of 'high-tech' equipment to keep all the fish in good condition. Here, banks of ultraviolet light filters efficiently clear the water of any bacteria and other microorganisms introduced from the wild.*

Above: *Large tanks and effective monitoring are essential features of a well-run holding station.*

Below: *Separate tanks for quarantine allow any damaged or unhealthy fish to be treated without risking the main stock.*

processes are also adopted, including the gradual lowering of salinity from the naturally occurring specific gravity of 1.024 down to 1.022. The lower specific gravity is beneficial in that it reduces osmotic stress, promotes higher levels of dissolved oxygen in the water and is more likely to correspond to the level to which the animals will be introduced when exported.

During transportation, the fish are individually packed in plastic bags, charged with oxygen, and placed in cardboard boxes lined with styrofoam. Food is withheld for a period before shipment – to prevent high ammonia levels building up during transit – and shipping is arranged with the minimum of delay. Airline companies provide specially designed heated holds on the aircraft into which the fish boxes are placed and, barring delays, transported fish are easily able to withstand an air journey across the world with the minimum of fatalities.

Fish-collecting methods are equally impressive and could act as a model for any country keen to apply this trade on a caring and sustainable basis. Joining a small group of collectors on one of their trips to a fish-collecting reef, reveals fascinating details of the techniques involved. One of the small, submerged reefs regularly used for fish collecting is less than a 10-minute journey in a motorized Arab dhow from the holding facility. Such areas are designated for the purpose by the Maldivian government as part of their overall management strategy.

Using SCUBA equipment, two divers enter the water and pass through curtains of brightly coloured jewelfish (*Anthias squamipinnis*) as they fin down a coral slope, densely populated with tiny marine tropicals, to a natural sandy depression close to the reef at a depth of about 10m(33ft). One of the divers erects a barrier net 1m(3.3ft) or more high and 10m long across the base of the depression, giving the appearance of a subsea tennis court. Working either singly or in pairs, the diver-collectors herd selected fish down the slope towards the barrier. Each diver carries a number of handnets of various sizes and uses these to trap a selected fish against the barrier, before expertly transferring the catch to a plastic bag attached at the waist. The whole process is very quick and causes minimum stress to the fish.

In less than 30 minutes, the two divers collect 20 or 30 small fish and transfer them to a large plastic tub in a shaded part of the boat. (To avoid the 'bends', the divers take about 40 seconds to ascend from a depth of 10m and this rate of ascent also protects the fish from any decompression

damage.) The normal catch in the area includes butterflyfishes, wrasse, clownfishes and damsels. Collectors can choose from a number of similar designated collecting areas and this particular location had been used for a considerable time without showing any noticeable signs of a decline in the fish population.

Clearly, the Maldivian government is concerned about overexploitation of the marine environment and anxious to avoid any conflict between the ornamental fishery and other uses of the marine environment, such as tourism. Tourist islands in the Maldives offer a wide range of water sports, including SCUBA diving and snorkelling, and these have been designated specifically for these purposes. (It is government policy to protect the marine environment by designating islands and their environs for various purposes, such as tourism, fisheries, urbanization, etc. Although there are no formally assigned park areas as yet, these will surely be nominated in the near future.)

Fish collecting is not allowed within 1000m(3300ft) of these activity parks and such protected areas provide an abundant reserve of fish populations and larvae to replenish areas where fish are collected. Other measures to ensure fish collecting is conducted on a sustainable basis include annual quotas on the number of fish which

Above left: *These fish collectors carry a range of handnets and use each in the best way to herd a selected fish down to the main barrier net and/or trap it against the barrier. They work quickly and with great care.*

Above: *A collector carefully disentangles a spiny fish caught in the soft mesh of the barrier.*

Right: *The final stage of transferring the catch of fish into a large plastic bag carried at the waist.*

can be exported – based on maximum numbers set on earlier years' catches – to ensure that the trade does not expand. Fish counts and surveys of the Maldives reefs are currently being conducted by scientists for the Maldivian Government to provide better information to assist in conserving numbers and fixing quotas.

Adopting such precautions, the exploitation of coral reefs in the form of ornamental fish collecting need not be harmful and can operate on a truly sustainable basis. The methods adopted in the Maldives, with designated areas protecting fish populations and ensuring an abundant reserve of juvenile fish to replenish areas where fish are collected, shows how this can be accomplished in practice. Thus, exploitation need not mean devastation. In fact, as we have seen, conservation can work hand in hand with the sustainable use of a natural resource for commercial gain.

Above: *Proud Seychelles' fishermen display their catch. Overfishing of resident territorial species is all too easy and yet it is also very difficult to encourage local fishermen to fish on a sustainable basis if the sea is their major source of protein.*

Left: *Infestation of the reef by* Diadema *sea urchins often indicates that there is an imbalance in the delicate ecosystem. This may result from the elimination of one of the urchin's predators or from nitrate pollution that encourages the development of lush algal growths on which the sea urchins eagerly feed. This photograph was taken on a Red Sea coral reef.*

Marine parks – the way forward

For thousands of years, the coral reefs of the world were little affected by human impact. Apart from the few native fishermen, who made insignificant demands on the population of fish and other creatures, they were left virtually unscathed. Over the past 40 or so years, this situation has almost reversed, with huge demands being made on the world's reefs and their resources, demands which are damaging to the reefs and which are growing each year.

The exploited reefs

Reefs have become food bowls – exploited for their fish, lobster and other seafood products – and are sources of other consumer items from pearls and ornamental fish to trite mantleshelf curios. The tourist demand to visit coral reef areas is now tremendous; the Caribbean encourages $160 million worth of SCUBA diving tourism from the USA alone each year, attracting large numbers of divers and producing enormous economic benefits to these areas.

The impacts of such pressures can be measured in terms of gross overfishing and damage to the reefs which, in some instances, is total and

Below: *Once common in the Caribbean, the queen conch* (Strombus gigas) *is now severely depleted due to this kind of overfishing. Culture methods under development in the Turks and Caicos may help.*

irreversible. Unfortunately, overfishing is very easy to accomplish, as many of the fishes living on reefs are resident territorial species. Depleting fish populations by concentrated fishing over a large area will effectively prevent recruitment, i.e., the replenishment of the reef by fishes living on reefs adjacent to the affected area.

During the early 1970s, areas of formerly healthy coral reefs in the Egyptian Red Sea became infested with huge populations of *Diadema* sea urchins that damaged the living corals as they foraged for algae. Scientists studying this phenomenon believe that the urchin population explosion may have been caused by the almost total annihilation of a major predator of the urchin, the porcupinefish (*Diodon hystrix*), by collectors for the curio trade. Whatever the cause, the reefs destroyed by the urchins became large areas of algal turf and blue-green algae-covered coral rubble that inhibited the process of recolonization by reef-building corals. Herbivorous fish species were attracted to the area and reef fish normally associated with corals retreated, transforming the reef into a completely different type of habitat populated by an entirely new range of biological communities.

Equally devastating are changes caused in the balance between the species left on the reef following concentrated fishing of one species. Groupers, for example, may be fished out and their prey, safe from predators, will flourish. The prey animals previously controlled by the groupers, having become greater in numbers, then compete with other fish populations for food and living space. Some fishes, particularly the less aggressive species, will fail to respond to such competition. Very quickly the genetic diversity, i.e. the range of species contributing to the 'gene pool', will become smaller and the nature of the reef will inexorably change. It is vital to remember that the mix of the many different species of herbivorous and carnivorous fishes living on the reef is important in maintaining the balance of animals constructing the reef itself.

Scientists working in the Key Largo Coral Reef Marine Sanctuary off the Florida Keys are studying the effects of spearfishing, which in the past has decimated the populations of groupers, the natural predators of reef fishes. Spearfishing is no longer allowed and the authorities have closed parts of the marine sanctuary area to the public for periods to allow the reefs to recover from overuse. Regularly monitoring the reefs and assessing their biological resources has enabled the scientists to record the changes in fish populations and compare them with areas that have not suffered from the impacts of spearfishing. Studying the population diversity due to recruitment from other areas has shown that coral reef biological communities do not necessarily return as anticipated.

Damage to the reefs from tourism occurs in a number of ways. The presence of people in areas adjacent to the reefs, both as transitory tourist populations and those there permanently to cater for them, produces large amounts of waste. The easy way to dispense with this material is to discharge it into the sea, but this and other pollutants can easily spoil the aesthetic qualities of the reef and may cause permanent damage to the fragile ecosystem. Ironically, the very people who appreciate the beauty of the coral reef and its populations of exotic animals, often crossing halfway around the world to enjoy its wonders, may inadvertently become the most significant spoilers of their own paradise.

Diving tourism also inevitably results in minor unintentional damage as divers and snorkellers trample on corals or accidently break off pieces with their clumsy movements. Where controls are not in force, tourist divers are also able to collect trophies and can damage corals in their search for 'souvenirs'. Significant coral damage may also be caused by the anchors of boats carrying divers and snorkellers to the reef sites. Plough-type anchors can be particularly disruptive. Since some corals grow only a few millimetres in a year, the damage caused in moments can take a lifetime to repair.

International responsibility

There are no international bodies or groups with overall responsibility for conserving reefs, and little attention has been paid to protecting corals or other animals existing within the world's coral ecosystems. Not a single coral fish and only a handful of reef animals are listed as endangered species, despite evidence of massive depletion of some species. Many of the designated protected reef areas of the world are protected not for their natural beauty or to prevent any harm coming to them but solely for economic reasons. Since the coral reef has become a resource, it makes good business sense to manage such a resource on an economic and sustainable basis.

The economic and commercial benefits from coral reefs may have no connection with the higher principles of conserving ecological processes and life support systems or with preserving genetic diversity, but they can be the key in encouraging such thinking by politicians and planners and in alerting public attention to the need for conservation. Designated protected reefs with regulations that allow them to remain reasonably intact will therefore be preserved if they are well managed, despite – and even because of – the economic motive.

There are always alternative exploitations of most resources, and reefs are no exception. Far worse pressures than tourism include coral mining for building materials, drilling for oil, and using reefs and cays as a dumping ground for toxic and other wastes. The increasing awareness of the need to protect the natural wonders of the reef from such impacts caused an outcry in Australia during

Below: *As diving tourism grows in popularity, many tropical areas are reaping the economic benefits of the boom. Far from threatening the reefs, such developments help to keep them in pristine condition. Since many of the best diving locations have marine parks, these areas are now being protected from exploitation – for now and into the future.*

the late 1960s and early 1970s when proposals to drill for oil on the Great Barrier Reef moved sufficiently strong public opinion to cancel the proposed operation.

Coral reef parks can benefit both reefs and people, the benefits to man translating roughly into recreational tourism and fishery management. Less obvious benefits are the preventative effect of reefs on coastal erosion and the value of reef parks in providing opportunities for research and education. The major benefit coincides with the main objective of a coral reef park, i.e. to maintain the quality of the environment and to ensure sustainable uses of its resources.

The benefits of marine parks

Managing coral reef areas under the protective umbrella of marine park regulations has arrested the deterioration of coral reefs in many parts of the world. Hanauma Bay on the island of Oahu in the Hawaiian Islands (see page 194) and the John

Above: *Scientists play an vital role in conducting biological surveys of the reefs before marine parks are designated. Using an electric mini-sub, these marine biologists are collecting 'benchmark' data on current status.*

Below: *Using SCUBA equipment to collect crayfish to satisfy the demands for gourmet seafood at tourist hotels can quickly deplete the crayfish population of the reef – a prime example of deliberate overfishing.*

Pennekamp Coral Reef State Park in Florida are good examples of the benefits of marine park regulations. Reefs throughout the Indo-Pacific, including the Red Sea, Indian Ocean locations such as Kenya and the Seychelles, and far eastern reefs, including the coastal reefs of Singapore and the Great Barrier Reef of Australia, are included in extensive marine national parks. There is quite a race on in the Caribbean to locate and designate marine parks and more than 80 percent of the diving tourism is now attracted to islands with coral reef park status.

Fortunately, many of the impacts caused in the past by overfishing and tourism are being addressed and rectified. Managing reefs in the manner that a farmer would manage his fields

reaps real benefits. The farmer does not kill off all of his stock in one year or heap trash on his fields. Regrettably, fishermen traditionally do not leave any fish they could possibly catch because this would just be leaving them for another to take. And using the sea as a dumping ground has always been considered fair, adopting the 'out of sight out of mind' philosophy and citing the large dilution factor the sea represents as equal to dealing with any amount of solid or liquid waste tipped into it.

Parks allow fisheries zones to be applied which can be regulated in order that some zones can be laid 'fallow', using the farmer's terminology, to allow the fish populations time to recover. Replenishment can be brought about by planned recruitment of fish stocks and animals from

Above: *A diver drills a hole in the reef at the Princess Alexandra Park in the Turks and Caicos as part of a scheme to install permanent mooring buoys. These will provide a positive way of preventing anchor damage by tourist boats, a system first developed in the John Pennekamp Coral Reef State Park in Florida.*

Right: *The permanent buoy system is designed to avoid damage to the reef by offering surface mooring buoys linked to these stainless steel bolts anchored deep into the coral rock. These and the attached lines are capable of holding a large boat, even in high winds – just one of many schemes to protect the coral reefs.*

adjacent areas, or it may involve deliberate seeding of the area with juveniles produced from mariculture schemes or relocation from other areas that are good natural 'nurseries' but are not able to support large adult populations.

Tourist impacts have been largely overcome by regulating waste disposal to avoid pollution and by a package of measures to avoid diver tourism damage. (Hanauma Bay is a good example of this.) Swimming, diving and snorkelling are encouraged, but a number of activities that would stress the reef are prohibited. Anchoring on the reef is replaced by the option of using permanently buoyed sites, where boats can attach to a buoy rather than dropping an anchor. Extensive programmes to provide permanent buoys are in operation all over the world. These involve drilling holes on the reef, away from living corals, securing stainless steel eye bolts and attaching buoyed lines to a surface buoy.

Regulations prohibit the removal or damage of any natural reef features and visitors to the parks are given guidance to enable them to 'leave the marine park as beautiful as they find it'. At any one time, perhaps 20 percent of a reef park may be

Above: *Coastal strip development can often be very detrimental to the coral reef communities immediately adjacent. Here in Indonesia, this aerial photo shows that the reef is being destroyed by dredging and harbour building. There will be a risk of further damage by pollution and the effects of changing the water flow around the reef.*

closed to the public to allow the living resources to recover from overuse. By tourist education and constraints on the use of the park, lush underwater scenery can be maintained.

Before designation, scientists play a vital role by conducting marine biological surveys of the reefs to provide valuable benchmark information on their current status, the location of the best areas and those most under threat. Sites are chosen for continuous environmental monitoring studies to keep a check for any changes, good or detrimental.

The future of the world's coral reefs is certainly improved with the introduction of marine parks and, more importantly, there is a greater awareness of the value of these wonderful natural areas. Reef resources can be tapped and utilized in a sustainable manner and provide a bounty for the foreseeable future. It is in our hands!

Creating a Coral Reef Aquarium

Above: *A fully established tropical marine aquarium can be a magnificent display of colourful reef fishes and invertebrates.*

It is easy to understand how, in the enclosed system of a home aquarium, it is difficult to simulate the exacting requirements of many coral reef fishes and invertebrates and why there is an ever-present need to maintain high water quality in order to succeed. For example, despite all the advances in keeping coral reef invertebrates in captivity, attempts to keep stony corals successfully have met with relatively limited success. It must be said that, even using the most sophisticated marine life-support systems, it is by no means easy to keep stony corals alive and healthy for prolonged periods in the home aquarium. With this in mind, it seems inadvisable to take them from their natural environment in the first place, since many stony corals take a long time to establish colonies in the wild and suffer accordingly when they are disrupted. In the interests of

conserving these animals and the beautiful reefs they build, it seems only right not to encourage their collection for the hobbyist market. There are plenty of other fascinating reef fishes and invertebrates, including soft corals and anemones, that will prosper in captivity and provide a truly rewarding and long-lasting display in a home aquarium.

Here, we review some of the important practical points to consider when setting up an aquarium to house reef fishes, suitable corals, anemones and a wide range of other reef invertebrates.

Selecting a tank
To reduce any problems of water management, the sensible first step is to select as large an aquarium as you can accommodate, and certainly one not less than 90cm long x 45cm deep x 30cm wide

(36x18x12in) holding approximately 104 litres(23 Imp. gallons/27 US gallons). Alternatively, the aquarium need not be over large if you can connect it to a separate reservoir that would effectively increase the working volume of water. In simple terms, the larger the amount of water, the more stable the conditions will remain and the more closely you will be able to duplicate the natural reef environment in the aquarium.

Water temperature
The ideal temperature range for the home aquarium containing coral reef fishes and invertebrates is 23-25°C(73-77°F). This is compatible with the majority of tropical

creatures and modern heating systems are well able to maintain these conditions. Temperatures above the optimum range can easily cause distress to sessile invertebrates, such as anemones, in the aquarium. This arises because oxygen levels fall as water temperature increases and, without the optimum levels of dissolved oxygen found in their natural environment, the creatures are affected by respiratory distress. This can be a problem during the summer, when high ambient temperatures and the warmth from bright tank lighting can raise the water temperature to 32°C(90°F) and beyond. To guard against these temperature surges, site the aquarium out of direct sunlight and arrange some form of ventilation system to cool the lights. The small extractor fans primarily designed to cool computers and other electronic equipment are ideal for this purpose. Fitted with a suitable thermostatic control, these are excellent for ventilating an aquarium hood containing lights.

Salinity of the water

It is vital to establish and maintain the correct salinity in the aquarium. Salinity is normally quoted in terms of specific gravity, which is simply the ratio of the density of a solution compared to the density of distilled water at the same temperature. Specific gravity readings between 1.020 and 1.025 are typical for the marine aquarium, but remember that the higher the specific gravity the greater the impact upon the metabolism of the creatures because they lose water from the body tissues by osmosis. (Osmosis is the natural process that strives to 'even up' the concentration of a solution on both sides of a thin membrane – in this case, the gill membranes or similar 'biological boundaries' – by the passage of pure water. The more concentrated the solution surrounding the creatures, the more tendency there is for water to pass out of them to even up the osmotic balance. The physical and physiological systems that animals use to cope with these gradients can be grouped under the umbrella term of osmoregulation.)

Be sure to test the salinity regularly with a hydrometer (the swing-needle types are convenient and accurate), as salt concentrations can rise rapidly through evaporation if a good seal is not formed between the sliding covers or condensation tray fitted in the top of the tank. Keep a constant watch on the situation and do not wait until the water recedes several centimetres or more before topping up with fresh (not saline) water; salinity changes must be made gradually to avoid stressing most invertebrates kept in the aquarium.

The ideal pH level

Maintaining the correct pH level (degree of acidity or alkalinity) is another important consideration for the well-being of most reef fishes and invertebrates. It is critical in the case of shelled molluscs, echinoderms and crustaceans, which must have a ready supply of calcium carbonate in the water. (The pH scale is a logarithmic one from 0 to 14, with the neutral point at 7 and values below 7 being acidic and above 7 being alkaline. The logarithmic nature of the scale means, for example, that pH5 is ten times more acidic than pH6 but one hundred times more acidic than pH7.) If possible, maintain the pH level between 8.0 and 8.3. As the normal tendency is for the pH level to fall, when setting up the aquarium include a calcium-rich substrate of coral sand over a layer of crushed sea mollusc shell or commercial equivalent.

As a lowering of the pH is often due to the acid reaction of dissolved carbon dioxide or to the decomposition of organic matter overloading the system, try to avoid this at all costs and maintain strict hygiene.

Below: *An orange dwarf angelfish and a bright blue damsel share their tank with soft corals and other invertebrates. To maintain these marine creatures in good health needs high standards of water management and very careful attention to lighting.*

Making regular water changes of 25 percent of the tank volume each month will stave off the permanent lowering of pH that occurs as the water ages, but do not attempt to make amends more quickly by changing larger proportions of water at any one time. Add the new (saline) water slowly.

Filtration of the water

The value of various filtration systems has been debated long and hard in aquarium circles, and there is no doubt that effective filtration is really essential in keeping water in peak condition. Several types of filtration can be employed in a marine aquarium and, as many invertebrates are extremely sensitive to water conditions, this aspect of water management is perhaps the main secret of success.

Methods of filtration fall into three main categories: mechanical, chemical and biological. Most aquariums need to use all of these methods in one form or another.

Mechanical filters trap and remove suspended matter from the aquarium and prevent chemical and biological filters clogging. Spun nylon floss and dacron are commonly used as a filter medium, often with a prefilter of ceramic pieces, plastic sheeting or netting in advance of the floss to prevent larger debris carried in the water from blocking up the main filter.

Chemical filters are commonly based on activated carbon, which removes dissolved waste from the water by adsorbing the ions onto its large surface area. (Adsorption is a kind of chemical 'attraction' process, as opposed to the simple mechanical process of absorption.) Other chemical filtration media include synthetic adsorption pads custom-made to fit inside canister-type filters. Both mechanical and chemical media are often placed in alternate layers in the body of a canister filter. It is essential to renew these regularly to avoid toxic materials building up and dissolving back into the water.

Biological filters cleanse the water by harnessing the biochemical action of living bacteria to break down toxic substances. Ammonia (NH_3/NH_4^+) and nitrite (NO_2^-) are the main culprits, resulting as waste from the invertebrates or fish in the aquarium. Anemones and crustaceans, particularly, are capable of producing large quantities of these harmful chemicals.

The most widely used form of biological filter uses the tank substrate as a filter medium. A plate at the bottom of the tank allows water to flow downwards (or upwards in so-called 'reverse-flow' systems) through the substrate and be 'purified' by the colonies of bacteria that develop naturally on the surface of the substrate particles. Other designs involve enclosing a similarly 'biologically active' medium in the body of a canister filter or in trays above or below the tank.

Whichever form of biological filtration you install, it is most important that the filter medium receives a constant flow of well-oxygenated water. This is because the bacteria involved in the breakdown process are aerobic, i.e. require oxygen to thrive, and will die if insufficient oxygen is present. Submersible impeller-driven pumps are

excellent for setting up a suitable water flow. Advanced forms of biological filtration often employ an above-water, trickle-fed system that allows a free flow of atmospheric oxygen to reach the bacteria. In these trickle filters, a much larger bacterial population can be maintained than would be possible using a similarly sized filter bed below water.

Although not widely used in the home aquarium, algal filters are a type of biological filter that has proved to be highly efficient in public aquariums, where highly sensitive marine invertebrates have been

Below: Sabellid fanworms are fascinating subjects for the aquarium, but choose any fish with care – they may eat the worms!

Above: *These bushy gorgonian sea whips from the Caribbean are adapted to thrive in the relatively hostile conditions of turbid shallow water subject to changes in temperature and salinity. Not surprisingly, this soft coral is ideal for the aquarium.*

successfully established. Some installations have dispensed entirely with conventional bacterial filtration and aeration and instead circulate the aquarium water through shallow trays sometimes referred to as 'algal turf scrubbers'. These trays contain plastic screens that support matlike growths of filamentous algae and are illuminated each night for several hours. The plants photosynthesize and rapidly remove ammonia and carbon dioxide, while adding oxygen and restoring pH to its optimum level. Such a system has similarities with natural conditions on coral reefs, where chemical and nutrient exchanges occur between open-ocean reef and adjacent lagoon/mangrove areas.

Providing water movement
Many marine invertebrates are relatively immobile and need strong water movement to provide the high oxygen levels they require. As food is normally also carried to them by this means, water movement in the aquarium performs a vital function. A powerful air pump supplying a number of airstones, or a well-placed submersible pump delivering water from a spray bar above the surface, can provide the necessary kind of movement and keep the water surface turbulent. Although the

fine mist of bubbles from an airstone looks impressive, it is water movement at the surface that provides the most efficient way of introducing oxygen into the water.

Lighting the aquarium

The final ingredient we need to add is the correct type of lighting. It is very important to the well-being of a large number of invertebrates, such as anemones and clams, with zooxanthellae in their tissues, that they receive adequate light levels. Adequate in this context means light of sufficient intensity and of the correct spectral wavelength. There is still a lot of experimentation taking place to determine the optimum levels for both these parameters in the aquarium. What is certain is that by using artificial light sources it is virtually impossible to get anywhere close to the brilliance and quality of light found in a natural tropical marine environment.

Research so far shows that high-pressure mercury vapour and metal-halide lamps provide the kind of light intensity required and are close to the spectral range of daylight. With a beam angle of about 20°, mercury vapour lamps offer an intense light

source over a small area. This means that you will need to mount these lamps close to the water, and a 90-watt lamp will illuminate an area of only about $900cm^2(1ft^2)$. As you might imagine, the number of lamps required to completely illuminate an aquarium is, in most cases, impractical, and normally they are used for spotlighting light-loving animals in one part of the aquarium. Supplementary lighting in the form of balanced daylight and actinic blue fluorescent tubes are often used in conjunction with high-pressure mercury vapour lamps to provide overall lighting that will show colours to best advantage.

Metal-halide lights must be regarded as the ultimate light source for our purpose as technology stands at the moment. They deliver almost one and a half times the light output of high-pressure mercury vapour lamps and radiate light close to the daylight spectrum. A 150-watt lamp will illuminate an area of approximately $1800cm^2(2ft^2)$ with very high-quality light.

Research into new lighting systems continues at a great pace and in contrast to the past, when developments were mainly linked to research associated with the quest

for ideal illumination in commercial greenhouses, research now also concentrates on lighting systems specifically for aquarium use. These developments are generally geared towards finding fluorescent tubes that will provide bright, correctly balanced light over a long time without fading. In this connection, a new fluorescent tube has been developed using a unique blend of the most efficient rare-earth-activated phosphors that promises all of these features and could prove to be ideal for aquarium, and especially marine aquarium, lighting.

Light intensity is only part of the equation, however, as this must be balanced with the correct duration, whatever system you choose. Trial and error is the only way of determining your exact requirements, but it is likely to be in the order of 12 hours a day at least to be adequate to sustain your reef aquarium.

Below: *Large* Heteractis *anemones such as this invariably play host to a number of clownfishes in the wild. This symbiotic relationship can be transferred to the aquarium and makes an ideal centrepiece.*

INTRODUCTION

Part Two: Coral Reefs of the World

In Part One, we discovered that coral reefs are constructed by tiny anemonelike animals and the immense structures they build are mainly the limestone remains of earlier generations covered with a thin veneer of living coral polyps. We also discovered that in the past, changes in the relationship of the sea level to adjacent land masses and the topography of the seabed have resulted in reefs of a variety of forms, from offshore barriers to doughnut-shaped atolls. We learned that the wide diversity of life forms on coral reefs interact, one with another, to produce a living web of life. This can be likened to a huge and complicated jigsaw in which all the pieces fit together to form a picture – literally, the coral reef ecosystem.

Armed with this clearer understanding of the miracle of nature we call a coral reef, we widen our horizons in Part Two of the book and embark upon a voyage of discovery around the world. Here, we glimpse in more detail the many spectacular examples of coral reefs and the rich variety of life they sustain. Our journey takes us to six locations: The Caribbean, The Maldives, The Red Sea, Kenya, The Great Barrier Reef and Hawaii. This is by no means a comprehensive selection of the world's coral reef areas, but it is representative enough to allow us to compare and contrast the marine life beneath the warm waters in six different spots in the major oceans. These regional chapters are presented in five sections:

The **main text** provides an overview of the reef location, its geography and the features that are interesting or unique to the area. The text also explores the fascinating interactions taking place between the wide range of life forms typical of the region. Early on in each section, a large map shows the region under review, marked with appropriate place names, the location of the major reefs and where marine parks are planned or already designated.

A **diving profile** summarises details of the weather conditions throughout the year (including sea temperature ranges at different seasons), the facilities available for tourist divers, the quality and range of diving opportunities the area has to offer, plus a word about any relevant conservation measures, particularly with respect to marine parks and any rules that apply.

The **dive location reports** reflect the experience of diving in specific locations within the area. Many of these are written in firsthand terms and are based on the author's own dives in these places. These reports feature appropriate photographs and sketch maps linked in style to the large area maps. These reports reflect the sensations of discovery and excitement that exploring the undersea world offers everyone who literally takes the plunge.

Each section includes two **aquarium care** panels that examine individual fish families in turn and offer practical advice on keeping a representative species successfully in the home aquarium. These panels build on the basic advice given in the section on 'Creating a Coral Reef Aquarium' on pages 68-71. Although these panels feature species found in the relevant geographical area, they also consider (and sometimes illustrate) other species of the family found in quite different locations.

Each chapter, except Hawaii, contains at least one **invertebrate life** panel. Here, we try to offset the imbalance we have knowingly introduced into the book by majoring on fishes. These panels not only explore the basic invertebrate groups in a biological sense, but also provide practical guidance for anyone seeking to keep a selection of invertebrates in a marine aquarium. Here, as in the aquarium care panels, we give due weight to the conservation angle.

The areas where coral reefs abound are marvellous places to visit. Tropical sunshine, blue skies, crystal waters and beautiful palm-fringed beaches are not merely fantasy images but the stuff of everyday life in these locations. If this book – and especially Part Two – does nothing else but instill in you the urge to visit these places, then our job is well done. For anyone able to don an aqualung, or even just fins, mask and snorkel, the coral world awaits your own personal journey of discovery. And for those who prefer a more leisurely exploration of the world's coral reefs – from the comfort of an armchair – Part Two provides a fascinating insight into one of the last frontiers left on earth. But remember, above all else, that the beauty of the coral reefs is mirrored in equal measure by their fragility. Let us strive to safeguard them for future generations to enjoy.

Above: *The very first impression of any coral reef is the bewildering array of colourful life.*

Right: *A closer look at these life forms reveals a wide diversity of fishes, here a Malabar grouper.*

Below: *Invertebrate life forms are just as colourful, but perhaps not all as easy to identify as this* Fromia *starfish.*

CORAL REEFS OF THE WORLD

Caribbean

'A unique storehouse of marine life'

The Caribbean has long been famous for its sun, sand and clear waters. With the advent of SCUBA diving tourism, what at one time would have been a beach holiday is now transformed into an exciting undersea excursion. Each season, more than $160 million is spent on diving tourism in this area in waters guaranteed to provide prolific and diverse life. This is due in no small part to the formation of the many marine national parks created to protect the coral reefs and maintain them in pristine condition.

In large parts of the Caribbean, the coral reefs are splendid examples of tropical West Atlantic reefs and present endless vistas of thriving stony corals, sea fans and sponges. A major feature of these reefs is the wide diversity of life forms that make up their structure. Multicoloured colonies of sponges are often as prominent as the stony corals they accompany, interspersed with peacock-hued sea fans and feathery sea whips.

A unique storehouse of marine life

The marine life of the Caribbean is particularly distinctive, with a large number of invertebrates and fish species being unique to the area. In fact, up to 90 hard coral species and twice that number of fish species are found only in the Caribbean.

To understand why the marine life of the Caribbean is so special, we need to venture a little into the origins of the area. The evolution of the Caribbean is a fascinating subject and started at an early stage in the development of the Earth as we know it today. The formation of the great continent of the Americas effectively prevented waterborne contact with the Pacific Ocean and, because many of the animals associated with tropical coral reefs are strictly territorial, the vast

Schooling blue-striped grunts.

distances across the Atlantic Ocean hindered contact with the tropical East Atlantic and Indo-Pacific. Cold sea conditions to the north and south also acted as an inhibiting factor to the growth of reef-building corals, and colonization by the tropical Caribbean fish species and the West Atlantic reefs became restricted to the relatively small area of today.

The fish that inhabit these reefs are its greatest attraction. Like their counterparts in other parts of the tropical world, Caribbean reefs are home to a wide range of fish species that are fascinating in their behaviour and range in appearance from the brilliantly colourful to the fascinatingly grotesque. They have evolved together with the coral to form an extremely complex and integrated system. As we have discovered, species and families of fishes can be grouped by their behaviour into those that are active during the day and those active by night. Feeding habits separate the herbivores from the predators and within these categories fishes are adapted to fully exploit the various food sources available on the reef. Here, we review the fishes typical of the Caribbean area.

Parrotfish, groupers and wrasses

The classic daytime grazers of the Caribbean reefs are undoubtedly the colourful parrotfish. Like 'marine cattle', they use their chisel-like teeth to scrape algae from the surface of the coral and in the process turn large amounts of coral into fine sand. These colourful herbivorous fishes abound in the shallows and are often the dominant members of the reef community. By their industrious efforts, parrotfishes have unwittingly become one of the principal causes of reef erosion and a major contributor to the beautiful white coral sand beaches that fringe the Caribbean waters.

Above: *The most common grouper found in Caribbean waters is the red hind* (Epinephelus guttatus). *This species, small by grouper standards, reaches less than 50cm(20in) when fully mature and is a favourite with fishermen.*

Left: *The Nassau grouper,* (Epinephelus striatus) *is a master of disguise, able to change colour and markings to match its surroundings. This beefy specimen is almost 1m(39in) long and weighs perhaps 20kg(44lb).*

Above: *The vibrant coney* (Cephalopholis fulva) *passes through a number of colour phases (one of them a bright yellow) before acquiring the adult coloration of red with blue spots as here.*

Among the carnivorous fishes, the groupers are permanent residents of most Caribbean reefs. They never stray far from the coral and are often found standing sentinel at the entrance to their lairs, hopeful of bagging a passing meal in the form of a small fish or crustacean. There are over 400 species in the grouper family (Serranidae) worldwide, the Caribbean species ranging in size from the 318kg(700lb) jewfish (*Epinephelus itajara*) to the diminutive royal gramma (*Gramma loreto*), weighing less than 28gm(1oz).

Groupers are remarkable for two reasons. Some groupers spend the first six or seven years of their lives as females, after which there follows a period when they are both male and female. The final years of their lives are spent as fully mature males, although they still have the remnants of egg-producing organs. The other unusual feature of groupers is their ability to rapidly change colour to match their surroundings. Some species, typified by the Nassau grouper (*Epinephelus striatus*), can pass through a number of colour phases, from white through brown to blue and, by darkening areas of the body, produce vertical stripes and bands. As in many other fishes, colour can vary at different stages of life. The coney (*Cephalopholis fulva*), for example, is beautifully marked red with bright blue spots as an adult but can pass through a bright yellow phase as a juvenile.

If the parrotfishes are the cattle of the reef then the wrasses are the sparrows, busily flitting from coral head to coral head. These opportunistic feeders are constantly in search of food and will follow divers in huge shoals, hopeful that a diver's fins might dislodge a piece of coral and reveal a meal in the form of small shrimps or worms.

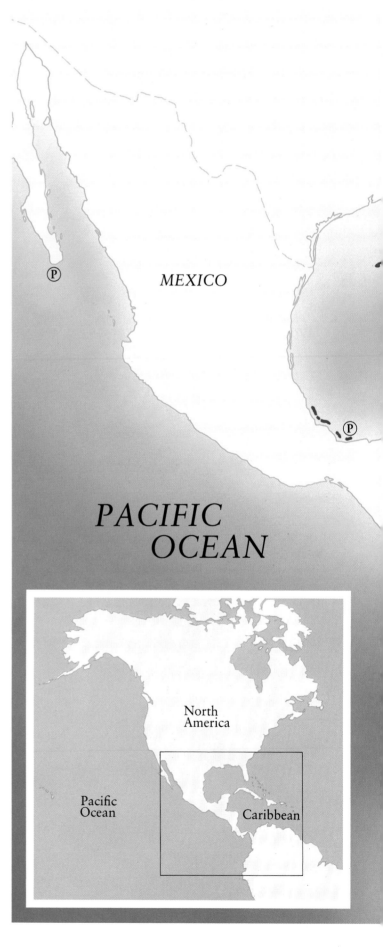

MEXICO

PACIFIC OCEAN

North America

Pacific Ocean

Caribbean

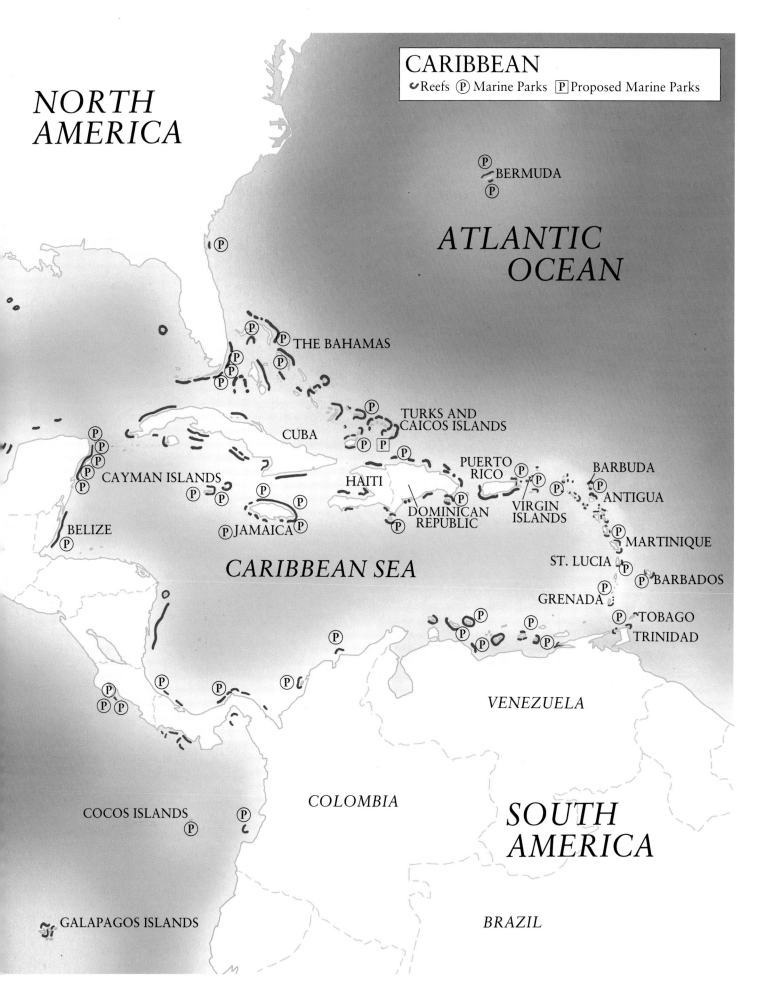

CARIBBEAN
Reefs ⓟ Marine Parks ⓟ Proposed Marine Parks

NORTH AMERICA

ATLANTIC OCEAN

BERMUDA

THE BAHAMAS

CUBA

TURKS AND CAICOS ISLANDS

CAYMAN ISLANDS

HAITI

PUERTO RICO

BARBUDA

ANTIGUA

BELIZE

JAMAICA

DOMINICAN REPUBLIC

VIRGIN ISLANDS

MARTINIQUE

ST. LUCIA

BARBADOS

GRENADA

TOBAGO

TRINIDAD

CARIBBEAN SEA

VENEZUELA

COCOS ISLANDS

COLOMBIA

SOUTH AMERICA

GALAPAGOS ISLANDS

BRAZIL

Angelfishes and butterflyfishes

Among the best-known of the Caribbean reef fishes are the angelfishes (Pomacanthidae family). All species have disc-shaped, laterally compressed bodies and are often very colourful. They differ from their close relatives the butterflyfishes in the presence of a distinctive stout spine at the base of the gill cover. All species are part of the daytime reef community. They are often highly territorial and are generally found in pairs, each pair occupying a specific territory. These territories are fairly small, and divers can usually encounter the same pair at a given location on each and every visit. Although adult angelfishes are common on the reef, few juveniles are encountered there. Mangroves close to reefs commonly form the nursery area for many reef fish species, as well as the juveniles of their predators. Juvenile angelfish are not usually observed in large numbers in such locations, however. The largest numbers occur in channels passing through cays and in association with small coral outcrops in the back reef lagoon.

Seven species of angelfish are common to the Caribbean and tropical West Atlantic reefs, all of them unique to the area. The grey angelfish (*Pomacanthus arcuatus*), named for its muted grey coloration, is the largest and most common species and a feature of many Caribbean reefs. It is superficially similar to the French angelfish (*P. paru*), a much more handsome species sporting black scales edged with gold.

Above: *A French angelfish displaying full adult coloration. Angelfish are very bold and inquisitive reef fishes. They often approach close to divers and make admirable subjects for photography.*

DIVING PROFILE Caribbean

CLIMATE

Air temperature range:
  23-30°C(73-86°F)
Sea temperature range:
  16-21°C(61-70°F)

The climate varies considerably, from the Bahamas in the north to Trinidad in the south. The northern Caribbean, from the Bahamas to the Turks and Caicos Islands, is affected by winter cold fronts from the Atlantic Ocean. Air temperatures can fall to 23°C(73°F) in winter and sea temperatures can be down to a chilly 16°C(61°F). The southern Caribbean enjoys fairly constant conditions all year around, with air temperatures of 28-30°C(82-86°F) and a comfortable sea temperature of 21°C(70°F). Generally speaking, low flat islands tend to be hot and dry; mountainous islands, wet and humid.

FACILITIES

Facilities in the north reflect the strong American diving tourism market and are excellent, if a little crowded at times. Major decompression chambers are located at Miami Florida, Grand Bahama, and Providenciales in the Turks and Caicos Islands. In the south, the facilities are not so well organized, but the diving more than makes up for any shortcomings.

DIVE RATING

It is very difficult to rate such a large and variable area but, at its best, Caribbean diving can be excellent, with a number of dive sites that rate among the best in the world. Wall diving, drift diving and wreck diving sites are available. The Turks and Caicos wall dives, for example, are perhaps the finest available. (See the dive location report, DIVING THE WALL, on page 88.)

CONSERVATION

The Caribbean island governments are starting to realize that the most popular diving areas are those based on marine parks, causing quite a race to install parks and conserve areas for divers. Established parks can be found in Tobago and Belize in the south, and in the Cayman Islands, Bahamas and the Turks and Caicos in the north of the region. Marine parks are undoubtedly the best locations to dive in Caribbean waters.

Above: *The muted colour of the grey angelfish contrasts with the yellow reverse of the pectoral fins, which it uses to signal its mate of any approaching danger.*

Left: *The rock beauty (Holacanthus tricolor) has vivid, easily recognizable markings. Although small, it is highly territoral and generally occurs singly.*

The lovely queen angel (*Holacanthus ciliaris*), beautifully garbed in brilliant colours, derives its royal status from the electric blue crown it carries majestically on its head. This angelfish has the most lavish colouring of the Caribbean species and is often sought after as a photographic subject. Two other *Holacanthus* species are also represented, the delightful rock beauty (*H. tricolor*), with its bright yellow-orange head and tail contrasting with the velvety black of the body, and the blue angel (*H. isabelita*), a less brilliant and rare cousin of the queen angel.

Two pygmy angelfishes complete the numbers, the flameback pygmy angelfish (*Centropyge aurantonotus*) and the cherubfish (*C. argi*). Both of these species are relatively recent finds due to their retiring nature and distribution, deep in the recesses of vertical cliffs 15 or more metres (over 50ft) below the surface.

Angelfish are curious and fearless creatures, invariably discovered nibbling at sponges and seemingly unconcerned at the diver's approach. Unfortunately, this lack of fear has contributed to their extermination in areas where spearfishing is allowed, and the marine parks are the best locations to view these beautiful fishes. (See pages 63-67 for more information on marine parks.)

The attractive butterflyfishes are equally popular with fish-watching snorkellers and divers visiting Caribbean reefs. The four-eyed butterflyfish (*Chaetodon capistratus*) is the most common species. It is an expert in the art of deception, employing bold black-and-white stripes to break up its body outline. A large ocellated black spot at the base of the tail is presumed to be a false eye which, combined with an obliterative black bar through the true eye, helps to confuse an attacking predator. The banded butterflyfish (*C. striatus*) also successfully obscures its outline with a series of vertical, bold, zebralike black stripes, one of which runs through the eye.

Above: *The bold markings of banded butterflyfishes disrupt their outlines to confuse would-be predators.*

Below: *The secretive long snout butterflyfish (Prognathodes aculeatus) is regarded as rare in shallow Caribbean waters.*

AQUARIUM CARE

Angelfishes

Angelfishes belong to the family Pomacanthidae, which is closely related to the butterflyfish family (Chaetodontidae) and provides some of the most attractive additions to the aquarium, with aristocratic names such as queen, emperor, regal and royal empress aptly describing their majestic bearing.

Angelfishes are not for beginners. Although easier to keep than butterflyfishes, for example, they still demand good water quality and many can be finicky feeders if conditions are not to their liking. The ground rules for keeping these species must include their intolerance of their own kind. This limits the number that can be kept together, although dwarf *Centropyge* species are easier in this respect than other genera.

The queen angel (*Holacanthus ciliaris*) makes a stunning addition to the larger aquarium, where it can easily reach 30cm(12in) or more in length. Unlike many angelfishes, it is not difficult to feed, quickly responding to a mixed diet of frozen meaty foods supplemented with live *Tubifex* worms (thoroughly cleaned) and brineshrimp, plus some green foodstuffs. Ensure that the water quality is good and aquarium conditions are stable to enable this species to develop its best colours for you to enjoy. Like many angelfishes, however, the queen angel is extremely intolerant of its own kind and is best kept as a single specimen or in twosomes, if you should be lucky enough to be offered a mated pair for your aquarium.

Finally, remember that fishes imported from the Caribbean are accustomed to sea water with a specific gravity of 1.026 and need to be acclimatized to the much lower 1.022 normally found in aquariums maintained for Indo-Pacific species. Also, fishes from the Caribbean may not have resistance to some viral diseases common to fishes originating from the Indo-Pacific.

Below: *The Queen angelfish (Holacanthus ciliaris) is without doubt the most eye-catching of the angelfish for the aquarium. It is easy to keep and rewards care with brilliant coloration and constant activity. As with many tropical fishes kept in the aquarium, the lighting conditions can change the appearance of the body colours. The juveniles of this stately species are equally attractive as this adult, adorned with royal blue lines on a dark blue, gold-finned body.*

Above: *Angelfishes, such as this elegant Pacific lemonpeel angelfish (Centropyge flavissimus), often make ideal aquarium subjects. Be sure to provide good water conditions and an ample supply of algae.*

Left: *The Indo-Pacific regal angelfish (Pygoplites diacanthus) requires top water conditions in the aquarium and is really only suitable for experienced aquarists.*

The nocturnal soldierfishes

Like other tropical reef areas of the world, the Caribbean is home to fishes adapted to feeding at night and resting during the day. Of the nocturnal species, the blackbar soldierfish (*Myripristis jacobus*) is most notable. As we found earlier on page 52, soldierfishes have large eyes to cope with living and finding food in dimly lit conditions and bright red coloration to act as low-light-level camouflage. Clear tropical sea water is not colourless, as you would imagine, but blue in colour, changing red wavelengths of the spectrum into dark muddy tones that appear black. This is especially true at low light levels and under shady coral overhangs and caves in the reef, where soldierfishes spend the daylight hours. Soldierfishes have earned their descriptive name because they appear to be acting as sentinels to such openings.

Below: *Longjaw squirrelfish* (Holocentrus ascensionis). *Note the spines on the edge of the gill cover, a feature not seen in the soldierfishes.*

Right: *A dense shoal of blackbar soldierfishes* (Myripristis jacobus). *Their large eyes and red coloration are typical of nocturnal feeders.*

AQUARIUM CARE

Butterflyfishes

Butterflyfishes (family Chaetodontidae) rank among the most beautiful of the reef fishes and are similar in appearance to the closely related angelfishes (Pomacanthidae). Angelfishes are usually much larger and can be aggressive members of a community aquarium, featuring at the top of the pecking order, whereas butterflyfishes are timid, nervous fishes that will be subject to bullying if accompanied by other boisterous species in the aquarium.

The family characteristics of butterflyfishes include a deep, laterally compressed body with a small projecting mouth containing brushlike teeth. The single dorsal fin has 6-16 spines and further spines, usually 3-5, project from the front part of the anal fin. Body coloration and markings are often adapted to disguise features such as eyes, with obliterating stripes being combined with false eye-spots at the base of the tail to confuse predators. Bold stripes and bars are also used to break up the body outline, allowing butterflyfishes to show a high profile on the reef while blending in with their vividly marked surroundings. The four-eyed butterflyfish, *Chaetodon capistratus*, is a master of these techniques, exhibiting a combination of effective camouflage markings.

Butterflyfishes are not the easiest of fishes to keep in the aquarium because of their intolerance to poor water quality and changes in conditions. Their nervous disposition can also easily cause them to become stressed, usually leading to difficulties in encouraging them to feed. Members of this family are typically feeders on coral polyps and other coelenterates in the wild and are difficult to acclimatize to an aquarium diet. Thus, a combination of poor water quality and stress can easily transform reluctance to feed into full-blown anorexia.

Fortunately, maintaining good water quality is not the chore it used to be. Modern forms of filtration can easily produce the optimum conditions for keeping butterflyfishes, and this is reflected in the current success in keeping species which at one time were regarded as impossible subjects. Of course, their natural feeding regime effectively bars them from inclusion in an aquarium with live corals and other small invertebrates. In no time, butterflyfishes will browse away any small polyps and damage or kill other small invertebrates in the tank.

Although a little difficult initially, the four-eyed butterflyfish is the easiest of the Caribbean species to keep in the aquarium.

This success is due to its adaptability to aquarium conditions and feeding regimes and is probably the main reason why this species is so widely distributed and common on West Atlantic reefs. Its abundance there clearly suggests that it is able to adapt its feeding behaviour to a variety of habitats. In the aquarium, a diet of frozen foods combined with live *Tubifex* worms and *Mysis* shrimps suits it best, and this species will also nibble at algae growing naturally in the aquarium.

A quite small species, rarely attaining 10cm(4in) in the wild, the four-eyed butterflyfish is peaceful towards other fish.

In common with other butterflyfishes, however, it can be intolerant of its own species or members of other similar species. The 'one butterflyfish per tank' rule is best applied to prevent problems.

Below: *The striking four-eyed butterflyfish is familiar to both divers and aquarists. In the wild, this species is one of the most commonly encountered reef fishes.*

Bottom: *The handsome yellowhead or goldrim butterflyfish (C. xanthocephalus) from the Indian Ocean makes a hardy and peaceful aquarium subject once settled in.*

Sponges

Any account of Caribbean reefs would be incomplete without a mention of the vast array of sponges to be found there. Few groups of marine animals are able to equal the wide diversity of shape and colour found in the sponges and nowhere in the world are they a more prominent feature than in the Caribbean. In fact, they are so abundant in some locations that it would be more correct to use the term sponge reefs rather than coral reefs.

Sponges consist of aggregations of cells but, unlike higher animals, there are no defined organs or systems, such as a heart or stomach; instead, the body mass acts as a co-ordinated collection of self-contained units. Incredibly, this has allowed sponges in laboratory experiments to be passed through a liquidizer and then returned to their environment, where they immediately started to reform back into the original 'colonial' animal. Such amazing powers of regeneration and adaptability not only enable sponges to quickly repair damage to themselves but also to vary in size, shape and colour dependent upon the circumstances.

Although simply a collection of cells, the sponge 'colony' is equipped to filter vast quantities of water to obtain food and oxygen. The entire outer surface of the sponge is covered with a matrix of small holes through which water is drawn by the action of tiny specialized cells, each equipped with a whiplike flagellum. As the water passes towards the hollow centre of the colony, other cells trap and digest food particles and absorb oxygen from the constant flow. The water, plus any waste products, leaves the colony through much larger openings, clearly visible to the eye.

Some sponge colonies can assume a variety of fascinating shapes, but their main attraction is their striking range of brilliant colours. Few sponges in tropical waters are drab, and many are brightly arrayed in gaudy shades of orange, red, yellow and blue. Some species, such as the Caribbean sponge *Callyspongia plicifera*, also fluoresce, glowing bright pink or peach at depths where these colours would not otherwise exist. Here, we show a few examples of sponges found among the reefs in the Caribbean region.

Below: *The diversity in shape and colour of sponges is vividly displayed here. The red, pink and blue fingers of* Haliclona *species contrast with the yellow exhalant openings (oscules) of* Siphodictyon coralliphagum. *The mass of this burrowing sponge is concealed.*

Sponges in the aquarium

There is no doubt that sponges can be attractive, offering a combination of brilliant colours and fascinating forms, and many appear to be an ideal choice for the aquarium. Unfortunately, most species are very difficult to keep in captivity and many of those imported will only live for a matter of weeks in the home aquarium. It is difficult to generalize about these animals because individual species have adapted to a wide range of conditions in the wild.

There are species, mainly encrusting forms, which live in very shallow, brightly lit exposed positions and which have a similar association with zooxanthellae as do corals and thus require bright lighting. A much larger proportion, however, avoid high light levels and are found on the undersides of coral ledges, beneath coral rubble or at depths where the light intensity is low. It is mainly members of this last group that are the most commonly imported, coveted for their bright orange, purple and red coloration. Belonging primarily to the Demospongiae class of sponges, these particular sponges come in a variety of forms from rigid urn or fan shapes to spongy fingers or ornate candelabra.

That they avoid high-intensity lighting is logical because the main difficulty confronting many of these species is a lack of any means to prevent encrusting algae colonizing their exterior surfaces. If this is allowed to occur, the algae slowly block the tiny pores through which large amounts of water are drawn to provide oxygen and food for these filter-feeding animals. Good lighting is a prerequisite for most algal growth and by avoiding such conditions these sponges are not troubled by the algae. Other sessile life forms, hard corals for example, release large amounts of mucus to free themselves of debris and deter algal invasion, but sponges have no such deterrent system.

Aquarium conditions usually favour algal growth, with strong lighting and a plentiful supply of nitrates to aid growth, and these are just the conditions that can inhibit sponges. Therefore, sponges do not make very good subjects in a typical marine aquarium and will slowly die, producing a potential risk of polluting the aquarium in the process. Keeping them successfully requires low-light intensity of the correct wavelength to discourage algae but show off the sponge's colours to best advantage.

Experimentation with actinic fluorescent tube lighting may be the answer, but at the present time no recommendation can be made. Based on current experience, perhaps it would be better to avoid keeping sponges in the home aquarium.

There is not the same threat to the conservation of these animals from collectors as there is with hard corals, because sponges have amazing powers of regeneration and animals collected from the wild are probably quickly replaced. There is a potential risk of damage to the reef, however, when sponges are detached or coral heads turned over during the search for specimens. It is also true to say that in many reef areas sponges are an integral part of the reef and therefore the reef could be weakened if they are removed.

Above: *The sponge* Aplysina archeri *uses its large, trumpetlike openings to expel water and rid itself of wastes.*

Below: *The sponges in this aquarium are being engulfed by algae, which will soon deprive them of food and oxygen.*

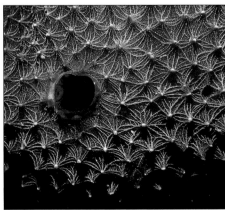

Above: *The oscula of the stinker sponge* (Iricinia fasciculata) *are widely spread. When removed from the water, the sponge emits an unpleasant odour.*

Above: *This branching sponge,* Gelloides ramosa, *often plays host to symbiotic zoanthid anemones, visible here. Brittle stars also entwine with it.*

DIVING THE WALL

The Turks and Caicos Islands are a scattering of small sandy cays and islands south of the Bahamas that offer remarkably clear water and spectacular reef drop-offs, or walls, as they are usually called. These tiny, flat limestone islands are perched on the edge of a great submerged canyon that plunges into the clear, blue waters of the Atlantic Ocean.

The Grand Turk Wall is a classic example. Only a few hundred metres from the sloping sandy shoreline, the reef edge plummets from a water depth of 15m(50ft) down to the seabed of the Turks Island Passage, 3,000m(10,000ft) below. This wall runs the entire 11km(7mile)-length of the west side of the island of Grand Turk. Similar walls occur off West Caicos, South Caicos and Providenciales (at Northwest Point), the other major vacation islands in the Turks and Caicos group.

These extraordinary dive locations – the result of a huge geological fault – offer unique and spectacular coral reef scenery. The coral colonization of the walls usually begins on the very edge, with shallow-water, spur-and-groove coral formations interspersed with sandy areas. Approaching the rim of the wall and peering down can be an awesome sight – the incredible 60-70m(200-230ft)-visibility can give you a case of underwater vertigo! The sheer cliffs are festooned with huge hard coral massives of star coral, fanlike gorgonians, feathery sea whips and a magnificent array of brightly coloured sponges. Silvery pelagic predators patrol the wall, including large barracuda, mackerel and jacks, accompanied by the occasional open-water shark.

The walls off South Caicos are exceptional. Located on a windward shore, they attract armadas of delta wing eagle rays and huge plankton-feeding Atlantic manta rays that swim inshore from deeper waters. Large shoals of grunts and snappers mill about in the shallows and spill over the wall into the depths, where Nassau groupers and Jewfishes stand sentinel at the entrances to their lairs, patiently waiting for the next opportunity for a meal. The whole

Above: *The Grand Turk Wall is festooned with brightly coloured sponges, including many fluorescent ones, such as this* Callyspongia plicifera.

Right: *Poised at the edge of a huge chasm, the divers pause before exploring the Grand Turk Wall, one of the most awesome reef dives.*

The Turks and Caicos Islands

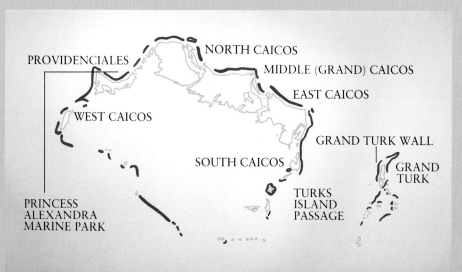

wall can often seem alive with the movement of colourful fish as they flit among the corals and sponges crowded onto the vertical faces.

If you would like to experience the feeling of floating in space surrounded by dramatic and exciting undersea scenery, why not join the privileged group of divers who have sampled the delights of exploring these magnificent walls.

Right: *Predatory horse-eye jacks* (Caranx latus) *hang in huge shoals. They show no fear of divers, allowing them to approach to within touching distance before veering away in a flash of silvery bodies.*

Fanworms

Over 600 million years ago, the erosion of the major continents formed great expanses of sand and mud on the seabed. This produced an environment abundant in food in the form of organic detritus and offered a protective means of concealment for a group of evolving invertebrates that are now known as polychaetes, or bristleworms. Their tubular segmented bodies were perfectly designed for burrowing through mud in search of food and it is a little surprising in the circumstances that two polychaete families, the Serpulidae and the Sabellidae, should have taken what appears to be a backward step in evolutionary terms. They evolved as tube-dwelling creatures, wholly dependent upon filtering food from the surrounding water through tiny cilia located on filaments around their mouths. These two families of worms became the fanworms so familiar to marine aquarists today, and the success of their life style is evident in their abundance and wide distribution in almost all the oceans of the world.

The biology of fanworms
Fanworms are among the most delicate and beautiful creatures any visitor to the reef is likely to find. It is hard to miss them, as their graceful, brightly coloured plumes, which give the fanworm its common name, occur in every colour of the rainbow. To the uninitiated, they can also seem to have mystical qualities, as individuals scattered like flowers among the reef terraces can suddenly disappear, almost as if by magic, when approached. This ability to withdraw instantly is well known by aquarists but often little understood. These very simple creatures can react up to 100 times faster than a human, yet they have no eyes or brain, only a simple network of nerve fibres. Their reaction on the approach of would-be predators is due to a well-developed network of muscles linked to a remarkable nervous system served by pressure- and light-sensitive cells in the filaments of the fan. The speed of the reaction appears to be determined by the size and thickness of the nerve fibres; the larger and thicker the nerve, the faster the reaction.

Most fanworms have two fans, one arranged on either side of the mouth opening. As well as serving as an early warning device and filter-feeding mechanism, these also act as gills for respiration. Marine biologists often refer to them as gill plumes. The fanworm's 'plumage' appears to be designed to attract, being decked out in an amazing range of colours and patterns. Probably the reverse is more correct, however, because the bright colours displayed on the gills may well be a warning device. This is undoubtedly the case in *Spirobranchus*, or Christmas tree worm, as the gaudy markings draw attention to the sharp projecting spur waiting to ensnare any fish attempting to snap at the plumes.

Serpulids and sabellids differ in a number of ways. Serpulids form cone-shaped gills arranged in a spiral and resemble miniature Christmas trees. They confine themselves within a hard calcareous tube and in the case of the most common species, *Spirobranchus giganteus*, attach permanently to a convenient stony coral host. The host species varies in different areas of the world. In the Red Sea and Indo-Pacific, for example, this species prefers growths of finger coral (*Porites*), whereas in the Caribbean it takes up residence in boulder corals such as brain coral (*Diploria*) and star coral (*Montastrea*). Fanworms of the family Sabellidae, on the other hand, construct soft tubes of mucus and detritus and are embedded in the sand and mud of the seabed. Their gill plumes are larger than those in serpulid worms and are arranged in stunning classic fan shapes.

All fanworms spend most of the daylight hours gathering food and building materials in their fine, remarkably efficient sievelike fans. Thousands of tiny cilia, each with its own set of micro muscles, sway back and forth, trapping small particles from the water. These particles are passed from cilium to cilium down 'food grooves' to the mouth opening, where they are sorted into three categories. The large particles are discarded and often mixed with lighter-than-water saliva to allow them to float freely upwards, the medium-sized pieces are ingested into the digestive system and the small particles are mixed with mucus to repair or extend their tubes.

Keeping fanworms in the aquarium
Ask any marine aquarists and they are sure to admit to having purchased a fanworm at some time or another, but few will readily agree that they have been successful in keeping them. The classic mistake seems to be to try to keep fanworms in a mixed fish/invertebrate system with fish that are natural fanworm predators. Angelfishes, butterflyfishes and triggerfishes can all be responsible for causing the untimely demise of a newly acquired fanworm.

Below: *The fans on either side of this serpulid's mouth opening are visible here. This plumage is controlled by a remarkable network of muscles, triggered by highly sensitive nerve fibres that react instantly to pressure and light.*

Porcupinefishes, boxfishes and pufferfishes are particularly partial to fanworms, especially the diminutive sharpnosed pufferfish (*Canthigaster solandri*), which is easily capable of tackling and eating a fanworm its own size (up to about 5cm/2in in the aquarium). Therefore, it is better to restrict fanworms to an invertebrate-only system or keep them with small fishes such as clownfishes, basslets, gobies, jawfishes and seahorses.

Otherwise, fanworms are easy to keep. They are not dependent on the high levels of light many other invertebrates require and will happily settle down to a wide range of lighting conditions. Water quality is also not as critical as it is for most other invertebrates, with the proviso that sudden wide variations in temperature appear to stress them badly, often to the point where the worm will discard the gill plumes. In fact, discarding the gill plumes is a common sign of stress and is a natural defence mechanism in case of attack. Although the worm may regrow its plumes, unless the cause of stress is discovered and overcome, it will finally succumb.

Some of the recent advances in aquarium systems have proved unfortunate for the fanworm. These include powerful filtration systems that are easily capable of completely stripping small particles of food and plankton from the water. Under such conditions, fanworms can quickly starve unless they are given additional liquid feeds and the water dosed with supplements that encourage natural plankton populations to develop. Given these simple precautions and a little care, fanworms can be the longest living of aquarium invertebrates and provide a real feature in any marine display.

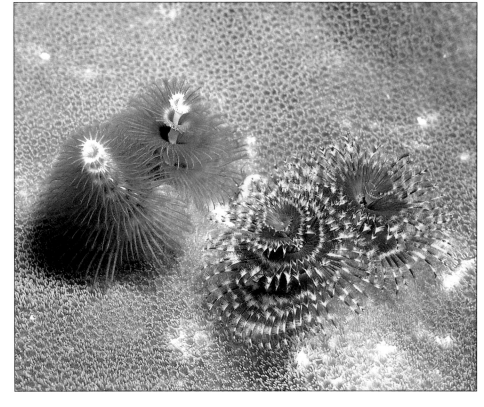

Above: *Christmas tree worms* (Spirobranchus sp.) *attached to a hard coral host. They show a clear preference for certain corals; here* Porites *coral.*

Below: Spirobranchus giganteus, *the Caribbean Christmas tree worm, is a showy species, varying in colour from pale lemon through brown to rich red.*

Above: *Sabellid worms often occur in groups. With enough suspended matter on which to feed, they are equally at home on muddy seabeds and coral reefs. When one is stimulated into retracting, the others follow instantly.*

DIVE LOCATION REPORT: Tobago

FLYING THE REEF

The lush green foliage and colourful flowers of the beautiful island of Tobago are not its only assets. A delightful world awaits below the warm, crystal-clear waters that lap its tropical shores. The hilly countryside above water is idyllic, with scented fruit trees laden with oranges, mangoes and papaya. Long winding roads spiral down to incredibly beautiful coves of clear water and white sand, with trees almost sweeping an ocean which is a tapestry of blues and turquoise.

From little coves, just such as these, it is possible to join small groups of divers putting out to sea in Tobago-built fishing pirogues to dive some amazing sites. Many have descriptive names such as The Black Forest, Shark Bank and Japanese Garden, this last location being perhaps one of the most beautiful dives in the whole Caribbean. It is not even necessary to be a SCUBA diver to experience some of the joys of this underwater world because Tobago's National Marine Park at Buccoo Reef provides enchanting vistas of submarine coral gardens in water often only knee deep.

For divers who like to feel the adrenalin pumping, an essential dive must be the Flying Reef at Crown Point on the southwestern tip of the island. The dive starts from a boat launched from Pigeon Point, a more beautiful beach you could not imagine. Passing around a headland onto the island's windward side, the pirogue hugs the coast, the native boat cutting smoothly through the swell as white-capped waves beat against its bow. A couple of kilometres along the coast, the divers prepare to exit the boat in a group led by a dive master trailing a surface marker buoy.

If you were to join such a group you would find yourself 10m(33ft) below the surface, flying along the reef in a 3- to 4-knot current through dramatic scenery of elkhorn coral and star coral set in waving fields of fan-shaped gorgonians. Fish are all around, seemingly unperturbed by the current. Yellowtail snapper and striped porkfish sweep by and a large queen angel peers from the cover of feathery sea whips. Awakened from its resting place beneath a coral head, a nurse shark speeds towards the deep water, followed by a shoal of rainbow parrotfish, each weighing more than 20kg(44lb). Weightless, you marvel at the exciting vistas unfolding around you, the boat tracking your course by following the marker buoy moving along at the surface. All too soon, the dive draws to a close, but a look at the watch reveals that almost an hour has past while you have been effortlessly gliding among the rich marine life on the Flying Reef of Tobago.

Right: *Swept along by currents, the divers fly effortlessly over the reef, passing vistas of dramatic coral canyons. The currents constantly provide nutrients that encourage rich growths of stony corals and sponges.*

Below: *Dense schools of striped porkfish (Anisotremus virginicus) shelter from the current in the lee of a coral head. When darkness falls, they will disperse to feed on crustaceans in the grassy areas of the lagoon floor. Porkfish form schools only during the spawning season.*

The island of Tobago

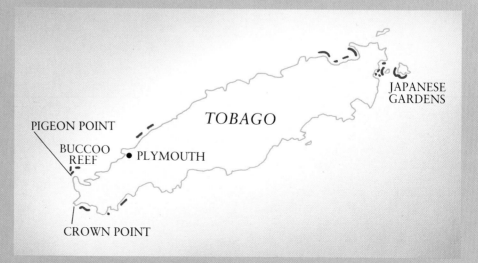

Maldives

'Life in the lagoon'

Picture the translucent blue waters of the Indian Ocean with hundreds of tiny sun-soaked coral islands stretching as far as the eye can see, and you have the Maldives. Seen from the air, this small republic 800km(500 miles) south of Sri Lanka is a tapestry of atolls and islands forming beautiful patterns in the deep blue of the ocean. Counts differ, but most people agree that there are over 1100 of these islands covering an area measuring 800km north to south by some 130km(about 80 miles) across at the greatest width. Only about 200 are inhabited.

As we have described on page 35, the Maldives consist of a long chain of coral atolls formed on a series of extinct submerged volcanoes extending northwards from the Equator. Examples of the classic atoll, based on a doughnut-shaped island with a central lagoon, abound in this area. Many of the atoll formations are much larger in scale, however, with some measuring 10km(about 6 miles) or more in diameter and consisting of a series of islands formed into a circle. A typical island in these larger formations is moulded by exposure to wind and currents into a tear-drop shape and is encircled by dazzling white beaches and coral formations. Most islands are low and flat, and heavily forested with coconut palms. Many are so small that it may take less than 20 minutes to walk around the entire coastline.

Life in the lagoon

An underwater excursion from the sugar-white beach of one of these islands would reveal a gently sloping seabed to the reef crest, 100m(330ft) or so from the shoreline, with depths seldom attaining more than 1.5m(5ft) along the way. This lagoon, formed in the lee of the reef, completely encircles the island. In this mainly sandy area, isolated

Unique blackfooted clownfishes.

outcrops of staghorn (*Acropora* spp.) and boulder corals (*Porites* spp.) act as a focus for a surprisingly rich diversity of colourful reef fishes.

Many of the familiar fish species common to shallow Indo-Pacific reefs are represented here, especially the brightly coloured members of the damselfish and clownfish (anemonefish) family (Pomacentridae). The humbug and domino damselfishes (*Dascyllus aruanus* and *trimaculatus*) shoal in close proximity to protective coral heads. Clownfishes, including the skunk clownfish (*Amphiprion akallopisos*), and the appealing blackfooted clownfish (*A. nigripes*), unique to the Maldives area, nestle in the large *Heteractis* anemones dotted among the corals, sometimes in water depths of little more than 1m(3.3ft).

Juveniles of a wide range of small wrasses, triggerfishes and surgeonfishes use this as a nursery area, darting in and out of small crannies and holes in the sandy bottom. Juveniles of the Picasso triggerfish (*Rhinecanthus aculeatus*) and the yellow-and-white striped sailfin surgeonfish (*Zebrasoma veliferum*), no larger than postage stamps, mingle with tiny *Coris* and *Anampses* wrasses as they dart about, sporting their brilliant juvenile coloration. One metre-long whitetip reef sharks (*Triaenodon obesus*), mere youngsters, coast between the coral heads, causing quite a disturbance among the local fish populations, signifying that this is a regular hunting ground for these young predators.

Beyond the reef crest

On approaching the reef crest, the lagoon becomes much shallower and the reef presents an almost continuous barrier of living coral between the lagoon and the open sea. Progress through this

barrier out onto the seaward face of the reef is provided by occasional surge channels and breaks in the coral growth. Once outside into the open sea, the reef becomes a spectacular, steeply shelving slope with small cliffs and canyons undercut to form caves and gullies. Swarms of fish – all zooplankton feeders – gather in large mixed shoals, forming tiers from just below the surface to depths of 20-30m(66-100ft). Territorial reef species, more integrated with the reef itself, move singly, in pairs or in small shoals between the coral growths. The overall impression of this reef zone is of large numbers of fish, tremendous diversity, movement and colour.

Zooplankton-feeding fishes include the pennant butterflyfish (*Heniochus diphreutes*), which parade in open water along the reef in schools sometimes numbering many hundreds – an amazing phenomenon more or less restricted to the reefs in this part of the world. Mixed shoals of spotted unicornfish (*Naso brevirostris*) and black pyramid butterflyfishes (*Hemitaurichthys zoster*) dash hither and thither, snapping up morsels from the zooplankton soup as they themselves are harassed by the solitary jack (*Carangoides* sp.) and schools of trevally (*Caranx* sp.). Clouds of golden jewelfish (*Anthias squamipinnis*) swarm in these crowded waters. These tiny golden zooplankton feeders are territorial and thus restricted to a given coral head on the reef edge, where, conveniently, wave action draws plankton up from the depths.

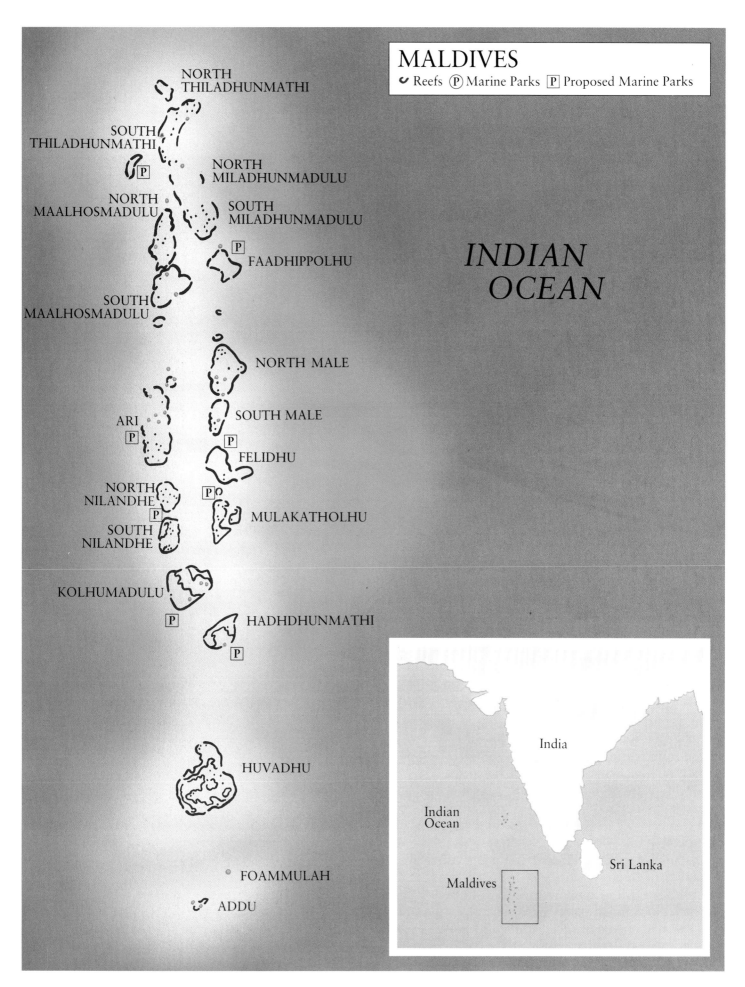

MALDIVES

꒰ Reefs Ⓟ Marine Parks ⯐P⯑ Proposed Marine Parks

NORTH
THILADHUNMATHI

SOUTH
THILADHUNMATHI

Ⓟ

NORTH
MILADHUNMADULU

NORTH
MAALHOSMADULU

SOUTH
MILADHUNMADULU

Ⓟ FAADHIPPOLHU

SOUTH
MAALHOSMADULU

INDIAN
OCEAN

NORTH MALE

ARI

Ⓟ

SOUTH MALE

Ⓟ

FELIDHU

NORTH
NILANDHE

Ⓟ

Ⓟ

MULAKATHOLHU

SOUTH
NILANDHE

KOLHUMADULU

Ⓟ HADHDHUNMATHI

Ⓟ

HUVADHU

● FOAMMULAH

꒛ ADDU

India

Indian
Ocean

Sri Lanka

Maldives

99

Unicornfish species are distinguished by sporting one, or occasionally two, unicornlike projections on the forehead. The spotted unicornfish has a very well-developed horn and is unusual in that it feeds as a herbivore during its juvenile and subadult stages before the horn develops. As an adult, it feeds on zooplankton and is often encountered speeding along the reef edge in small shoals. The Vlaming's unicornfish (*Naso vlamingii*) is a spectacular species fairly common to the Maldives but rare elsewhere. The males of this species are more colourful than the females, with long filaments trailing from each lobe of the tail. These exquisitely beautiful males are capable of bright displays when in breeding condition, and this species is perhaps the most distinctive member of the family. In place of the horn, there is a large hump decorated with a splash of bright blue.

The range of territorial reef species in this zone is phenomenal, with over 1000 fish species common to the atoll group. With such a wide diversity, fish watching can be bewildering, and each underwater excursion is spiced with many unexpected and spectacular surprises.

Just such a spectacular surprise is provided by the cowfish (*Lactoria cornuta*). This aptly named and unusual fish is a member of that family of eccentrically shaped fishes – the Ostraciidae – that also includes the boxfishes. Admirably suited to survive the competitive world of the coral reef, the cowfish has a hard exterior armed with 'horns'

strategically placed to resist attack from the front and rear. A further defence mechanism common to this group is perhaps one of the biggest drawbacks to keeping them in the aquarium. When alarmed or frightened, some species are capable of secreting a skin poison called ostracitoxin. In the confines of the aquarium, such secretions are capable of killing all the fish in the system.

Top: Caranx sexfasciatus, *the predatory big-eye trevally, may form into huge menacing schools, as shown here. They cruise along the reef, preying upon zooplankton feeders with deadly efficiency.*

Above: *It would be hard to imagine a more unusual fish than the spectacular Vlaming's unicornfish. The male shown here sports long trailing tail filaments and colourful markings.*

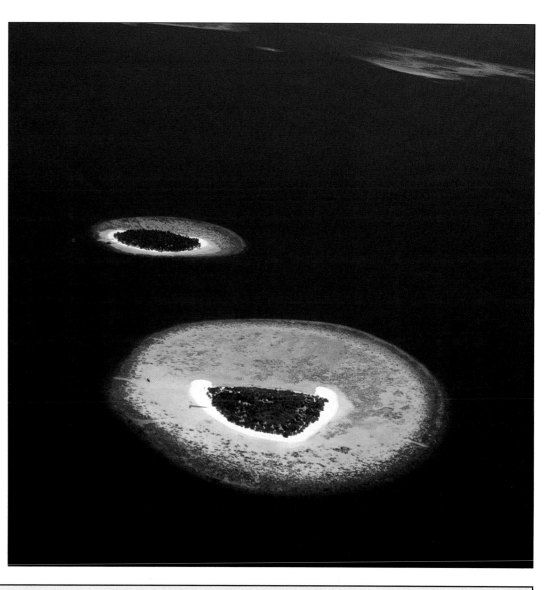

Above: *A long-horned cowfish* (Lactoria cornuta), *one of a group of slow-moving fishes that have evolved some novel defence mechanisms, such as the secretion of a deadly poison. A closer inspection of this unusual fish reveals that the rigid body is made up of hexagonal plates.*

Right: *A typical Maldivian island moulded by wind and current to form a tear-drop shape. Underwater excursions from the sugar-white beaches of such islands can be spiced with spectacular surprises, including large creatures.*

DIVING PROFILE *The Maldives*

CLIMATE

Mean air temperature: 30°C(86°F)
Mean sea temperature: 21°C(70°F)

The Maldivian weather is determined by the phases of the southwest and northeast monsoons. High winds and rainfall usually coincide with the northeast monsoon in December and January, but these conditions tend to be localized. In July, August and in October, rainfall can reach 30cm(12in) in any of these months, with attendant high humidity, but sea conditions are usually good. The period February to May is the driest, with hot, sunny, calm days that herald the change from the winter northeast to the summer southwest monsoon period. In broad terms, the climate is as near perfect as you are likely to find, with few periods in the year when diving is not possible.

FACILITIES

Facilities are second to none, with 53 major resort islands providing SCUBA diving facilities. Decompression chamber facilities are available on the islands of Faruklohufushi and Bandos.

DIVE RATING

Based on the quality of reefs, diversity of marine life, range of dive locations and variety of dives, the rating is high. This is one of the few parts of the world where it is easily possible to glimpse large sharks, manta rays and dolphins. A variety of dives is possible, including wall dives, drift dives in the channels and a good wreck dive near the airport. The airport is on a separate small island close to the island of Male, where the Maldives capital town of Male is located.

CONSERVATION

The Maldivian Government is concerned about safeguarding the marine environment and large areas are protected for conservation purposes. Spearfishing is not allowed and fish collecting within 1km(0.6 mile) of resort islands is forbidden. A programme of research currently underway should provide valuable indicators as to where marine parks can be established and information on the designation of protected areas.

One of the major attractions of diving in the Maldives is the opportunity to observe not only spectacularly unusual, but also spectacularly large marine creatures. Nowhere else in the world is it so easy to swim among and glimpse large fishes such as manta rays and sharks. (See the dive location report on page 108).The largest members of many fish families are represented and the wrasses are no exception, with the huge humphead wrasse (*Cheilinus undulatus*) attaining a length of 2m(6.6ft) or more and weighing in at a sturdy 190kg(420lb).

At the diminutive end of the scale, the gobies rarely attain more than a few centimetres in length. Despite its tiny size, however, the fire goby (*Nemateleotris magnifica*) is unlikely to be overlooked, with its brilliant fiery coloration and graceful swimming behaviour. The fire goby is a free-swimming species usually found singly or in pairs close to the reef wall, where it quickly darts for cover when approached. Most other goby species do not have a conventional swimbladder and are restricted to living close to the seabed. Some of these more sedentary gobies, of which the watchman goby (*Crytocentrus lutheri*) is a good example, have set up home in small burrows with pistol shrimps (Alpheidae). These two creatures

live symbiotically in close association, the shrimp excavating and maintaining the burrow while the goby acts as a lookout. If danger threatens, the goby quickly takes refuge in the burrow, alerting and warning the poor-sighted shrimp.

Above: *The huge humphead wrasse is a familiar sight on reefs from the Red Sea to the Eastern Pacific. The Maldives are home to the biggest specimens.*

Below: *Glimpses of large marine creatures, such as this massive manta ray, are not unusual. Plankton-rich waters provide a banquet for these gentle giants.*

AQUARIUM CARE

Gobies

The gobies are members of the largest family of fishes (Gobiidae) in the tropical seas, a family that contains over 500 species. Not confined solely to tropical waters, these tiny fishes have adapted to a wide range of habitats in both temperate and tropical environments and can be found everywhere from brightly lit seashore rockpools down to the sunless depths over 200m(656ft) below the surface. Some species live in fresh water.

The main characteristics of gobies are a long, thin tapering body with a sucking disc formed by the fusion of the pelvic fins. The swimbladder is normally absent, swimming being confined to short bursts followed by a quick return to the seabed. The eyes are arranged on the top of the head and on the same plane to provide the fish with binocular, three-dimensional vision. Their keen eyesight and alert manner is undoubtedly a major defence mechanism against predators.

Including members of the genus *Nemateleotris* into the goby ranks does upset these simple distinctions a little. Nemateleotrids, including the fire goby

(*Nemateleotris magnifica*), are free swimming and do not have a sucking disc, preferring to hover in open water or hide in small burrows in the reef face.

The diminutive fire goby, reaching a maximum length of 8cm(3.2in), is one of the most brilliantly coloured fish available for the aquarium. Its rich, creamy peach body coloration, fiery burnt-orange tail and pennant-like dorsal fin accentuated with orange make this an outstanding species likely to set off any aquarium to perfection. It will be quite happy kept as a single specimen, but it is far more attractive as a pair or in a small shoal, when the fish can often be seen displaying to each other by flicking their conspicuous dorsal fins back and forth.

To care for this species properly, it is vital to take into account its naturally nervous disposition. If there are boisterous or aggressive fish sharing the aquarium, this little goby will spend most of the time hiding. There are no further difficulties related to care and feeding. It will readily accept flake foods, as well as a wide range of live and frozen foods. To really enhance

and maintain the fire goby's brilliant coloration, provide a high-protein diet of fresh or frozen squid, mussel or fish, supplemented with regular feeds of live brineshrimp and *Mysis* shrimp.

It is not surprising that such gobies are aquarium favourites, having all the attributes of a good marine aquarium fish. They are small, colourful and peaceful with other fish species, and easy to feed and care for. As a bonus, they can be a safe addition to an invertebrate system, where they pose no threat to a wide range of inverts and add a welcome dash of colour and movement.

Below: *Few marine fish can rival the brilliant colours of the fire goby* (Nemateleotris magnifica). *This beautiful species makes an ideal aquarium fish; it is compact, attractive and easy to care for. Its fiery colours can be maintained with regular feeds of live shrimps. Here, a pair flick up their long dorsal fins in a streamlined and appealing synchronized display. In the aquarium, these fishes will only settle down when they have organized a convenient 'bolthole' in the substrate.*

DIVING INTO DARKNESS

We decided to set out at dusk. This would give us time to find our way through the reef before darkness fell. The sun was setting, a deep red glow filling the sky and reflecting the colour of Burgundy wine on the still ocean, as we waded into the warm, clear water from the sugar-white beach of our tiny resort on the island of Bandos. As we immersed ourselves in the sea, the weight of our cameras and diving equipment simply melted away. The sandy lagoon, only a matter of a 100 metres(330ft) or so from the reef crest, was a white sandy wonderland peppered with isolated outcrops of intricately shaped corals. Safe for the night, tiny blackfooted clownfishes (*Amphiprion nigripes*), a species unique to the Maldives area, nestled deep down into the partly closed tentacled mass of a large *Heteractis* anemone, and colourful damselfishes nervously peered out from within the spiky protective branches of staghorn corals as we approached.

Minutes later, we reached the reef crest and located a surge channel to give us easy access to the outside of the reef and our destination, the reef slope. Along the reef edge, daytime species were making for their night-time refuges; a Moorish idol (*Zanclus canescens*) swam by, its colours starting to darken from white and lemon to a muted grey; shy oriental sweetlips (*Plectorhynchus orientalis*) broke formation from their shoal and disappeared in ones and twos into clefts in the reef. The evening predators were already active; small groups of lionfish (*Pterois volitans*), pectoral fins spread, felt their way across the reef face, and a lone big-eye (*Priacanthus hamrur*) disguised with rich tawny red, melted in and out of the coral outcrops.

The natural light was now all but faded and we were enveloped in a midnight-blue ocean with our torch's stabbing beam picking up a fish here and a coral outcrop there. Crinoids were perched on the top of most coral heads, spreading their feathery arms like open fans. Soft *Xeniidae* corals with expanded polyps were waiting to ensnare the minute zooplankton passing by, the circles of tentacles opening and closing rhythmically like small grasping hands. Photographic opportunities were everywhere, as one unusual creature after another came into view. Nerves jangled with a mixture of excitement and fear of the unknown beyond our torch beam. We were not able to easily erase memories of our dive earlier that day only 500 metres(1640ft) along the reef at the location called Shark Point, where we were within touching distance of six or seven large ocean whitetip sharks (see page 124). Apart from the small area illuminated by our torch, being effectively blinded by the darkness can soon cause the imagination to conjure up all manner of possible situations, which usually culminate in the diver featuring as the main course.

The wreck of a small sloop festooned with brightly coloured sponges, hydroids and corals appeared eerily from the darkness, a large moray eel slithering back into the shadows of the fo'c'sle, startled by the harsh beam of our torch. The rigging, still intact, was covered with growths and what, at first sight, appeared to be a gigantic spider's web. We quickly recognized this as a basket star, a big cousin of the crinoids.

Bandos in the Maldives

NORTH MALE ATOLL

BANDOS

MALE

These large filter feeders, with impressive fan-shaped bodies, impale their prey on tiny hooks, periodically passing the catch to the central mouth. (For more information on this and other echinoderms, see the panel starting on page 109.)   The cameras had been busily clicking and in no time our film was exhausted. A glance at our air pressure gauges showed that they were close to the safety margin for our return to the surface and, grudgingly, we emerged from the beguiling darkness into the bright moonlight of a tropic night.

Right: *Wreck diving can often be charged with excitement, but nothing surpasses the nerve-tingling experience of diving a wreck at night, enveloped in eerie darkness.*

Top: *As darkness falls, spidery crinoids emerge from their hiding places to find vantage points on the reef. Other filter-feeders also appear, eager to feed on the plankton soup rising from the depths. All hard surfaces are exploited, each tiny animal having its own niche.*

Above: *Oriental sweetlips gather in shoals below coral overhangs during the day, but at night become lone nocturnal hunters, searching for their prey of crabs, shrimps and occasional small fish. Hunting grounds are sandy areas or reef clefts.*

Left: *The sun sets and the time arrives to immerse ourselves in the warm waters of the wine-dark sea to explore the reef at night.*

Exploiting all food sources

The shallower sections of the reef are rich in filamentous algae. Such a food source is eagerly consumed by herbivorous fishes that feed exclusively on this abundant plant life. The surgeonfishes are such a group well represented in the Maldives, and the powder blue surgeonfish (*Acanthurus leucosternon*) is one of the most striking, with a brilliant blue body edged in yellow. To see a large shoal browsing on the reef flat is an amazing sight.

A distinctive feature in a number of surgeonfish species is their striking yellow juvenile coloration. Juveniles of *Acanthurus pyroferus*, an Indo-Pacific species, begin life with bright yellow coloration, but this completely changes to brown and blue in the adult form. (The same sequence occurs in the blue tang, *Acanthurus coeruleus*, a West Atlantic species, whereas the yellow tang, *Zebrasoma flavescens*, from the Pacific Ocean is unusual in this respect in that it retains its vivid yellow coloration as an adult.)

The brilliant yellow saddle goatfish (*Parupeneus cyclostomus*) is a further delightful species that is colourful as a juvenile but becomes quite drab in colour as it matures. Shoals of these unusual creatures can be observed probing the sandy patches of the reef, using their long sensory barbels to locate their prey of small worms and crustaceans. The goatfish family (Mullidae) is well represented on these reefs by at least six more species, namely the long barbel goatfish (*Parupeneus macronema*), the beautiful rosy goatfish (*P. rubescens*), the cinnabar goatfish (*P. cinnabarinus*), the barred goatfish (*P. bifasciatus*) and the two *Mulloides* species, the yellowstripe goatfish (*M. flavolineatus*) and the schooling yellowfin goatfish (*M. vanicolensis*).

Deep recesses in the reef and the shadows formed by coral overhangs are the daytime abode

of the nocturnal blotcheye soldierfish (*Myripristis murdjan*). Often, huge shoals of soldierfishes and the closely related squirrelfishes can be found massing together beneath the protecting coral. The force of gravity is not a great influence in the aqueous medium of the sea and it is not unusual to find soldierfishes swimming upside down close to the roof of a cave, mistaking this for the sea floor.

The coral trout (*Cephalopholis miniata*) is a common and beautiful member of the grouper family (Serranidae) found mainly in well-developed reef areas in clear waters and particularly abundant in this area. Mature adults are brilliant red or orange with numerous blue spots on the body and fins. This wily predator swims out in the open, appearing to be unaware of other fish close by but in reality carefully manoeuvring itself in readiness to attack a potential prey. A lightning-fast lunge, and the hapless prey disappears into the recesses of its cavernous mouth.

Other members of the grouper family are 'lie-in-wait' predators and the Maldives are home to a number of species that fall into this category. The slender grouper (*Anyperdon leucogrammicus*), the peacock grouper (*Cephalopholis argus*) and the beautiful lyretail grouper (*Variola louti*) are common on the upper reef slope, while the black-saddled coral trout (*Plectropomus laevis*) favours the lower reef slope as a habitat.

Below left: *The camera follows a shoal of bright yellowfin goatfish* (Mulloides vanicolensis) *gliding over the reef. Each fish systematically probes any patches of sand with the sensory barbels near its mouth, as it searches for small invertebrates.*

Below: *Mixed shoals of fish, consisting mainly of various soldierfish species in typical red livery, throng beneath a coral ledge at night. Some 'defy' gravity and swim upside down among growths of feathery crinoids clinging to the cave roof.*

JOINING THE SHARK CIRCUS

To many divers, the Maldives is the most thrilling place to visit, simply because nowhere is it easier to dive in close proximity to large sharks. The person we decided to see to make this a reality was Herwarth Voigtmann, a celebrated German diver who managed a diving school on the island of Bandos. Herwarth organized dives to visit what he referred to as his 'shark circus'. He regarded himself as a kind of lion tamer who had substituted large oceanic white-tip sharks for his lions. I was lucky enough to be able to join him and a German television camera crew who were attempting to record the amazing association Herwarth had built up with the large oceanic sharks living close to the island.

The site Herwarth had chosen was 20m(66ft) below the surface, at a point where the reef slope was undercut, forming dark caverns. The sharks performed around a pinnacle of dead coral perched precariously on the edge of a sheer underwater chasm. We were all designated positions in relative safety, with our backs to the reef close to where Hewarth took up his position on top of the pinnacle. Shark Point, as the pinnacle had inevitably been called, was seething with life, including large numbers of red-faced batfishes (*Platax pinnatus*). The reason for this abundance of sea life quickly became apparent when Herwarth started to chum the water to summon the sharks. Chumming involves chopping up fish to release the taste into the water, acting as a sort of underwater dinner bell for the sharks and incidently encouraging masses of other fishes to share in the feast being provided for them.

In no time, the first shark appeared, a nervous youngster 2m(6.6ft) or so long, followed quickly by three or four more. Our adrenalin levels started to rise as the sharks circled and closed in on Herwarth, who was crouched on the pinnacle holding out a fish and looking quite unperturbed. The largest shark shot in, snatched the fish and quickly sped away. This procedure was repeated a number of times, the sharks becoming quite excited and Herwarth choreographing the proceedings exactly like a lion tamer, occasionally fending off the more adventurous sharks with a push on the snout. The piece de resistance entailed Herwarth gripping a fish between his teeth and inviting a shark to take it. There then followed the remarkable sight of the German diver with his head almost in the shark's mouth and so close to those rows and rows of teeth!

It is difficult to imagine a more exciting and memorable dive. As we sped back to shore, the faces of the other divers reflected my own sentiments exactly, as, in silence, we savoured the thoughts of our recent experience with the sharks of Shark Point off the island of Bandos.

Bandos in the Maldives

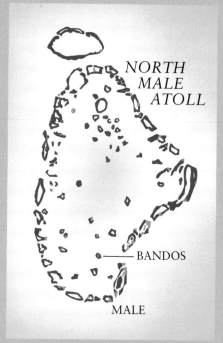

Below: *Herwarth Voigtmann offers a shark a fish gripped between his teeth. It has taken many years for Herwarth to reach this level of mutual trust with these sharks.*

INVERTEBRATE LIFE

Echinoderms

Among the earliest forms of life to be recorded as fossilized remains were members of the phylum Echinodermata. These creatures, called crinoids, lived in the newly forming oceans of the world over 500 million years ago. They were not the feathery, starfishlike animals we know as crinoids today, however, but an earlier form which attached to the seabed, similar in appearance to 'modern' sea lilies. These crinoids were abundant in fossil times but are now represented by only a handful of species. Despite this apparent blind alley in evolutionary terms, other echinoderms evolved that now make up an important group of marine animals well represented in all the world oceans and which are conspicuous and colourful members of many coral reef communities.

The biology of echinoderms
Echinoderms are easily recognized by a number of characteristic features. In keeping with their descriptive scientific name of 'echinoderm', meaning spiny skin, they have a rough, often spiny, exterior. Another feature typical of all echinoderms is an unusual form of locomotion incorporating tiny tube feet connected to a unique water vascular system. The underlying principle involves the distribution of water along a series of internal canals to hydraulically operate muscular sacs connected to the tube feet to allow movement and other muscular actions to take place. Finally, many echinoderms have a five-fold symmetry, meaning that the body consists of five or multiples of five identical parts. This is by no means universal, however, since even the most representative group, the starfishes (*Asteroidea*), includes many species that do not conform to the five-fold pattern. The crown-of-thorns starfish (*Acanthaster planci*), for example, may have up to 23 arms.

The main subdivisions, or classes, into which the echinoderms can be divided also number five. These are the starfishes, or seastars (*Asteroidea*); the brittle stars (*Ophiuroidea*); the feather stars (*Crinoidea*); the sea urchins (*Echinoidea*); and the sea cucumbers (*Holothuroidea*).

Starfishes
The starfishes are perhaps the most familiar star-shaped creatures, with five or more arms radiating from a central round body. The body plan is radially symmetrical, with each of the arms supplied with its own organs for locomotion, respiration, digestion and reproduction. The combination of this form of replication of organs within a single animal, together with amazing powers of regeneration, allows a complete new individual to grow from a detached arm. Many species use this strategy to reproduce asexually by division. Sexual reproduction also takes place by the release of huge quantities of eggs and sperm into the water. It is often reasoned that millions of eggs are released to reduce the risk that a random release may occur where and when large amounts of sperm are not available to come into contact with the eggs. In practice, the release of eggs and sperm are often coordinated, with large numbers of a species being 'triggered' simultaneously by chemical 'messages' passed between them.

Of the brightly coloured reef starfishes, a number are suitable for the aquarium, especially those from the genera *Linkia* and *Fromia*. The Indo-Pacific blue seastar (*Linkia laevigata*) is a typical example, a beautiful blue species that would appear to be reasonably free from predators as it can often be found out in the open on the reef. In the aquarium, it is equally conspicuous as it slowly creeps around in search of food. Like all starfishes, this species is carnivorous and feeds on encrusting organisms on the seabed. It also performs a useful function on the reef by acting as a scavenger and devouring the remains of any dead creatures. In fact, many starfishes are content to feed on the bacteria that form a rich layer in the nooks and crannies in the reef.

Some asteroids are more specialized feeders. These include *Fromia monilis*, an attractive Indo-Pacific species with a bright orange-mottled coloration that grazes on sponges. It is important to determine the feeding habits of any starfish that you intend to keep in a marine aquarium in order to avoid mixing one of these carnivorous echinoderms with other invertebrates that may form a part of its diet.

There is one specialized feeder among the starfishes that there is no difficulty in recognizing. This is the crown-of-thorns

Left: Fromia monilis, *a starfish highly recommended for the aquarium because of its brilliant orange and red coloration and hardy nature. Although it feeds mainly on sponges in the wild, it adapts to become an excellent scavenger in the aquarium. It can reach up to 10cm (4in) across, but rarely exceeds 6cm (2.4in).*

starfish, which feeds on live coral polyps. This menacing, spiny creature can reach a diameter of 30cm(12in) or more and feeds by everting its stomach onto a suitable area of coral, secreting digestive juices and then withdrawing the stomach, together with the dissolved coral tissues, up into its body cavity. This species became quite notorious in the late 1960s and early 1970s, when populations in a number of Indo-Pacific areas almost simultaneously reached plague proportions. This led to the destruction of large areas of coral on the Great Barrier Reef, before these huge concentrations disappeared in late 1973. There was a great deal of conjecture at the time regarding the reason for such a huge population explosion in a species normally found only in small numbers, and concern was voiced as to whether the damage would be permanent. The fear was that some manmade impact was to blame and that total destruction of the reefs might result. Among the causes put forward to explain the phenomenon were pollution and the collection of triton (*Charonia tritonis*), a shelled mollusc which is a major predator of the crown-of-thorns starfish. The plague began to diminish even as the debate still raged and, with the passage of time, the crown-of-thorns populations reduced to their previous levels. There is some evidence to suggest that populations of these animals can rise and fall in a cyclical fashion and that the plague was probably a natural occurrence. The reefs are now slowly being recolonized by new coral growths.

Brittle stars

The brittle stars are related to and closely resemble the starfishes. Delicate spiny arms are attached to a small, central disc and a high degree of mobility is a characteristic of most species. Brittle stars are generally inconspicuous animals that lurk beneath coral rubble or hang entwined among coral or gorgonian branches. They are mainly suspension feeders that collect zooplankton in their spiny arms, but some species coil their arms like springs and shoot these out to grasp passing prey.

Basket stars, cousins of the brittle stars, are also suspension feeders. They rely on sharp hooks and a lightning reflex action to engulf and impale the small invertebrates on which they feed.

Feather stars

Feather stars are beautiful creatures, with feathery, ostrich-plume-like arms. They perch on high vantage points at night to feed on the rich plankton, but remain

Above: *Their architectural elegance makes featherstars highly desirable aquarium subjects. Sadly, keeping them in captivity has not proved to be very successful. In their own environment, these fragile crinoids are the most successful of all the echinoderms.*

Below: *This delicate brittle star* (Ophiomyxa sp.) *is a suspension feeder that busily filters its prey of tiny zooplankton from the water currents sweeping by. Other species are less conspicuous detrital feeders, lurking below coral rubble in warm shallows.*

hidden away in recesses in the coral during the day. They differ from starfishes in a number of ways. The mouth, for example, is located on the upper surface of the disc rather than underneath. A feather star feeds by trapping small planktonic animals in sticky mucus on its feathery arms and transporting these tiny parcels by the action of microscopic cilia along grooves in the upper surface of each arm to the central mouth opening. Arms can number 200 or more in some species. In addition to these feathery appendages, tiny sharp hooks called cirri are located around the underside of the animal to allow it to cling to its vantage point. These animals are the most numerous of the echinoderms on the reef and there are species in a wide range of brilliant colours. Some Indo-Pacific species are imported for the aquarium, including the black *Lamprometra klunzinger*, the crimson *Himerometra robustipinna* and the brilliant yellow *Comanthus bennetti*. Keeping these animals in captivity has not proved to be successful in the past due, perhaps, to their stringent dietary requirements and easily stressed nature, which often leads to them casting arms. They will also shed their arms as a defence against predation.

Sea urchins
Sea urchins are an unusual form of echinoderm. It is easier to recognize them as such if you imagine a starfish with the arms curled upwards and joined together to form a hard fragile ball. Their body plan is similar to that of a starfish, with the mouth located below and tube feet being used for slowly moving over the reef. The mouth contains a complex structure known as Aristotle's lantern that incorporates five teeth and is used to scrape algae from rocky surfaces. In large numbers, such grazing can lead to erosion and reef damage.

The *Diadema* sea urchins have a particularly effective defence mechanism in the form of long, black spines that can be tipped with a toxic mucus capable of causing painful wounds. Even this means of protection has been broached by the triggerfishes, however. These fishes flip the urchin over with a sharp jet of water and feed upon the unprotected underparts. Even so, triggerfishes often become victims of the spines during this procedure, and it is not unusual to find the occasional large titan triggerfish (*Balistoides viridescens*) on Indo-Pacific reefs with a number of *Diadema* spines projecting from its snout.

Sea cucumbers
The final echinoderm group, the holothurians, or sea cucumbers, are sausage-shaped versions of the sea urchins. They have no spines but have projections called spicules and a rough exterior as protection from predators. Many species rely on releasing extremely distasteful chemicals called holothurins through the skin to deter predators, or they may release long, white strings of

Above: *The colourful sea apple feeds by placing each large tentacle in turn into the mouth and consuming captured particles, mainly diatoms, adhering to the mucus-covered surfaces.*

tubules from the anus, which are highly adhesive and poisonous.

There are two basic feeding methods, the most common being simply to pass sand and detritus through the body, digesting any organic matter in the process. A more elaborate method involves using the sticky, feathery tentacles around the mouth to trap suspended food. Many species have a matrix of these branching tentacles and can be observed placing each tentacle in turn into the mouth opening as they feed on the trapped particles.

A number of sea cucumber species are imported for the aquarium, and perhaps the best known is the Indo-Pacific sea apple (*Pseudocolochirus axiologus*), an attractive lilac species with rows of bright red tube feet along the body and delicate mauve and red feeding tentacles. This beautiful species feeds mainly on diatoms and can be kept quite successfully in the aquarium. Avoid using filtration systems that strip the water of the food this species needs; otherwise, you will need to add suitable food supplements.

Left: *The sea urchin* Asthenosoma varium *is common in the Indo-Pacific and the scourge of any unsuspecting diver. The urchin is covered in long, transparent, needle-sharp spines, each one tipped with a poison sac. Wounds from these can be painful and so this is one of a number of species not suitable (or widely available) for the aquarium. The Indo-Pacific common urchin (*Echinomelia mathaei*) is a much safer and more reliable choice.*

The friendly batfishes

There is one fish that all visitors to these waters like to meet because of its friendly disposition. The red-faced batfish (*Platax pinnatus*) has built up quite a rapport with divers in many parts of the Maldives and it is not unusual to have one or even a number of these sleek creatures tagging on behind during a dive. Just like a friendly stray dog, the batfish follows behind, hopeful of picking up a tidbit or even simply seeking companionship. The graceful disc-shaped, almost circular body, black with silvery stripes and with a permanently smiling face and expressive eyes, is an attraction which most divers look out for. The back reef mangrove areas form the nursery grounds of young batfishes. Here, they feed greedily on the abundant brineshrimp and crustaceans floating in the zooplankton and grow at a phenomenal rate. An interesting – and highly protective – feature of juvenile batfishes is their ability to mimic dead mangrove leaves by floating on the surface, curled up like a leaf. Their gold and brown coloration matches the leaf colours exactly.

Below: *Accompanied by a shoal of red-faced batfish* (Platax pinnatus), *a young diver eagerly joins in an impromptu underwater ballet. Not many other members of the coral kingdom are quite as responsive and personable as these friendly creatures.*

AQUARIUM CARE

Surgeonfishes

The Surgeonfishes (family Acanthuridae) are well represented in the Indo-Pacific and provide some of the hardiest and most amenable species for the marine aquarium. Surgeonfishes, or tangs as they are sometimes called, are distinguished by a laterally compressed body and steeply rising forehead, which gives them a permanent 'raised-eyebrow' expression of surprise. Many species are brightly coloured, with eye-catching markings.

A common characteristic of this family is the presence of sharp spines, or 'scalpels' (hence the name 'surgeons'), on either side of the base of the tail. Some species have a single spine that can be raised or folded back into a groove, while other species have two or three fixed spines arranged on a bony plate. Armed so effectively, it is not surprising that members of this family normally have little difficulty in defending themselves or their territory.

A number of species are delightful and easy to keep, provided you follow a few general rules. Surgeonfishes are generally sensitive to temperature changes, for example, and can be easily stressed by other than gradual fluctuations. They also prefer relatively high temperatures, thriving at around 26°C(79°F). Although many species shoal in the wild, they tend to be mutually intolerant of each other in captivity and so it is best to keep only a single specimen in a community aquarium.

Like all members of this family, the powder blue surgeonfish (*Acanthurus leucosternon*) is an energetic swimmer and is happiest in a large aquarium with strongly aerated water and plenty of swimming space, as well as some cover. Generally herbivorous in feeding habits, it will thrive on a basic diet of natural algae growing in the aquarium. Where this is not available, be sure to provide supplements of algae,

Above: *The brilliant blue coloration of the powder blue surgeonfish is seldom as vivid in aquarium conditions as it is in the wild. It is quite a sensitive species; to succeed with it, pay close attention to water quality and temperature. Make any changes gradually.*

spinach or lettuce. These fishes will readily accept *Tubifex* worms and frozen meaty foods, but be careful to ensure that any live foods are clean and disease free.

Powder blue surgeonfishes are sometimes considered to be prone to disease. Undoubtedly, this can often be due to their high sensitivity to temperature changes during transportation. The resulting stress can discourage them from feeding and lower their resistance to disease. More care taken at this stage, plus gradual acclimation to aquarium temperatures before introduction, should forestall many of these problems at the outset.

CORAL REEFS OF THE WORLD
Red Sea

'A rich profusion of fish'

The Red Sea is the continuation of the huge fault that first split the continent of Africa, and in doing so created the African Rift Valley, before extending northwards to produce the Red Sea and the Gulfs of Aqaba and Suez. The fringing coral reefs bordering the Red Sea are generally narrow, positioned on the edge of a huge chasm often many thousands of metres deep. The steeply shelving continental slope has literally forced light-loving marine life, such as corals, to crowd into a very narrow band. The depth zonation, i.e. the various zones of non-moving animals fixed to the seabed, is markedly compressed. Moving from one zone to another can be accomplished by finning only a few metres down the steep slope into the depths. In such a situation, it is easy to understand how competition for space has resulted in such a profusion of marine animals in a small area, creating a huge aquarium-like effect teeming with life.

Red Sea reefs are among the most beautifully developed reefs in the world and contain a wide range of coral species. Sometimes 20 or more species can be found within the span of a few metres and their dense growth provides an ideal habitat for a wide range of animals.

The contrast between the vibrant reefs beneath the surface and the stark desert landscapes above water never ceases to amaze. It emphasizes how successful the corals have been in transforming an equally sterile environment below the water into a thriving ecosystem. Their association with the tiny zooxanthellae – single-celled plants that thrive in the tissues of many coelenterates and some other marine animals – has allowed corals to harness the energy of the sun to provide food and enabled them to act as a vital catalyst for other creatures by producing these magnificent reef structures.

A silver shoal in a Red Sea cave.

A rich profusion of fish

The most spectacular feature of Red Sea reefs is undoubtedly the wide variety of fish species they support. Over 1,000 species, varying enormously in colour shape and behaviour, have been identified as indigenous to the Red Sea and of these perhaps 30 percent are specific to this area, an amazingly high proportion considering the time usually taken for new species to evolve and the relatively short period, in evolutionary terms, since the area was first invaded by the waters of the Indian Ocean.

If we were to immerse ourselves below the clear blue waters, the first impressions would be of colour and movement as multitudes of brightly coloured fish mingle with the coral. Aquarists would easily recognize many small damselfish species, including humbugs (*Dascyllus aruanus*), dominoes (*D. trimaculatus*) and green chromis (*Chromis caerulea*), and the Red Sea clown (*Amphiprion bicinctus*) nestling among the tentacles of the large *Stoichactis gigas* anemone. Attractively shaped angelfish and butterflyfish are common to the reefs, and familiar favourites such as the regal angel (*Pygoplites diacanthus*) and the emperor angel (*Pomacanthus imperator*) are easily encountered, together with a much less common aquarium fish, the Red Sea half moon angelfish (*P. maculosus*). Many of the Red Sea butterflyfishes are strictly specific to the area and are not generally exported for the aquarist hobby, but *Chaetodon semilarvatus* and *C. fasciatus*, the Red Sea version of the Indo-Pacific species *C. lunula*, would not be strangers to marine fishkeepers.

The prolific wrasses

A prominent feature of most Red Sea reefs is the large number and wide diversity of members of the

116

Left: *The beautiful crown butterflyfish* (Chaetodon paucifasciatus) *is one of many fish species found exclusively in the Red Sea. The Indo-Pacific species* C. mertensii *and* C. xanthurus *are similar and closely related to it.*

Below: *The seaward faces of the reef crest and upper reef slope are rich in life, as golden jewelfish* (Anthias squamipinnnis) *and other zooplankton feeders harvest the rich upwellings of plankton from deeper waters.*

wrasse family, Labridae. There are over 50 species in the Red Sea area, varying in size from the diminutive sixstripe wrasse (*Pseudocheilinus hexataenia*) at only 3-4cm(1.2-1.6in) up to the massive humphead wrasse (*Cheilinus undulatus*), which can reach 2m(6.6ft) or more in length.

Many species undergo spectacular changes in colour and shape as they mature from juvenile to adult. The clown twin-spot wrasse (*Coris aygula*), for example, is a real gem as a juvenile, with creamy white coloration handsomely marked with small black spots and two vivid orange dorsal spots. Aquarists are very fond of this species but would not recognize it as a 90cm(36in)-adult sporting a large hump on its forehead and muted grey body coloration. The broomtail wrasse (*Cheilinus lunulatus*), on the other hand, is a beautiful fish throughout its life and is aptly named for its long ragged tail edged with deep blue. Large males can reach 50cm(20in) in length, with a dark green body suffused with blue and yellow, and attractively marked with spots and bars. An impressive sight on the reef.

On maturity, male and female wrasses are usually quite dissimilar. This has caused difficulties for biologists in the past, with a single species often being mistakenly described as a number of different species. And complications over sex do not stop there because, in common with many reef fish, labrids have the ability to change sex during their adult lives; they mature as one sex first, then may change to the other.

The sex life of some species can be very complicated, with most males occurring as a result of a sex change from a mature female. These males are known as 'super males' and are generally larger and develop gaudier colour patterns compared with their former female coloration. There are also a small number of 'natural' males, i.e. born as males; these maintain a similar appearance to females on maturity and are much smaller than the 'super males'. During spawning, the 'super males' establish breeding stations, to which the females come to spawn. The super males drive other super males away from their breeding sites but can easily overlook female-lookalike naturally born males, which are able to gain access and spawn with the females.

This unusual behaviour interests scientists because it demonstrates the rare phenomenon of

Below: *A flamboyant male broomtail wrasse* (Cheilinus lunulatus) *sporting the ragged tail that so aptly reflects its common name. It is closely related to the larger humphead wrasse* (Cheilinus undulatus) *and is equally inquisitive, boldly approaching divers entering its territory.*

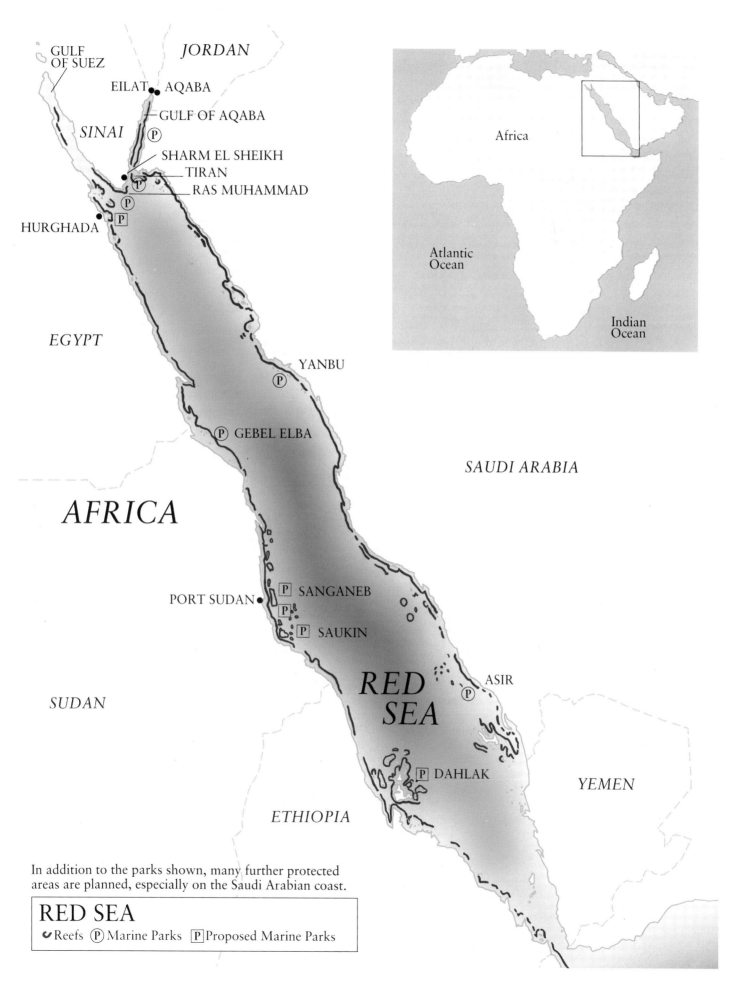

GULF
OF SUEZ

JORDAN

EILAT • AQABA

GULF OF AQABA

SINAI

Ⓟ

SHARM EL SHEIKH
TIRAN
RAS MUHAMMAD

Ⓟ

ⓅP

HURGHADA •

EGYPT

Africa

Atlantic
Ocean

Indian
Ocean

YANBU

Ⓟ

Ⓟ GEBEL ELBA

SAUDI ARABIA

AFRICA

P SANGANEB

PORT SUDAN •

P

P SAUKIN

*RED
SEA*

ASIR

Ⓟ

SUDAN

P DAHLAK

YEMEN

ETHIOPIA

In addition to the parks shown, many further protected
areas are planned, especially on the Saudi Arabian coast.

RED SEA

↝ Reefs Ⓟ Marine Parks P Proposed Marine Parks

two quite different reproductive strategies displayed by a single species. The significance of this in terms of input to the genetic pot is that the dominance of the super male is short circuited and the apparently inferior naturally born males are able to provide their contribution. Examples of such a contradiction of the natural law of evolution based upon the principle of 'survival of the fittest' seldom occur.

One wrasse which can be easily recognized is the cleaner wrasse (*Labroides dimidiatus*), a fascinating species to watch as it maintains a fixed station on the reef acting as a focal point for fish to congregate to be cleaned of parasites and minor irritations. The flashing of the cleaner's electric blue body stripe acts as an unmistakable beacon to nearby fishes. The cleaning symbiosis of the cleaner wrasse must have been in existence for a very long time because another fish species, a small blenny, the predatory false cleaner fish (*Aspidontus taeniatus*), has evolved similar body markings to *Labroides dimidiatus* and even mimics the dancing motion the wrasse uses to summon its customers. The unsuspecting 'client' arrives to be cleaned and the deceiving blenny darts forward, attacking its victim and tearing off small pieces of living tissue.

Above: *At the diminutive end of the wrasse size scale is the pretty, but secretive sixstripe wrasse.*

Left: *A cleaner wrasse busy attending a 'client' fish, a routine pursuit both seem to find beneficial and pleasurable.*

DIVING PROFILE *The Red Sea*

CLIMATE

Air temperature range:
North 20°-30°C(68-86°F)
South 21°-32°C(70-90°F)

Sea temperature range:
North 20°-22°C(68-72°F)
South 20°-24°C(68-75°F)

Not surprisingly, the Red Sea resorts in the Gulf of Aqaba experience slightly cooler conditions than those at Djibouti, 1,200km(750miles) to the south. Winter temperatures are still very pleasant, however, in the north, and the large numbers of sunny days combined with excellent year-round sea conditions means little more discomfort than wearing a light wet suit to ward off the chilly water. Desert climate conditions apply throughout the Red Sea, with hot daytime conditions contrasting with relatively low night-time temperatures of 12°-16°C(54°-61°F).

FACILITIES

The north is dominated by the Israeli town of Eilat, which has large hotels and offers a wide variety of sea sports, including extensive facilities for snorkelling and diving. Complementary, if not as extensive, facilities are available over the border into Jordan at Aqaba. Dive safaris are also arranged across the Egyptian border along the Sinai Peninsula, from Eilat south to Sharm-el-Sheikh. These include cross-country trips from Cairo to Sharm-el-Sheikh. Diving activity along the main Egyptian coast of the Red Sea centres on the resort of Hurghada, just south of the point at which the Red Sea divides into the Gulfs of Suez and Aqaba.

Djibouti and Port Sudan in Sudan provide facilities for resort-type diving and are embarkation points for live-aboard dive boat operations. Live-aboard arrangements are also available from Eilat in Israel and Sharm-el-Sheikh in Sinai, providing access to the region.

DIVE RATING

The diving from all the Red Sea centres is excellent, providing varied opportunities to dive some of the most well-developed and pristine reefs in the Indo-Pacific. Reefs are at their best in the Straits of Tiran (at the entrance to the Gulf of Aqaba) and wall diving is supreme at Ras Muhammad (at the tip of the Sinai Peninsula). Wreck diving on the wreck of the *Umbria*, close to Port Sudan, defies description.

CONSERVATION

The governments of Israel, Egypt, Jordan and Saudi Arabia have all made provisions to conserve the reefs and their associated sea life. The most popular of these is the marine conservation area established at Ras Muhammad, which protects some of the best reefs for SCUBA diving in the whole of the Red Sea region.

AQUARIUM CARE

Damselfishes

The large Pomacentridae family has a wide distribution over all the tropical oceans of the world. It can be divided into two groups: the anemonefishes, or clownfishes, (*Amphiprion* and *Premnas* spp.) and the damselfishes. Members of both groups are a familiar feature of reefs in many parts of the world, where they are usually found hovering close to coral heads, ready to dart instantly into the protective coral branches when disturbed. Many species display strong territorial behaviour and aggressively attack or drive other fishes away from their small fixed stations on the reef.

There are no clear distinctions between the sexes but some species form into pairs on maturity. Anemonefishes and damselfishes lay elliptical eggs, which adhere to a previously cleaned coral surface chosen as the nest site. The nest is guarded by both parents or, in some instances, only by the male, and parental protection is sometimes extended to the newly hatched fry before they eventually disperse.

Members of this family are also common in the aquarium hobby, being prized for their attractive colours and patterns and their convenient small size. They are the hardiest of fishes for the marine aquarium and a very popular choice for beginners. Among many popular members of the

Above: *The vivid blue damsel from the Indo-Pacific* (Abudefduf cyaneus) *is not as territorially defensive as other damsels.*

Above: *The humbug* (Dascyllus aruanus) *is often the first introduction many aquarists have to marine fishkeeping. It is a hardy beginner's fish, but beware – it's a bully.*

damselfish group are the electric blue and brilliant green *Chromis* and *Pomacentrus* species, the striking *Abudefduf* species (including the aptly named striped sergeant major, *Abudefduf saxatilis*) and members of the *Dascyllus* genus. Notable aquarium favourites among *Dascyllus* species are the attractive humbug (*D. aruanus*), with humbug-like, black-and-white stripes, and the velvety black, bouncy little domino (*D. trimaculatus*), instantly recognizable by its three white spots. Damsels of this genus are all very active and hardy fish, rarely reaching more than 10cm(4in) in nature. They are carnivorous, feeding on the minute zooplankton in the water column above their selected coral head. Most *Dascyllus* species show their aggression by making audible clicking noises with the small teeth lining the throat.

Humbug damsels are easy to obtain and make very amenable aquarium subjects. They tolerate less than perfect water conditions and thrive on a diet of dried foods and fresh or frozen meaty foods. There is a hitch, unfortunately, in that they are the most territorially possessive of all the damselfishes and will pugnaciously defend their area of the aquarium from other fishes. They form aggregations in the wild but in the aquarium can show intolerance of their own kind as they mature. A small humbug can quite quickly establish a reign of terror in a small aquarium and will attack much larger fish by nipping at their fins and flanks. To establish harmony in the aquarium and avoid problems as the humbug grows older, use a large tank and take care in choosing and introducing other fish. Fish that have grown up with the humbug, for example, are far more likely to be left unmolested than new introductions to the aquarium.

Below: *The iridescent green* Chromis caerulea *is a common Indo-Pacific species and settles well to aquarium life. It is a peaceful fish and thrives in small shoals.*

DIVING WITH THE HATCHETFISH

To many of us, a visit to a tropical coral reef remains an unattainable paradise or the substance of pipedreams conjured up in front of the television on a cold winter's evening. However, this dream has now become more of a reality with the discovery of the Red Sea as a holiday destination. It all started when a few European skin divers first experienced the delights of diving the Gulf of Aqaba, at the most northerly end of the Red Sea. Tourism increased and, finally, package tour companies began to offer cheap inclusive tours to the area. This improved access and now it is possible for divers and non-divers (after a little snorkel instruction) to share and enjoy the pleasures of exploring the beautiful underwater scenery of Red Sea reefs.

Situated just south of the 30° parallel, it is perhaps surprising to find tropical reefs flourishing so far to the north. Despite this, the Red Sea is a truly tropical sea and the Gulf of Aqaba is one of the most northerly coral reef zones in the northern hemisphere. The coral reefs of the Gulf owe their existence to the Red Sea's unique position, almost totally enclosed by surrounding land masses and within an area which enjoys a large number of hot, clear sunny days all year around. This combination allows the waters of the Gulf to warm up sufficiently to permit coral not only to succeed but also to flourish and produce high-quality reefs of massive proportions.

Nevertheless, visitors to the area are still a little amazed by the relatively low sea temperatures, which can fall to 20°C(68°F) in winter – only marginally within the acknowledged lower limit for normal coral growth. When combined with a further feature of the area – high salinity at around 41 parts per thousand – such cool conditions seem to provide an unlikely recipe for coral reef development and would certainly be cause for concern if duplicated in the aquarium. Conditions are ideal, however, and reflected in the breathtaking beauty of the luxuriant reefs and the equally astounding diversity of sea life.

Here, we follow the exploits of a typical dive group exploring the waters of the Gulf. The dive site, a few kilometres from Aqaba towards the Saudi Arabian border, provided a perfect setting on a small, crescent-shaped bay between low sand bluffs. Across a deep blue sea and under a blue sky, visibility extended to the mountains of the Sinai Peninsula.

The briefing from our dive guide completed, we followed his instructions and snorkelled for a hundred metres or so over sand and scattered outcrops of coral until we reached the reef crest, passing a large coral outcrop and finally arriving at the drop-off. This vertical cliff was incredible; dramatic crags thronging with clouds of small fish plummeted 50m(164ft) vertically into the depths. A huge school of surgeonfishes passed by with two cornetfishes in attendance hoping to surprise small fish by disguising themselves as members of this harmless shoal of herbivores.

Three large humphead wrasse (*Cheilinus undulatus*), each 2m(6.6ft) long and weighing over 150kg(330lb), materialized from the blue and swam through clouds of golden jewelfish (*Anthias squamipinnis*) fading away from the reef into the depths. Following them down the cliff face to a depth of 30m(100ft), we discovered an impressive crag of coral – like a huge stalagmite thrusting upwards from the depths – covered in life. On top of this mini seamount, a large *Heteractis* anemone provided a home for two large Red Sea clownfishes (*Amphiprion bicinctus*), which pugnaciously attacked us to defend their clutch of eggs nestled

Above: *Hatchetfish, or sweepers, are nocturnal hunters that rest during the day in deep recesses in the reef. Large shoals often return to the same cave after each night's excursions. They form dense silvery curtains that part as the divers approach, reacting instantly to any disturbance.*

below the anemone's protective tentacles. We passed by a fan-shaped gorgonian, looking like a spider's web and appropriately adorned with three black, spiderlike crinoids. Below a ledge, a large basket star clung to the coral surface, awaiting darkness to join the crinoids and feed by using its feathery arms to filter out rising zooplankton from the water current.

Moving back up the cliff, patrolled by bristling lionfishes and a small pack of 1m(3.3ft)-long barracudas, we came across a large coral head

The Gulf of Aqaba

EILAT
ISRAEL
AQABA
GULF OF AQABA
JORDAN

Above: *Simply investigating the underside of a coral overhang can damage the reef, since the exhaust bubbles from the SCUBA equipment can become trapped and strand marine life in air spaces.*

Left: *Thousands of fish fry mass in swirling iridescent shoals. These tiny midwater feeders thrive on the abundant plankton and in turn provide rich pickings for predators such as lionfishes and groupers.*

the size of a small cottage covered in bright pink *Dendronephthya* soft corals. On one side at the base a man-sized tunnel was alive with lionfishes, large groupers and thousands of tiny fish fry, each bright silver and 2-3cm(0.8-1.2in) long. A large shoal of dark brown hatchetfish, or sweepers, (*Pempheris vanicolensis*) poured in and out of the opening. As I swam into the tunnel mouth, the fish closed in behind me and almost completely obscured my view in a living curtain of fish. Wherever I moved, the hatchetfish parted on my approach and closed ranks again behind me. Further down the tunnel, the mass of fish suddenly disappeared with amazing speed, leaving me guessing what would happen next. Perhaps a large shark would join me in the tunnel or a predatory grouper with an appetite for small fish? Suddenly, a large dark form blundered up the cliff, spewing out silver mushrooms of bubbles – the sure sign of the approach of the ultimate predator and spoiler of the reef – man.

Dangers of the reef

Although very attractive, the Red Sea reefs are not without their dangers. Visitors to reef areas in any part of the world need to be cautious and although the risks may sometimes be exaggerated, they are real. However, a little knowledge of each area can help to distinguish the real dangers from the imaginary and, once properly informed, it is easy to avoid many of the risks involved. To put this into proper perspective, the maxim 'look don't touch' will help in most situations and this applies not only to the marine animals you can see but also to others that may be cunningly camouflaged as a piece of dead coral or a patch of sand. It is best to snorkel or dive out of touching distance of the reef and to avoid standing on living reefs wherever possible, both for your own safety and to assist in the conservation of the reef itself, which can easily be damaged by trampling.

Sharks and barracudas

The principal danger most people associate with swimming or diving among coral reefs is the possibility of a shark attack. Dangerous sharks are a fact of life in some parts of the world and most of us are acquainted with the reports of attacks in Australia and California. Films and television programmes have glorified the gruesome aspects of such attacks and have branded the shark as an evil and primitive creature charging from the depths to attack with merciless ferocity.

Sharks *can* attack people, and do, but these attacks are extremely rare and confined to a handful of locations around the world. To most divers, the experience of observing a shark in its natural surroundings is exhilarating and unforgettable. No marine animal is quite so graceful or beautiful and none so successful. For millions of years, the shark has commanded a high position at the top of the food chain without any need to evolve further. It remains one of the earliest forms of life still living today.

In the Red Sea, there are three common species all classed as dangerous to man; the whitetip reef shark (*Triaenodon obesus*); the blacktip reef shark(*Carcharhinus melanopterus*); and, living close to reefs, the shortnose blacktip shark (*C. wheeleri*). These are all relatively small sharks, seldom reaching more than 1.5m(5ft) in length, which feed on small fish and crustaceans. Of these, whitetips are the most commonly observed, but a diver needs to be pretty lucky to approach close to

Above: *A whitetip reef shark* (Triaenodon obesus), *the most common of the Indo-Pacific species. There are no reliable records of attacks, but this species is regarded as dangerous.*

Left: *Shoals of juvenile barracudas such as these are generally quite harmless, although lone adults may sometimes attack in murky waters.*

Left: *A deceptively pretty scorpionfish – in this case, the common Red Sea species* Scorpaenopsis oxycephalus – *lies in camouflaged concealment, ready to surprise its prey. Its venomous spines are only used in self defence.*

Below: *A* morose stonefish (Synanceia verrucosa), *one of the most venomous fishes likely to be encountered on the reef. It is difficult to see, even close up. Take care not to blunder into this one by mistake!*

this nervous species. Other sharks can also be seen at certain times of the year. In specific areas, Ras Muhammad on the Sinai Peninsula for example, hammerhead sharks (*Sphyrna lewini*) form into large aggregations in spring to breed, but for most of the time these oceanic sharks are confined to deep water. The oceanic whitetip or silvertip (*Carcharhinus albimarginatus*) is common in deep water but is rarely seen inshore in the Red Sea.

Barracudas are also large carnivores and are often categorized along with sharks as vicious killers. There have been attacks on man in the past but the dangers are generally exaggerated. The great barracuda (*Sphyraena barracuda*) is found in the Red Sea and other parts of the Indo-Pacific (and also in the Atlantic) and can reach over 2m(6.6ft) in length. This solitary hunter is fearless and will approach quite close if its curiosity is aroused. Attacks have been generally confined to murky water, where a leg or arm has been mistaken for prey, or as retaliation when a fish has been hooked or speared by a fisherman.

Spines, stings and venom

On occasion, divers may see sharks and barracudas, but they are far more likely to encounter dangerous fish that rely on venomous stings for defence and aggression. The lionfishes, scorpionfishes and stonefishes, of the family Scorpaenidae, are bristling with sharp venomous spines. The most outstanding Red Sea species must be the lionfish (*Pterois volitans*), a widely distributed Indo-Pacific species which, despite its needle-sharp venomous dorsal, anal and pelvic spines, is one of the most unusual and attractive fishes. The behaviour of this fish is both

fascinating and menacing. On being approached, it erects its winglike pectoral fins and finally assumes a head-down position in the manner of a bull about to charge. Despite its reputation in the Gulf of Aqaba for being inclined to be aggressive, the lionfish uses its venomous spines essentially as a means of defence against larger predators that would otherwise snap up this slow-moving species.

The stonefish (*Synanceia verrucosa*), closely related to scorpionfishes, is one of the most venomous creatures in the sea. Wounds from the dorsal spines are extremely painful and deaths have been reported. The danger with this species, is that it will be stepped on or touched by accident. Its coral-like camouflage is so perfect and matches its surroundings so well that it can be undetectable, even at close range.

The spines of the stingray are generally not considered venomous, but they are capable of delivering a painful wound that invariably becomes infected from the mucus covering each spine. There is a difference of opinion on this, however, since research has shown that for part of their lives some stingray species have tissue surrounding the base of the sting that produces venom. Stingrays carry one or more of these very sharp spines, which can measure up to 10cm(4in) long in larger specimens. Although not aggressive creatures, they can injure anyone who inadvertently steps on them as purely a defensive reaction. Rays enjoy basking in shallow water covered by a loose covering of sand and a surprising number of visitors to reef areas have been injured by stepping on these superbly camouflaged creatures.

The most common Red Sea species (but also widely distributed in the Indo-Pacific) is the blue-spotted stingray (*Taeniura lymna*), a very beautiful ray with numerous bright blue spots. This ray bears one or two spines at the base of a tail, which is longer than the disc-shaped body. It is often encountered in reef areas, hiding in small caves and on sandy patches beneath overhanging projections in the reef.

The treatment for stings ranges from immediate medical treatment in the case of stonefish and lionfish venom, where antivenin and heat treatment can effect relief, to cleaning the wound caused by a stingray barb and soaking the area in hot salt water. Even stingray wounds can be unbearably painful, however, and may require painkilling injections.

Although venomous sea snakes are not found in the Red Sea, they can be found in other parts of the Indo-Pacific and so it is appropriate to broaden our discussion and mention them here. Divers are likely to come in close proximity to dangerous sea snakes only in locations on the Australian Barrier Reef and adjoining Coral Sea (see page 167). The reputation of these Australian snakes is based on their possession of a virulent venom and on their behaviour during breeding times, when they can be aggressive. Again, the myth has taken over from reality to a large extent and most divers in that area find them to be inoffensive, curious creatures that are gentle enough to be handled.

Experience has shown that many potentially dangerous marine animals are quite safe, but to avoid harm always show a healthy respect for venomous marine creatures and large carnivores. These fascinating animals should also be respected for their ingenuity in adapting to their environment so successfully. Until man arrived on the scene, many of them had nothing to fear. Unfortunately, the revulsion often felt for animals labelled 'dangerous', fuelled by myths and hearsay, has often lead to their total extinction in some areas (such as big cats in parts of Africa and India, and sharks off some parts of the Australian coast). The biological consequences of removing such important predators from the marine ecosystem cannot be overlooked. It is a pity that we cannot appreciate the role they play and marvel at their ingenuity rather than blindly fear it.

Left: *The twin spines on this blue-spotted stingray* (Taeniura lymna) *are just visible, laid flat against the tail. These can be erected in self defence. Take care not to step on this ray; it may not be very visible as it lies partly buried in sandy patches.*

AQUARIUM CARE

Lionfishes

It must seem a little unusual to be recommending fishes as aquarium subjects that are potentially lethal to their owners. Without doubt, the venomous spines of a number of lionfish species can be dangerous, varying from bee-sting proportions to a powerful injection of a venom that can cause excruciating pain or even death. Thankfully, most of the highly venomous species do not make popular aquarium subjects, not because of their dangerous reputation but quite simply because they are too ugly to appeal to marine aquarists.

There are, however, several members of this family that make attractive and unusual aquarium subjects. The members of the genus *Pterois* fall into this category and, despite a pretty virulent sting, they are very popular. The Red Sea and the Indo-Pacific are well endowed with *Pterois* species, of which the best-known and most attractive is *Pterois volitans*, the lionfish or turkeyfish. The form, colour and pattern of this species are very striking and it is hard to imagine that their main purpose is to camouflage the fish. On the reef, it is a cunning predator of small fish and uses two quite distinct means of catching prey. In the open, it can remain motionless, blending perfectly with its surroundings by varying the intensity of its colouring, ready to gulp down any unsuspecting passerby.

Alternatively, it spreads its winglike pectoral fins and sweeps small fish into an area of no escape on the reef and simply swallows them with ruthless efficiency.

The dorsal, anal and pelvic fins of *P. volitans* are all venomous and the toxin is potent but not as lethal as a stonefish (*Synanceia verrucosa*) or scorpionfish (*Scorpaenopsis oxycephalus*). Anchor-shaped spines are fed by adjacent grooves running from a large gland attached to the spine. A sting usually results only from careless handling, as this species is not aggressive. Symptoms can vary, but a large fish is capable of a sting that will be unbelievably painful and may have lethal consequences. The recommended treatment is to immerse the injured part in water as hot as can be borne to alleviate the pain by clotting the venom – much in the same way as the white of an egg solidifies when hard boiled. An anti-venin serum is available from specialist dealers but requires to be administered by a qualified medical practitioner.

Despite – or perhaps because of – this notoriety, the lionfish appears in the top ten list of marine fishes commonly available to the hobby. It is an ideal aquarium subject, seldom reaching more than 35cm(14in) in the wild and perhaps half this size in captivity. Since it spends most of the daytime in clefts or below coral overhangs,

Above: *Lionfishes – in this case,* Pterois volitans *– are very handsome, despite their venomous spines. They make good aquarium subjects, but they will hunt down and devour any smaller fish or crustaceans in the tank. Note that the dorsal fin rays are quite separate, while the pectoral fin rays are partially joined by thin tissue. This helps to create effective 'wings' that the fish uses to 'corner' prey before engulfing them.*

it is naturally adaptable to the confines of an aquarium. It is a very hardy species and is not choosy as to water quality, having a known nitrate tolerance of up to 55ppm.

Feeding can be a problem with some newly introduced specimens and there may be a need to coax these fish to feed by offering live foods such as guppies or mollies. Once this species starts to eat regularly it becomes a gross feeder, accepting non-living foods, such as fresh or frozen shrimp, fish and shellfish meat, and quickly puts on weight. Lionfishes are generally sociable in a community aquarium but, of course, they will attack and devour any fish smaller than themselves, as well as cleaner shrimps and other small crustaceans. These predatory carnivores have deceptively large mouths, enabling them to engulf quite sizeable prey. A good rule is to keep them with their own species or with larger fish of other species.

DIVING THE UMBRIA

A dive on the wreck of the *Umbria* has been described as the ultimate wreck dive. Ever since Hans Hass introduced the world to this exciting dive location with his book 'Under the Red Sea' in the early 1950s, and later in a film of the same name, diving enthusiasts and photographers have regarded the site as an underwater Mecca.

Situated close to Port Sudan, the *Umbria*, an Italian registered vessel carrying a load of munitions, was scuttled in 1940 in an effort to prevent the British Authorities in Port Sudan impounding her, following Italy's entry into the Second World War. The vessel settled down in 30m(100ft) of water, almost upright, but with a list to her port side. The bows of the vessel rest in the coral, with the portside obscured and the starboard side facing upwards, the starboard screw clear of the seabed. At one time, large parts of her superstructure, including the funnel and main mast, broke the surface but now only small sections and the starboard davits are showing above the water.

Approaching the *Umbria* is relatively easy and the area is protected by reefs surrounding the whole site. The visibility can vary but is generally in the order of 30m(100ft) or more.

The wreck is swept by currents loaded with nutrients and this, combined with the clear water and intense sunlight, has caused the wreck to be extensively colonized by light-seeking sea life, including prolific growths of corals and all manner of marine creatures. In the well-lit sections, the wreck structure has been totally covered in hard corals, mostly *Acropora, Millepora* stinging coral and *Montipora*, in shades of blue, mauve, pink and yellow. It can be uncanny to swim along the external companionways running down the starboard side, still largely recognizable, with the guard rails facing the surface and the

Right: *Diving the wreck of the Umbria near Port Sudan, perhaps the most photographed wreck dive since its discovery by Hans Hass.*

door openings and ports appearing as gaping black holes. Clouds of golden jewelfish (*Anthias squamipinnis*) shoal in the sunlight, accompanied by stripy sergeant major damsels (*Abudefduf saxatilis*). A large humphead wrasse (*Cheilinus undulatus*), a permanent resident, stands sentinel to the wreck, first disappearing then reappearing from the blue depths. The *Umbria* appears to harbour larger than average-sized fishes, including blue-spotted squaretail groupers (*Plectropomus truncatus*) with protruding canine teeth. These lurk in the depths of the hold, together with large brown moray eels (*Gymnothorax* spp.).

Fish crowding over the wreck can appear like the contents of a 'Red Sea Fishwatchers Guide'. Brightly coloured half moon angels (*Pomacanthus maculosus*), emperor angelfish (*P. imperator*) and the delicate regal angelfish (*Pygoplites diacanthus*) are common on the site, as are the exquisite (*Chaetodon austriacus*) and orange-face (*Gonochaetodon larvatus*) butterflyfishes. Large lionfish flit down the companionways and shoals of triggerfishes and surgeonfishes are an everyday feature. In the winter months, manta rays pass close by the site in huge and impressive aggregations.

For wreck explorers, the interior of the ship and the holds are still largely intact, with a major part of the cargo strewn around. The site is designated a dangerous wreck and the potentially lethal bombs, shells and bullets should be left well alone. The silt-covered engines look capable of springing back to life and parts of the crews' quarters and communal areas still contain many interesting artifacts of everyday life.

The main feature of the wreck is its magnificent sea life. This is protected by the Sudanese Government, who have banned spearfishing and the collection of corals and shells within its waters, thus safeguarding the future of the *Umbria* experience for new generations of divers who have yet to discover its fascination.

Below: *Cardinalfishes, here* Apogon leptacanthus, *are active at night as they feed on zooplankton. A wreck forms an ideal daytime retreat for them.*

Below: *A number of emperor angelfish* (Pomacanthus imperator) *live close to the Umbria wreck. Hand feeding has made them bold.*

Below: *Regal angelfish* (Pygoplites diacanthus) *are a common sight around the wreck of the Umbria. The Red Sea strain of this species is much richer in coloration than its counterparts in the waters around Singapore and the Philippines.*

The wreck of the Umbria

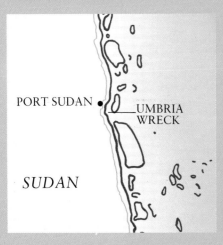

PORT SUDAN

UMBRIA WRECK

SUDAN

DIVING RAS MUHAMMAD

Ras Muhammad, or Mohammed's Head, is located at the point at which the Red Sea divides, with the Gulf of Aqaba to the east and the approaches to the Gulf of Suez to the west. This barren finger of land points out into the Red Sea at the southernmost tip of the Sinai Peninsula, the sun-baked land seemingly devoid of life sharply contrasting with the rich and diverse marine life to be found beneath the sea lapping its shores. The land may not have the necessary ingredients for life but the sea certainly does, supporting one of the Earth's most prolific sources of marine life.

The continental slope at Ras Muhammad is very close inshore and often vertical, even undercut in places. Located as it is on a Ras, or peninsula, projecting into deep water, the reefs plunge precipitously to great depths. Diving this area usually means encounters with large pelagic fish, visitors to the reef from the open sea or the depths. Large sharks are common and hammerheads gather in large aggregations to breed in early spring. Shoals of 1m(39in)-long barracuda and silvery jacks are frequent visitors and graceful eagle rays coast along about 20m(66ft) below the surface close to the drop-off to deeper and darker waters.

Diving at Ras Muhammad usually gets under way from a boat, although it is easy for a diver to swim out from the shore in many places. Passing over the shallow reef crest into deep water immediately produces a kind of free-fall sensation as, surrounded by shoals of golden jewelfish (*Anthias squamipinnis*), an awesome sight unfolds. Suspended in the clear water above such great depths, the impression of hanging in space or falling feels very real. A quick adjustment of buoyancy to a more neutral state arrests any uncontrolled downward movement and provides the opportunity to take a closer look at the immediate surroundings. The strong light above the surface is transformed to blue and the pastel colours of the corals and brightly coloured jewelfish quickly fade with increasing depth.

Above: *Ras Muhammad is one of the few places where you will find the tiny Fridman's fish* (Pseudochromis fridmanni). *This species was discovered in the 1970s by David Fridman of the Marine Laboratory in Eilat.*

Centre: *The rocky promontory of Ras Muhammad juts out from the Sinai towards the Straits of Tiran. The stark desert scenery contrasts with the rich marine life that thrives below water.*

But, in the relative shallows, only 6-8m(20-26ft) from the surface, the world is still colourful, with pink, peach, brown, and pale blue hard corals forming a backdrop to brightly coloured reef fish, tiny gems surrounded by the intricate filigree of the coral. Fiercely territorial striped surgeonfish (*Acanthurus sohal*) swim hither and thither, tending and protecting their gardens of algae. A cleaner wrasse (*Labroides dimidiatus*) holds surgery on a coral head, swimming in and out of the open gill plates of a bright red grouper (*Cephalopholis miniata*) as

Left: *The stately yellowbar angelfish* (Pomacanthus maculosus) *is endemic to the Red Sea and the East African coast south to Zanzibar.*

Below: *With increasing depth, the wall of colourful hard corals gives way to soft corals and gorgonians.*

it picks parasites and small pieces of dead skin from the fish's gills. A large anemone plays host to two small Red Sea clownfish (*Amphiprion bicinctus*), the only species of clownfish represented in the Red Sea and a common sight in shallow water.

Passing down the wall, the hard corals give way to fluffy soft corals and gorgonians. The huge bulk of a humphead wrasse (*Cheilinus undulatus*) appears from the blue, a 1.5m(5ft)-long specimen with a large humped forehead, on its way to keep an appointment with the tiny cleaner wrasse in the shallows above. Three spotted eagle rays (*Stoasodon narinari*) fly past in close formation, wings beating in unison as they change direction the instant they detect the diver's presence, and speed off gracefully into the open sea.

A not too infrequent experience is an encounter with a large scalloped hammerhead shark (*Sphyrna lewini*).

The unmistakable silhouette of this, the most recognizable of sharks, may suddenly appear from the depths below, the huge animal slowly swimming with a pronounced weaving motion of its tail. Although more than 15-20m(50-66ft) below, the shark can seem enormous and its movements menacing. Its deceptively slow swimming action nevertheless allows it to vanish into the depths as quickly as it appears. The feeling of vulnerability is very pronounced on such occasions in open oceanic conditions and it is reassuring to have the cover of the reef wall close by for protection. Divers have visited this site when the water has been filled with hammerheads during their breeding season! Ras Muhammad is thus able to provide some exciting and unforgettable experiences that add an extra dimension to Red Sea diving and certainly cause the adrenalin to flow more quickly!

Above: *Entering the twilight world of Ras Muhammad, the diver descends the sheer reef precipice.*

Ras Muhammad

SINAI

SAUDI ARABIA

RAS MUHAMMAD

EGYPT

Anemones and their allies

We discovered earlier in the book that anemones, together with corals, jellyfishes and sea fans, make up the group of animals called coelenterates. Anemones and corals are similar members of this group and share the same characteristic body structure, the polyp. The major features of this jellylike structure are a simple radial shape with a single opening serving both as a mouth and a means of liberating waste products. The opening is surrounded by tentacles liberally furnished with stinging cells called nematocysts. These can be discharged as a defence against predators or used to disable their prey, which is then grasped by the tentacles and fed into the central mouth opening.

Coelenterates are carnivorous. Some species feed on zooplankton, while the larger species take more substantial prey in the form of small fish or crustaceans. Like corals, anemones often contain within their tissues millions of single-celled plants known as zooxanthellae and require bright sunlight to allow these tiny plants to live and photosynthesize. Unlike most corals, however, anemones are solitary, although there are colonial species. These are really individual anemones, however, that live in aggregations.

Survival by reproduction
For a group of organisms to succeed and flourish for 500 million years almost unchanged by evolution, as coelenterates have, is remarkable and reserved for very few life forms. This kind of success in any group of animals and plants is based primarily on their means of survival. One basic survival technique is reproduction, and the coelenterates are superbly accomplished in this respect. They can employ a variety of reproductive methods. Numbers can be doubled instantly by division, or smaller versions of the parent can be produced as buds or offsets. Anemones can produce tiny complete replicas of themselves in their body cavity, to be spewed out when fully developed. Reef corals can also reproduce sexually, producing microscopic medusalike larvae that join the zooplankton and are swept by currents to settle on another suitable place and so establish a new reef. Some anemones also have this ability.

Beneficial partnerships
Anemones have succeeded well in their partnership with zooxanthellae and are often among the most conspicuous animals on the reef. Other organisms have also become reliant on anemones and such relationships commonly involve crustaceans and fishes. Many of these associations can be transferred from the reef to the aquarium and provide a fascinating feature. The anemone crab (*Neopetrolisthes ohshimai*) from the Indo-Pacific, for example, lives in association with

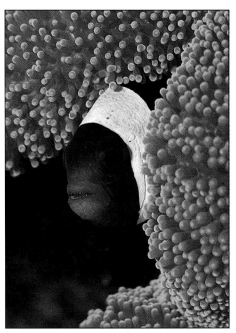

Left: *The large* Heteractis magnifica *is often included in shipments from Singapore. This beautiful anemone is a popular aquarium species. Under good lighting, it often changes colour due to the abundant zooxanthellae it fosters.*

Above: *A common clownfish* (Amphiprion ocellaris) *nestles in the tentacles of its host anemone,* Heteractis malu. *This association between two quite dissimilar life forms is a popular partnership for the aquarium.*

Top: *Clownfish species often choose a given type of anemone with which to associate and will disregard other types.* Stoichactis *anemones are preferred by some clownfish species, as shown here.*

Above: *This tiny anemone crab* (Neopetrolisthes ohshimai) *lives closely with anemones, especially* Stoichactis *species, which apparently receive no benefit from the association.*

Stoichactis and *Heteractis* anemones and this is just the type of alliance that can be fostered in the aquarium. *Lysmata amboinensis*, the cleaner shrimp, also associates with *Heteractis* anemones, and there are a number of shrimps from the genus *Periclimenes* that associate with *Bartholomea* species of anemone. The most popular partnership for the aquarium, however, is that between clownfishes and the large anemone species of the genera *Heteractis*, *Stoichactis* and *Dicosoma*. A well-known version of this association occurs between the Red Sea clownfish (*Amphiprion bicinctus*) and the large carpet anemone (*Stoichactis gigas*), a feature of many Red Sea reefs.

Types of anemones
Here, we consider a range of anemones under four headings: actiniarian anemones, corallimorpharians, cerianthid anemones and the zoanthid anemones (of a separate order).

Actiniarian anemones
Of the anemones regularly imported from the Indo-Pacific, members of the order Actiniaria are perhaps the most popular. *Heteractis malu* is a beautiful species of this order and ideal to associate with clownfishes. There are various colour forms, ranging from pure white through yellow to brown, but the main distinguishing feature is the bright purple tips to the tentacles. Under good lighting, most specimens will thrive and can reach 40cm(16in) in diameter in favourable conditions. This is a species that needs good lighting to encourage the development of the zooxanthellae on which it depends. The larger species *Heteractis magnifica* is another regular import; it may grow up to 70cm(27.5in) across. The Caribbean equivalent to these species is *Condylactis gigantea*, a beautiful white anemone blushed with pink or lilac and adorned with 10cm(4in)-long tentacles tipped in vivid pink-purple.

The carpet anemones, such as the Indo-Pacific *Stoichactis gigas* and the Caribbean *Stoichactis helianthus*, have hundreds of stubby tentacles and can vary in colour from bright green to pink or white. Imported specimens often measure up to 25cm(10in) in diameter, but *Stoichactis gigas* is capable of growing to three or four times this size in the wild. This species, particularly, associates well with clownfishes.

continued on next page

Above: *Mushroom anemones*
(Rhodactis *spp.*) *are ideal for the*
invertebrate tank and may reproduce.

Corallimorpharians
The corallimorpharians are a small
order of coral-like anemones that often
live in large colonies. Sometimes
referred to as mushroom anemones and
mostly of the *Rhodactis* genus, these are
found in clusters on rocky substrates,
each polyp resembling an inverted
umbrella with short tentacles radiating
like spokes from the centre. Depending
on the species, the expanded polyp can
vary in diameter from 2-20cm(0.8-8in).
The Caribbean species *Rhodactis*
sanctihomae is a typical example; it
may reach 10cm(4in) in diameter and
sports translucent green to brown
polyps with small tentacles. The closely
related *Ricordea* species are vivid green
and covered with tiny bubblelike
tentacles; these often occur in groups of
many hundreds of individuals. The
Caribbean *Ricordea florida* is a
particularly attractive species. These
anemones are good subjects for the
aquarium, being easy to keep, and they
may often reproduce in captivity.

Cerianthid anemones
The cerianthid anemones are an
unusual group that live on coarse,
sandy substrates in buried tubes
constructed of mucus and detritus. They
have a mass of very ornamental, long
thin tentacles that can vary in colour
from white to pink through to dark
brown. They are nocturnal feeders and
normally stay within their tubes during
the day, expanding at night to a
diameter of 20cm(8in) or more. The
tentacles are arranged in two groups; a
whorl of short tentacles surrounds the
mouth, with a series of much longer
tentacles on the margin of the oral disc.
Specimens imported from the Indo-

Pacific usually include *Pachycerianthus*
mana, but it rarely succeeds as an
aquarium subject. It is a very delicate
species and easily damaged during
transportation; most specimens fail to
survive the ordeal. The sting of this
species is particularly powerful, and it
does not play host to clownfishes.

Zoanthid anemones
Finally, we must mention the zoanthids.
Although these are part of a separate
order to the anemones, they are often
commonly referred to as zoanthid
anemones. These tiny anemonelike
polyps may live solitarily but are most
often found in groups. There are
symbiotic species, which associate with
other invertebrates such as sponges, and
free-living species. *Parazoanthus swiftii*
is a brilliant orange Caribbean species
that lives in association with a number
of sponge species. The bright coloration
may serve to advertise its toxic nature.
This species reproduces mainly by
budding, forming bandlike rows. The
yellow polyps of the Atlantic species
Parazoanthus dixoni are equally
spectacular. They are linked together by
stolons to form expansive matlike
growths only 2cm(0.8in) high on rocky
surfaces. Little is known about their
care in the aquarium.

Right: *This bright yellow tropical*
Atlantic zoanthid prefers shade and is
found under coral ledges in the wild.

Below: *Cerianthid anemones are not*
easy to establish, but Pachycerianthus
mana *is regularly imported.*

Basic aquarium care
Generally, anemones are admirable
subjects for the aquarium, as long as
you can meet their exacting
requirements. Simply stated, these are
good water conditions and the correct
level of lighting. Most species also
appreciate a strong flow of water to
provide food and oxygen and to rid
them of metabolic waste products. An
aquarium devoted solely to anemones
and other sessile or slow-moving
invertebrate animals, such as fanworms
and sea cucumbers, can be very
attractive in its own right. Such an
arrangement can often be improved by
introducing a few small fish, such as
clownfishes, or symbiotic crustaceans to
add colour and movement to the tank.

AQUARIUM CARE

Wrasses

The family of wrasses, Labridae, is one of the largest in the temperate and tropical seas of the world, embracing more than 400 species. On tropical reefs, where this family often features prominently, wrasses are amazingly diverse in size and form. However, they do share an elongated shape and a slightly compressed body, with a single continuous dorsal fin sporting 7-14 spines, and a mouth located terminally on the pointed head. The mouth is usually fairly small, with well-developed canine teeth at the front of the jaws.

Many wrasse species are spectacular in their brilliant coloration and often display sexual dimorphism, i.e. males are easily distinguishable from females by differences in form and/or colour. This is a rare feature among tropical marine fishes. Juvenile wrasses can be brightly coloured and are frequently quite different from their respective adults.

A number of species have a novel means of evading predators, by diving into the sandy seabed and disappearing from sight. This can happen when you introduce a newly purchased wrasse into the aquarium. Do not be alarmed, however; after a short while, it will reappear. Some wrasses bury themselves at night, while others, like the parrotfishes, manufacture a mucus cocoon within which they spend the night.

Wrasses are an ideal group of fishes for the aquarium and can be regarded as good subjects for beginners to marine fishkeeping. They are generally easy to keep and, with the odd exception, are not over-sensitive to small changes in water quality. It is worth mentioning that, when stressed on introduction to the aquarium, some wrasse species may lay on the bottom gasping. Left alone, the fish will soon recover. In fact, it is a good idea to switch off the aquarium lighting to allow wrasses a short settling-in period. Wrasses are opportunistic feeders in the wild, constantly nibbling the substrate and corals in search of small crustaceans or worms. Most species usually settle down in the aquarium and eagerly accept all kinds of food offered to them.

The twin-spot wrasse (*Coris aygula*) is a very accommodating species and, especially in its brilliant juvenile phase, makes a spectacular addition to any aquarium. Its natural diet consists largely of small crustaceans and shelled molluscs, which it has little difficulty in attacking and consuming, crushing the shells with its prominent canine teeth. Aquarium diet may

be varied but should feature fresh or frozen shrimps, crab meat and mussel or other shellfish.

The twin-spot wrasse loses it gaudy coloration with age, passing through two or three colour phases. The orange spots slowly fade and the body progressively darkens. Males develop a large hump on the head, turning a dark blue-green with a broad, pale blue vertical bar in the mid-section of the body. Often approaching 1m(39in) in length, males can be very territorially aggressive and even challenge an approaching diver, charging forward and veering off at the last second. They are strong animals and will turn over quite large coral boulders in search of food.

Top: *The juvenile form of the twin-spot wrasse is a spectacularly colourful fish, quite different in appearance from the adult. Juveniles, in particular, are very popular aquarium subjects, not only because of their beautiful coloration, but also because, like most wrasse species, they are relatively easy to keep in captivity.*

Above: *The same specimen – now a subadult – has lost its two orange spots and is dramatically different from its earlier juvenile form. In fact, this wrasse will pass through two or three colour phases. Adult males can grow as long as 1m(39in) in the wild but will rarely reach more than 30cm(12in) in the aquarium.*

CORAL REEFS OF THE WORLD

Kenya

'Life in the bright shallows'

To many people, Africa is Kenya, a place of stunning landscapes and vast wildlife reserves. The trackless heartland of the country attracts many visitors, drawn by the excitement of making overland safaris to view the magnificent wildlife, natural wonders and spectacular scenery. The coastland bordering the Kenyan countryside is every bit as exciting, providing visitors equivalent opportunities to observe wildlife just as spectacular below the inviting waters at the coral-fringed margin of the vast Indian Ocean.

The Kenyan coast offers 300km(188 miles) of reefs for diving and snorkelling, with excellent facilities provided by the many water sport-oriented hotels and resorts to the north and south of Mombasa. The quality of the reefs is excellent and the sea life at its best in the Watamu Marine National Park and the Malindi Marine National Park, both near Malindi, 80km(50 miles) north of Mombasa.

The gradual and even slope of the continental shelf has produced almost uniform conditions along the entire coast. White sandy beaches are lapped by a wide shallow sand and sea grass lagoon that extends for up to 2km (just over a mile) before reaching the reef crest running parallel to the straight unbroken coastline. Further submerged fringing reefs formed in parallel ridges extend to the seaward of the reef crest and, in some locations, as many as three or four of these ridge formations can occur.

Tidal differences can be measured in metres and at low tide it is often possible to walk out to rockpools formed in the lagoon and on the reef crest. The water clarity is variable, depending on the time of year and the prevailing weather conditions. During the wet seasons, from April to June and again in November, the rainfall can be

A trio of grazing wimplefishes.

quite high and sea conditions poor. Considerable amounts of sea grass are washed ashore and the water can be quite turbid for days on end. The nutrients washed into the sea during wet periods produce large blooms of plankton and this rich food source commonly encourages visits by huge filter-feeding animals, such as manta rays and whale sharks. During dry periods, skies are blue and the water visibility extends on average to about 20m(66ft).

Life in the bright shallows

Snorkelling along the edge of the reef crest in 2-3m(up to 10ft) of water can be a revelation. In these shallow well-lit conditions, corals abound and countless reef fishes can be spotted wending their way in and out of the growths as they graze on the algae-covered back reef flats. Among these, the longnose butterflyfish (*Forcipiger flavissimus*) and equally long-nosed copperband butterflyfish (*Chelmon rostratus*) can be found probing in holes or pecking at corals with forceps-like snouts in search of food. Butterflyfishes are well represented in these ideal conditions. Pairs of vagabond butterflyfish (*Chaetodon vagabundus*) and brilliant rainbow redfins (*Chaetodon trifasciatus*) as large as saucers flit among the *Acropora* corals. All of these are typically feeders on coral polyps and other small coelenterates. Only recently has it been discovered that, in addition to taking coral polyps, butterflyfishes also feed on the mucus liberated by the corals. This has a high nutritional value and may be an important part of these fishes' diet.

The wimplefish (*Heniochus acuminatus*) is an exception in that it grazes on algae and feeds on small polychaete worms and crustaceans on the bottom. Equipped with a long trailing dorsal fin, this species is often called the 'poor man's

Above: *Reef fishes that are predominantly red, such as this lyretail grouper (Variola louti), appear dark grey in deeper water, where they are camouflaged in the dimness of the turpid sea.*

Left: *Huge schools of blue-striped snappers (Lutjanus kasmira) often mass in the shallows. This important commercial species in many parts of the Indian Ocean is traditionally caught in nets or by hook and line.*

Moorish idol' and easily confused with the true Moorish idol (*Zanclus canescens*), the single species in the family Zanclidae closely allied to the surgeonfishes. The pennant butterflyfish (*Heniochus diphreutes*) also adopts a non-typical feeding pattern for butterflyfishes; it gathers in shoals and feeds in midwater on zooplankton.

The most successful reef species of any genera are those that are adaptable to a wide variety of food sources, since they are able to colonize a correspondingly wide range of habitats. The triggerfishes fall into this category; they are able to eat almost anything and thus they are among the most cosmopolitan of reef fish species.

Triggerfishes are often colourful and just a little bizarre in appearance. Their novel means of evading predators is to dash for cover into a small hole in the reef and erect a large spine with which

to jam themselves into positon. The large spine is one of three forming the first of two dorsal fins. The whole spine assembly fits into a groove and, once erect, can only be released either by the fish itself or by pressing down the third spine, or 'trigger', which locks the first in place.

The titan triggerfish (*Balistoides viridescens*) is common on these shallow Kenyan reef crest sites and is often large, reaching 50-60cm(20-24in) in length. Seemingly willing to tackle any food source, this species loves to feed on *Diadema* sea

Below: *The aristocratic Moorish idol can darken its body coloration to almost black as a form of night camouflage or to disguise itself in the gloomy conditions of deeper water. It is a familiar species to divers visiting many Indo-Pacific reefs. Its distribution ranges from Hawaii in the eastern Pacific to Kenya in the Indian Ocean.*

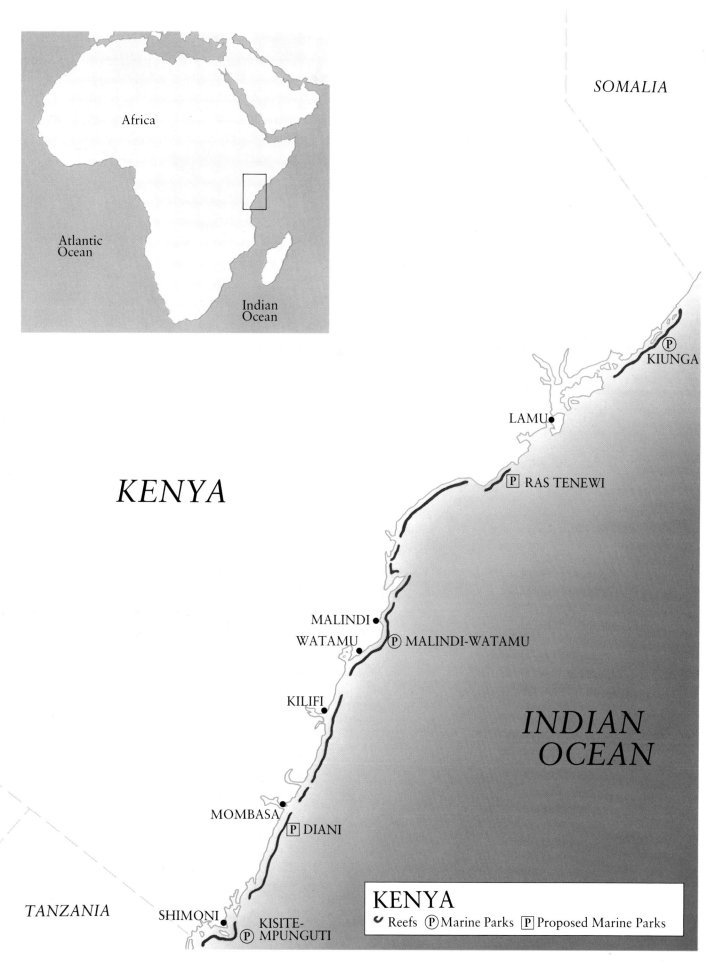

SOMALIA

Africa

Atlantic
Ocean

Indian
Ocean

KENYA

INDIAN
OCEAN

Ⓟ KIUNGA

LAMU •

Ⓟ RAS TENEWI

MALINDI •

WATAMU • Ⓟ MALINDI-WATAMU

KILIFI •

MOMBASA •

Ⓟ DIANI

TANZANIA

SHIMONI •

KISITE-
Ⓟ MPUNGUTI

KENYA
⤸ Reefs Ⓟ Marine Parks [P] Proposed Marine Parks

Above: *Facilities for diving are excellent on the Kenyan coast. Here, vacationing divers are going through their paces on a resort diving course at Watamu. Instruction is vital, not only for the safety of the divers, but also for the reefs, since advice is given on how to avoid causing damage.*

urchins. It is able to avoid the long spines by shooting jets of water to turn the urchin over before it feeds on the vulnerable underparts. As we mentioned on page 111, its success is a little in doubt as these fish are often seen with two or three spines projecting from the snout. Large titan triggerfishes can be aggressive and seem to delight in chasing snorkellers. This often occurs during the breeding season in November, when the male excavates a depression in the sand for the female to lay her eggs. The male aggressively defends the eggs and will attack anything or anyone approaching closer than a few metres.

At least four other triggerfish species are commonly found on East African reefs: the Picasso triggerfish (*Rhinecanthus aculeatus*); the beautiful orange-striped triggerfish (*Balistapus undulatus*) – both popular aquarium species; the white-lined triggerfish (*Balistes bursa*) and, in deeper waters, the clown triggerfish (*Balistoides conspicillum*), which with its distinctive white-spotted body is the most easily recognizable of all the triggerfishes.

In these shallow waters, herbivores are also well represented. Powder blue surgeons (*Acanthurus leucosternon*) browse in large shoal on the algae, moving together as if orchestrated by some unknown force. By contrast, the clown surgeonfish (*Acanthurus lineatus*) is a lone swimmer, busily flitting from one well-lit surface to the next in an endless search for any filamentous algae left uncropped. This species defends a territory from

---

DIVING PROFILE *Kenya*

CLIMATE

Air temperature range:
28-32°C(82-90°F)
Sea temperature range:
22-24°C(72-75°F)

From April to June and again in November the rainfall can be quite high, with up to 24cm(9.5in) of rain falling in one month. During these periods, sea conditions can be rough and the water turbid, restricting diving and other water sports. Despite the rainfall, daily sunshine amounts can still be in the region of 7-8 hours. Hotel prices are much lower during this period, if you are willing to take a chance. The best months for diving are January to March, and December, with little rain, lots of sunshine and calm seas.

FACILITIES

Facilities are excellent, with a decompression chamber in Mombasa and a dozen or so major dive centres along the coast. All the diving activities are administered by the Kenya Divers' Association. The resort of Turtle Bay is most conveniently located for the Watamu Marine National Park.

DIVE RATING

The quality of the reefs inshore is very high, providing ideal conditions for snorkelling; in fact, these waters are often too shallow to warrant SCUBA equipment. The diving is mainly conducted at depths of 20-30m(66-100ft) on offshore reefs that can be variable in quality due to the effects of turbidity on visibility. When visibility is restricted, however, there is a plentiful variety of small marine life that can be observed close up. Reef diving and drift dives are available.

CONSERVATION

The diving is operated on the 'look don't touch' basis and shell and coral collecting is discouraged. The Marine National Park at Watamu near Malindi offers opportunities to dive on undisturbed reefs where spearfishing and fish, shell and coral collecting are not permitted. The close cooperation between the diving tourism industry and the Marine National Park authorities is very evident. Dive tour guides rigorously enforce the Park's rules. Further Marine National Parks are currently in the process of designation.

literally keep the reef picked clean of plants, including the algal film adhering to dead corals and reef rock. Although the greenery is not noticeable, reefs do produce a tremendous amount of plant material, however, and this represents a principal food source, not only for herbivorous fish species but also for an enormous variety of other animals, including sea urchins, crustaceans and molluscs.

Into the gloom of deeper waters

The deeper water habitats of the outer reefs off Kenya are very different to the shallow well-lit snorkelling areas. Relatively poor light transmission does not encourage a wide range of corals and there is a shift in the depth-related zonation of species. Soft corals and gorgonians, which in clear waters would be found 30 or 40m(100-130ft) from the surface, are found at 20m(66ft) and sponges are much more conspicuous, growing out in the open rather than being restricted to sites below overhangs and shaded areas.

The main surprise is to find nocturnal animals at large on the open reef during daylight rather than hidden in caves and crevices. Large shoals of normally nocturnal golden cardinalfishes (*Apogon apogonides*) swim among gorgonian fan corals, both groups of animals feeding on the zooplankton. A solitary big-eye (*Priacanthus hamrur*), also a nocturnal zooplankton feeder, lies motionless, the dark brick red colour of its body set off by large expressionless eyes exhibiting an almost hypnotic quality. This nocturnal species rests during the day but does not sleep. When disturbed, such a fish will dart away and settle again. If the background is light in colour, the solid red of its body will fade in a matter of seconds to a mottled red over silver and finally to faint red bars on a silvery body and fins, matching its surroundings perfectly. In this hazy world, the normal order has become adapted to the particular environment of these East African reefs. The dim conditions allow nocturnal animals to use their low-light camouflage effectively during the day and their large eyes are advantageous in the poor visibility. Whereas on clear-water reefs the hours of darkness provide the best opportunity for zooplankton feeders to crop the harvest rising from the depths, on these turbid reefs, zooplankton-rich waters provide food in plenty throughout the twenty-four hour cycle. (The complex food web of the tropical oceans involves a wide range of predators, of which those on the zooplankton are perhaps the most varied.)

Above: *The big-eye is aptly named, since it has large eyes adapted to night vision. During the day, it hides by rapidly changing its body pattern.*

Below: *Unlike most of the surgeonfish family, the unicornfishes, such as this yellow-edged unicorn* (Naso lituratus), *are mainly plankton feeders.*

intrusion by other herbivores and becomes very excited when shoals of powder blue surgeons or parrotfishes try to invade its algal garden and overwhelm it by sheer weight of numbers.

The success of these herbivores is such that few of us think of plants in the context of coral reefs. The attentions of such typically voracious feeders

Not surprisingly, many diurnal, or daytime-active, species compete with these misplaced nocturnal species. Golden jewelfish (*Anthias squamipinnis*), for example, can be observed readily shoaling with cardinalfishes that would normally retire during the daylight hours. There is also some evidence that the daytime species are subject to natural selection based on their coloration. Thus, predominantly red species, such as the coral trout (*Cephalopholis miniata*), which appears black or dark grey in these light conditions, and patterned fishes, such as the Moorish idol, the clown trigger and lionfish (*Pterois volitans*), which have the ability to darken their coloration to almost black, are common. In this way, red fishes that appear black in low-light conditions and the muted tones of the other species provide effective camouflage in the dim conditions that prevail.

The fragile ecosystem of the reef

Habitat and environment have moulded the life on these reefs into a unique ecosystem. It is easy to appreciate how easily reefs can be changed by external factors such as the impacts caused by turbidity or pollution. The opening of a small channel through the reef, for example, can cause sediment to be deposited on the reef and produce perpetually turbid conditions as back reef lagoon silt is flushed out with each tide. The communities associated with the reef when it was pristine and clear become transformed, with adapting survivors from the former conditions being joined by outsiders naturally fitted to the new conditions.

Where this has occurred on shallow reefs, dying corals have often been taken over by filamentous algae that thrive in the high-nutrient conditions. Deprived of their food source, the coral-browsing fish species and other animals are quickly replaced by herbivores. Even if such impacts are discontinued, there is often little prospect of recolonization by corals, quite simply because the habitat becomes irreversibly damaged.

Above: *Golden jewelfish form huge aggregations in shallow water, mainly on the seaward face of the reef crest. This daytime species feeds on plankton that are drawn from the depths by the movement of water over the reef.*

Left: *The lionfish erects its fins and uses them to manoeuvre small fish into corners, where it gulps them down before they are able to escape. It will also adapt its coloration and body pattern to match its surroundings so that it can lie in wait and make surprise attacks on unsuspecting passing prey.*

AQUARIUM CARE

Triggerfishes

Triggerfishes belong to the order Tetraodontiformes, which also includes the filefish, puffer and boxfish families. The common feature drawing the members of this large group together is the possession of sharp chisel-like teeth. Accordingly, the name of the order is derived from the Greek word for 'four teeth'.

Triggerfishes are characterized by the development of a dorsal spine that can be erected and locked into place. The fish use this spine to jam themselves into crevices in the coral as a means of defence against predators. The 'trigger' refers to the method used by fishermen to lower the spine by pressing down the rearmost of two smaller spines located immediately behind the erect one.

Most members of the family are beautifully marked, but the triggerfishes specifically are generally regarded as distinctive rather than beautiful. The laterally compressed body is usually diamond shaped, with the head taking up more than a third of the total body length. This can give the impression of the fish consisting of a disembodied head with fins.

Triggerfish are not strong swimmers, using a waving action of the dorsal and anal fins rather than relying on the caudal. Although this does not bestow great power it does provide amazing manoeuvrability, allowing the fish to quickly weave in and out of holes and to swim backwards to extricate itself from any possible tight spot.

The jaws are strong, with four protruding teeth that enable the carnivorous triggerfishes to feed on a wide range of invertebrates, including crabs and shellfish, which they find little difficulty in crushing and devouring, shell and all. Triggerfishes are major predators of unlikely prey such as the long-spined *Diadema* sea urchin and the spiny crown of thorns starfish. The stomach contents of some species have also included live corals, sponges, brittle stars and small fishes.

Think carefully before buying a triggerfish for the aquarium because these colourful and hardy fishes can be quite aggressive towards other fish in the tank. They will often quickly outgrow their quarters and, apart from large coelenterates, will attack and devour any invertebrates. If you have a fish-only system and carefully choose other species to accompany them that can withstand their bullying, you are not likely to have problems. Triggerfishes are happy within a temperature range of 24-26°C (75-79°F) and are tolerant of gradual changes in water quality. Feeding is not difficult as these 'eating machines' will consume almost anything; they will thrive on frozen or fresh crab, clam or mussel.

The clown triggerfish (*Balistoides conspicillum*) is one of the most distinctive species and is understandably popular among marine fishkeepers. It is very difficult to resist its stunning coloration and bizarre appearance. Unfortunately, it is not the

easiest of fish to acclimatize and keep in aquarium conditions. This is possibly because very young juveniles of the species are the most sought after. These are only seasonally available and are thus expensive. Because they are so small, these juveniles are easily stressed by aquarium conditions. These are not fish for beginners; they need good water quality and a diet of small crustaceans, including shrimp and shellfish meat, during their settling-in period.

Above: *The bizarre clown triggerfish can hardly be described as beautiful, but is nevertheless very popular with aquarists who can cope with the hefty price tag. An adult specimen can provide a marvellous feature in a large marine aquarium, but other fish to accompany this aggressive species need to be chosen with care.*

Left: *Clown triggerfish have a reputation for being difficult to keep successfully. Unfortunately, juveniles, which are particularly sought after because of their attractive markings, are fragile and easily stressed. They require experienced care and precise water quality management.*

THE TWILIGHT REEFS

Shafts of weak sunlight shimmered on our expelled air bubbles, as they rose towards the surface, imparting a dreamlike quality to the blue-green realm that enveloped us. Diving Kenya's reefs can often be like this – a twilight world of hazy horizons limited to a visibility of 10m(33ft) in any direction. It is a warm, silent, comfortable world populated by exotic creatures that loom out of the haze, appearing as if by magic and just as quickly disappearing again.

At a depth of 20m(66ft), we reached a gently sloping reef of corals and sponges. Small shoals of painted grunts (*Plectorhynchus pictus*) approached inquisitively, seemingly curious to observe the visitors from the outside world above the surface. These benthic feeders nosed industriously among the sandy patches between the corals, searching for the small invertebrates on which they feed.

Camouflage is a common survival technique on these reefs and as our eyes became more accustomed, we began to pick out creatures blending with the colours and textures of the corals. A bright crimson eye betrayed a large scorpionfish, otherwise perfectly disguised by elaborate patterns and fleshy projections that broke up the outline of its body against the surrounding corals. We nearly overlooked this half-metre-long fish and, far worse, we could easily have blundered into its venomous dorsal spines, each capable of inflicting a sting of unbelievable agony. The scorpionfish had no such intentions, however, content to avoid the intruders as it faded into the distance with a quick sweep of its tail.

Our senses sharpened by this encounter, it was not surprising that we were more than prepared when we happened upon another large animal. Resting on the bottom, a huge loggerhead turtle was itself startled when, almost within touching distance, this wizened, ancient-looking marine reptile realized that it was not alone. The wrinkled head of the animal was as large as a human head and the carapace the proportions of a small coral outgrowth. In a flurry of sediment, the clumsy animal lumbered away, colliding with the nearest corals before disappearing rapidly into the relative safety of the depths.

Such large marine creatures are no strangers to these reefs. The day before, divers had found an immense shark and by comparing its overall length against the dive boat guessed its size to be 9m(30ft) or more from nose to tail. This huge but harmless whale shark had remained close to the boat for 20 minutes or more and allowed snorkellers to hitch a ride by gripping the metre-high dorsal fin. Encounters such as this are fairly common in Kenyan waters, as these mammoth creatures are attracted by the rich blooms of plankton and small schooling fishes on which they feed. The metre-wide mouth gapes

Below: *The reefs around Malindi provide exciting encounters with large animals, including marine reptiles, such as this loggerhead turtle. This is one of the largest species of sea turtle and is quite common on the Kenyan coast.*

open and water washes over the gills, leaving the plankton and small fish adhering to the throat and sievelike gill rakers. Countless rows of small teeth transfer this haul to the gullet, and large whale sharks have been observed standing on their tails head upwards to assist the process.

The conditions around Malindi often attract numbers of this, the largest living fish species in the world, and giants of 20m(66ft) have been recorded. This is only one of the large creatures you can find on this coastline, as large manta rays are also frequent visitors to these reefs. The manta ray cruises along the reef feeding just below the surface, using the large lobed horns to scoop plankton towards it enormous mouth. It is a remarkable sight to see one of these huge rays leaping out of the water and landing with a tremendous splash.

The coast of Kenya

The Malindi National park was designated in 1968 to protect the reefs of the area and no sport fishing or shell collecting is permitted. The park encompasses the North Reef and a long stretch of fringing reef, and within its boundaries gentle giants such as these sharks and rays are free to feed unmolested. The waters of the park are rich in life and care is taken to preserve the fragile reefs. The well-organized tourist diving is conducted from buoyed sites – to avoid anchor damage – and the professional tourist diving groups show a real regard for conservation.

However, nature is always at the mercy of man and often where there are conflicts of interests the outcome is not usually in nature's favour. Unfortunately, this is the case at Malindi. When Kenya became independent, the Government-owned land along the coastal strip was given to the people for cultivation. Land adjacent to rivers which the Government had formerly insisted should not be farmed – to prevent soil erosion into the rivers during the rainy season – was also cleared and cultivated. The inevitable result has been massive erosion capable of polluting reefs close to river mouths. The silt washed onto the reefs not only damages the corals by reducing light penetration due to turbidity but also directly clogs the delicate polyps. Malindi lies close to the mouth of the Sabaki (Galana) river in an area with just such a potential. Fortunately, steps are being taken to monitor the effect of these impacts on the park and, hopefully, measures can be applied

Top: *The sandy shores of Malindi slope gently to the sea. In remote places the beach provides a nesting area for a variety of sea turtles.*

Above: *Cultivation of land adjacent to the Sabaki river in Kenya has produced silt-laden waters that have a devastating effect on Malindi's reefs, choking the coral polyps.*

to preserve these vibrant reefs.

And there is a great deal worth preserving, as these reefs are home to a large variety of colourful reef fish, sponges and corals. Over 50 species of coral are found on Malindi's reefs and perhaps ten times that number of reef fish species. The coral reefs of the Kenyan coast are unique in many ways and form one of the remaining natural wild areas of the world. The conservation effort has traditionally centred on the terrestrial wildlife in the magnificent game parks; it would be a pity if the equally valuable marine life was overlooked.

Crustaceans

Some of our invertebrate panels have concentrated on sessile, or non-moving, marine invertebrates, but here we feature a class of highly mobile animals, the crustaceans. This group of animals encompasses approximately 30,000 species and includes some of the most spectacular inhabitants of the tropical reefs around the world.

After first evolving from segmented worms, the crustaceans developed into creatures classified as part of the phylum Arthropoda, a huge group that also includes the insects and spiders. In their aquatic environment, they flourished and became truly mobile.

Armoured denizens of the water
Crustaceans are characterized by a chitinous exoskeleton, a hard external skeleton that serves both as protection and support for their bodies. The external skeleton is very versatile and in each species the shape has become modified to suit its own individual requirements, from the tiny copepod to the giant Japanese spider crab, with a legspan measuring more than 3m(10ft) across. This external armour is very successful in protecting the animal, but such an unyielding material can represent problems since it completely encloses the body and makes no allowance for growth. The strategy that developed to overcome this difficulty was to shed the outer shell periodically. During the moulting process, the animal absorbs a large amount of calcium carbonate from its shell and forms a new but soft shell beneath the old one. The outgrown shell splits and the soft animal extricates itself, leaving a seemingly complete animal behind. There follows a very dangerous period for the now unprotected creature during which it hides to allow the new shell to stretch, swell and finally harden before the animal ventures once again into the hostile world.

The familiar decapods
Many of the crustaceans occurring on coral reefs belong to the order Decapoda (literally meaning 'ten legs'). The decapods have developed five pairs of walking legs on the thorax, the front pair of which is often equipped with large claws. Swimmerets (pleopods), leglike appendages, occur on the abdomen and similar appendages, generally five pairs, are present on the head and have become

modified as mouthparts. The decapods include shrimps and crabs, a group of marine invertebrates familiar to most of us because of their wide distribution and prominent position in our own food chain. Shrimps and crabs also provide many species suitable for the aquarium hobby, and an invertebrate aquarium would be incomplete without one of their number. Most species are very hardy and are among the easiest of invertebrates to feed; they make excellent scavengers, for example. They are real attentions seekers, either busily patrolling for food – appearing to leave no stone unturned in their quest for the next morsel – or display some other unusual and unique behaviour pattern.

Shrimps for the aquarium
Of the many decapod species, the wide variety of tiny, brightly coloured shrimps are perhaps the most attractive and deserving of a place in any invertebrate or mixed fish/invert system containing small, non-aggressive fish. There are difficulties in keeping shrimps with larger fish of course, as they form part of the diet of many fish species and in the enclosed environs of the aquarium cannot be safe from such predation. I will not easily forget the time early in my marine aquarium keeping days when I purchased six brightly coloured dancing shrimps (*Rhynococynetes* sp.), having been assured that their striking pattern and brilliant colours signified a nasty taste and prevented them being harmed by fish. Within minutes of placing them

in the tank, all six were consumed by a particularly voracious coral hopper (*Cirrhitichthys oxycephalus*), that, quite unconcerned, relished its very expensive and attractive supper.

As an aside on the dancing shrimp, it seems that the techniques used to catch this species in the Indo-Pacific are very destructive. It appears that large pieces of living coral are torn from the reef and taken ashore to be broken and destroyed to catch the shrimps hidden inside. This is a pity because this species, although one of the most attractive available to the aquarist, should not be imported if such damage to the reef is necessary to acquire it for the commercial trade.

Currently, the shrimp most popular with marine aquarists is without doubt the banded coral shrimp, or boxing shrimp (*Stenopus hispidus*). In the wild, this little red-and-white spindly crustacean spends most of its time on the reef, cleaning parasites off the resident and visiting fish populations and in the process providing itself with a meal. A cluster of white antennae waving from beneath a coral ledge usually signifies the cleaning station of one or more shrimps, and such is the popularity of the service they perform that it is not unusual to see fish actually queuing for attention.

The banded coral shrimp is a common inhabitant of coral reefs in shallow waters all over the world, its distribution including locations as far apart as the Indo-Pacific, tropical West Atlantic and northern New Zealand. Although often found in pairs in the wild, this little

Above: *These brightly coloured dancing shrimps (*Rhynococynetes *sp.) are best kept in small groups in the aquarium.*

Above: *The banded coral shrimp is sometimes known as the boxing shrimp because it weaves like a boxer sparring.*

Above: *The vividly marked red-backed shrimp* (Lysmata grabhami) *is perhaps the boldest of the cleaner shrimps.*

shrimp is not tolerant of other crustaceans and will fight to the death for its territory if placed in an aquarium with members of its own or other species. With such a pugnacious nature, it is not uncommon for this shrimp to loose one of its oversized claws. This does not appear to cause too much discomfort or handicap the shrimp, and at the next moult a brand new, albeit smaller claw appears that through successive moults grows back to its original size.

Perhaps the boldest of the cleaner shrimps, the red-backed, or painted lady, shrimp (*Lysmata grabhami*) will even pursue its cleaning activities on a person's hand carefully placed in the aquarium. Employing a similar technique to *Stenopus* to attract clients, the waving white antennae and brilliant white dorsal stripe of this shrimp contrast vividly with the red bands on either side of its body. This species prefers to live in small aggregations and is often encountered sharing a coral crevice with a large moray eel, clambering nimbly over the moray's head and even entering the mouth in search of food scraps and parasites. These and other shrimps also associate with large anemones, having been observed with *Stoichactis helianthus* and *Condylactis gigantea* in the Caribbean and with various Stoichactid anemones in the Indo-Pacific.

Several of these red-backed shrimps will happily live together in the same aquarium and may spend a large part of the year producing clusters of eggs, which

Below: *The Caribbean shrimp* Thor amboinensis *lives in association with the anemone* Bartholomea annulata.

Below: *The attractive* Periclimenes yucatanicus *is another commensal shrimp, associating with* Condylactis sp.

they carry between the swimmerets under the abdomen and tail. Little is known about the biology and reproductive behaviour of this species, but it would appear to be similar to many other coral reef inhabitants and capable of changing sex. Place any two shrimps of this species in the same aquarium and, within a short period, both may be found bearing egg clusters. This occurs because the shrimps have behaved both as male and female towards each other. Spawning occurs regularly at three- to four-week intervals after moults. The tiny shrimp nauplii carried for this period are liberated just before moulting occurs and a brand new brood is produced almost immediately after. (Although the young are relatively large, I have not yet succeeded in rearing them beyond about 13 days, despite experimentation with proprietary invert feeds, brineshrimp rearing food and rotifer cultures.)

There are several other notable shrimp species available, including the colourful *Thor amboinensis* and *Periclimenes yucatanicus*, both of which live commensally with anemones. Both also have basically transparent bodies with brightly coloured saddles of cream, white or pink and are often aptly called clown shrimps. *Lysmata rathbunae*, the beautiful red-veined shrimp, associates with sponges, but will adapt quite well to aquarium life without a sponge host.

Crabs for the aquarium
Crabs can be equally as colourful and fascinating as shrimps. Unfortunately, many species are either too large for the average aquarium or lead a secretive life based around nocturnal feeding, and thus

continued on next page

provide little interest for onlookers. Notable exceptions are the hermit crabs, which make admirable subjects and fulfil an important scavenging function in the aquarium. To some extent they have avoided the hazards of being shell-less at moulting time by protecting themselves in discarded mollusc shells and trundle about the aquarium executing all manner of acrobatics complete with this adopted protection. Their claws are shaped so that they conveniently form an armour-plated door to the shell when they withdraw. They spend a great deal of their time house hunting for a new slightly larger shell to replace the one they are rapidly outgrowing.

The red hairy hermit crab (*Dardanus megistos*) is often available to hobbyists and, although it tends to be a little on the large side for a small aquarium, can be a worthwhile addition where room is available. It is easily able to look after itself and is safe to include in mixed invertebrate/fish systems, even those containing quite large fish, with the exception of triggerfishes, which can make a meal out of quite a large hermit crab. Other *Dardanus* species are often sold complete with an anemone (*Calliactis tricolor*) attached to the shell, which the hermit crab actually places there and will transfer to later shell homes it may acquire. Despite this association with anemones, some large *Dardanus* species can be destructive and either damage or feed upon other inverts if they are not kept well fed.

The tiny bright red species *Calcinus tibicen* is a very attractive hermit crab with pale orange antennae and eye stalks topped with dark eyes rimmed in brilliant white. This species lives in small aggregations among rocks and coral reef formations of the tropical West Atlantic and Canary Islands. Although principally a nocturnal feeder, in the aquarium, it conveniently settles down well to a daytime feeding regime.

Finally, any list of crab species suitable for the aquarium would be incomplete without mentioning the arrow crab (*Stenorhynchus seticornis*). Extremely long spindly legs and a pointed conelike body make this interesting little crab an aquarium favourite. Despite its small size (up to 7cm/2.75in), this species can be rather aggressive and quite capable of making a gourmet meal out of any small fish which gets too close. It is highly recommended for an invertebrate-only system, however. If you should be lucky to chance upon a pair, it is often possible to encourage them to reproduce in the aquarium, the female bearing eggs for

long periods during the spring and summer. I have no knowledge of a breeder successfully rearing the young of this species, but I am sure it could be possible given a little of the right kind of dedication. Various species of shrimps, crabs and lobsters are now being commercially bred very successfully. Most of this work has concentrated on edible species, but the success of the enterprise does suggest that similar results

could be achieved with a range of suitable decorative aquarium species.

Of course, there are a number of tiny crustaceans that provide a valuable service in the aquarium as live food for the principal occupants. Brineshrimps (*Artemia salina*) are an excellent and nutritious food for marine fish and can be raised from eggs available at aquatic dealers. They can be used at the newly hatched stage or grown on for larger fish.

Top: *The tropical west Atlantic provides many crustaceans suitable for the aquarium. This red hairy hermit crab* (Dardanus megistos) *is ideal for a large tank and is a good scavenger.*

Above: *The extraordinary arrow crab is circumtropical in its distribution but most numerous in the tropical Atlantic. This interesting little crab settles down well in an invertebrate tank.*

AQUARIUM CARE

The Moorish Idol

There is a great deal of confusion regarding the lookalike group of fishes that includes the wimplefish, or poor man's Moorish idol (*Heniochus acuminatus*), the bannerfish (*Heniochus monoceros*), the pennant butterflyfish (*Heniochus diphreutes*) and the true Moorish idol (*Zanclus canescens*). Although quite dissimilar in many ways, all of these species are grouped together because they sport the classic lines and black-over-white markings popularly associated with the freshwater angelfishes of the cichlid family. None of these marine fish species belong to the cichlids, however, nor are they species of marine angelfishes (Pomacanthidae). The wimplefish, bannerfish and pennant butterflyfish all belong to a subfamily of the butterflyfishes (Chaetodontidae), while the Moorish idol is the sole member of the Zanclidae family and is closely related to the surgeonfishes (Acanthuridae).

The Moorish idol is the true aristocrat of the group. It can be easily distinguished from the rest of its fellow lookalikes by its surgeonfish features. The eyes are set high in the head, the snout is elongated and the teeth are in one row and denticulate along the edges. The caudal fin is forked, whereas other members of the group have a rounded tail fin. The elongated dorsal and anal fins are very distinctive, but quite often these are absent in aquarium specimens because of their fragile nature and the lack of careful handling during transportation. Older specimens can often develop preorbital spikes or horns and at one time were incorrectly distinguished by this feature as a separate species, *Z. cornutus*.

Despite a close relationship with the hardy and easy to keep surgeonfishes, the Moorish idol is not particularly easy to care for in the aquarium. It is more demanding than many species, requiring precise water management that does not allow nitrate levels to exceed 20ppm(mg/litre). This large species easily reaches 20cm(8in) in captivity and really appreciates plenty of space. Regard an aquarium of 180litres (40 Imp./47 US gallons) as the minimum; a typical tank of this volume measures 120x38x45cm (48x15x18in) in length, width and depth.

In the wild, the Moorish idol is a benthic feeder, browsing on small crustaceans and animals encrusting the reef. Such specialized feeders can be difficult to acclimatize to an aquarium diet and the Moorish idol needs live foods such as *Mysis* shrimps to encourage it to start feeding. As an easily stressed species, all aspects of its initial

acclimatization are very critical for its continued well-being. As part of this sensitivity it has an intolerance to most disease remedies, especially copper-based ones, and can easily be 'killed by the cure' if it is treated for diseases brought about by its stressed condition. Once settled into the aquarium environment, however, it will thrive on a wide range of fresh or frozen foods, including shrimp, mussel and cockle, and will browse on the natural greenery growing in the aquarium.

Above: *The true Moorish idol is the most sought-after species of the group, but it needs plenty of space and should only be considered by experienced aquarists.*

Left: *Although superficially similar to the Moorish idol, the pennant butterflyfish is not related. This species is a good choice for the inexperienced marine fishkeeper.*

Below: *A common Indo-Pacific species, the wimplefish is so named because its flowing dorsal fin resembles the nun's headwear. Note the plain yellow dorsal and tail fins.*

151

DRIFTING WITH THE CURRENT

Travel in either direction along the coastline from Mombasa and you will find large hotels, each offering facilities for a wide range of water sports, including diving. It was just one of these hotels 30km(19 miles) or so south of Mombasa that attracted our attention and had us early out of bed for the 40-minute drive to join the morning dive.

The road was crowded – school children in matching brightly coloured school shirts, old women with impossibly large loads balanced on their heads and queues of young women collecting water from roadside faucets. Delays were inevitable in this Kenyan coast version of the rush hour and the drive became a hot, dusty trial of patience. From past experience, I knew that the dive centre would not delay the dive boat's departure and I was not disappointed. The boat departed on the dot of 9.00am, with the last divers hurriedly assembling diving equipment and underwater cameras before climbing aboard.

Thirty minutes later, our fast dive boat arrived at the outer reef on a site which showed no detectable sign of the reef below apart from a swirling current and some dark blue patches beneath the opal-coloured veneer of the surface. It was to be a drift dive, and this was to be no exaggeration! Divers were jettisoned into the water in pairs, the boat keeping pace as it was carried by the current. In the grip of this strong current, each pair of divers was

The coast of Kenya

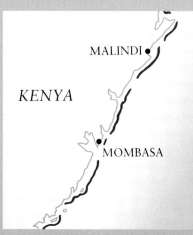

Above: *A dignified Koran angelfish forages on the reef. Note how subdued its markings are in comparison with the juvenile.*

Right: *The juvenile Koran angelfish is liberally marked with curved lines. As the fish matures, the tail markings are said to resemble Arabic script.*

Left: *Pennant butterflyfish gather in large shoals in the shallower sections of the reef to feed on plankton.*

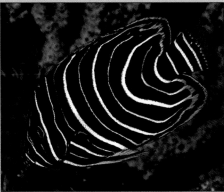

swept at what appeared to be breakneck speed, with little prospect of changing direction or arresting movement against the relentless surge. In clear waters, this can be quite a pleasant experience, effortlessly gliding along as the reef unfolds. In these waters, with visibility less than 10m(33ft), it was a different story, and obstacles such as coral heads loomed up suddenly, requiring extremely quick avoiding manoeuvres on our parts.

The reef reached within 10m(33ft) of the surface and was formed in elongated bars in line with the current and parallel with the distant coastline. The tops of these bars were 20-30m(66-100ft) across, with reef faces extending down into deeper water on both seaward and shoreward sides. The platform formed was scarred and etched with gullies and higher profile coral heads. Brightly coloured sponges mingled with hard and soft corals in a tightly packed matrix of marine life. The wide variety of attractive life forms

cried out for closer inspection and, with a little experimentation, it was possible to glide into the lee of a coral head or below the profile of the reef to find a spot where the current abated a little. An amazing number of spectacular invertebrates clung to the reef clamouring for space, especially the filter feeders – vivid purple and yellow sea cucumbers with feathery tentacles, sponges of all shapes and sizes and, below reef overhangs, bright orange *Tubastrea* corals sheltered from the light. *Tubastrea* coral colonies do not harbour microscopic algae in their tissues and rely entirely on zooplankton for food. The *Tubastrea's* big fleshy polyps in turn provide a meal for a range of carnivorous molluscs. In this location, these include striking egg cowries (*Ovula ovum*). This cowrie, with a pure white shell and contrasting black mantle spotted with gold, feeds almost exclusively on corals.

The prolific colonies of sponges encourages large numbers of sponge-feeding angelfishes. A beautiful emperor angelfish (*Pomacanthus imperator*) –

perhaps the most splendid of reef fishes – glides past, seemingly oblivious of intruders or the strong current. A Koran angelfish (*Pomacanthus semicirculatus*), much more subdued in coloration than its majestic cousins, busily forages close by. This adult has lost the Arabic lettering-like markings on its tail that have inspired its common name.

A movement in a small crevice drew our attention to two small candy-striped cleaner shrimps and a little troupe of dancing shrimps that had set up home together. Swimming over for a closer look instantly proved to be a bad decision because from the depths of the hole the head of a large moray eel appeared. The moray mouthed the water menacingly, disregarding the shrimps, which adeptly attended to their cleaning duties as they clambered all over its head, and posed for a series of memorable photographs. The moray's attention seemed riveted on our camera and it was often necessary to retire as the large head, followed by a huge body, started to emerge from the crevice in our direction. It was not until we were safely back onboard the dive boat that we discovered that this particular moray was used to hand feeding by divers and was merely looking for its accustomed tidbit and not poised for attack at all!

Below: *The large head of a moray appeared from the depths of a crevice in the reef. But its menacing actions were not a prelude to attack; it was simply used to hand feeding by divers and seeking satisfaction!*

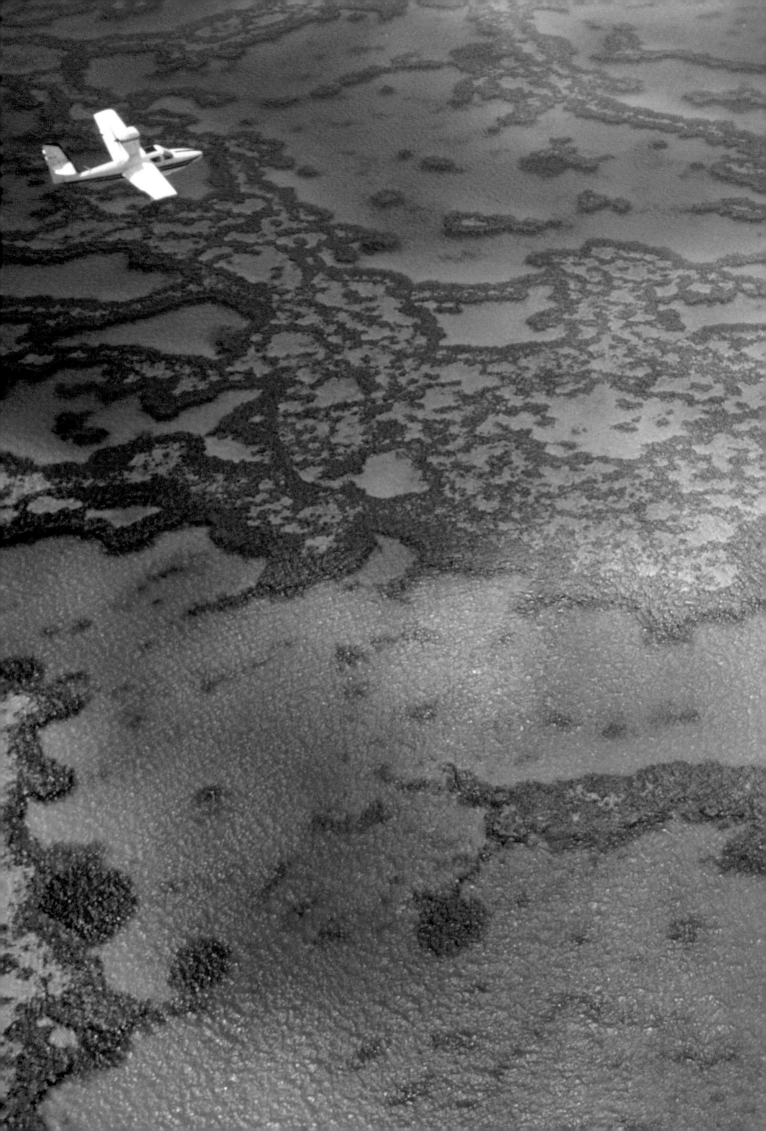

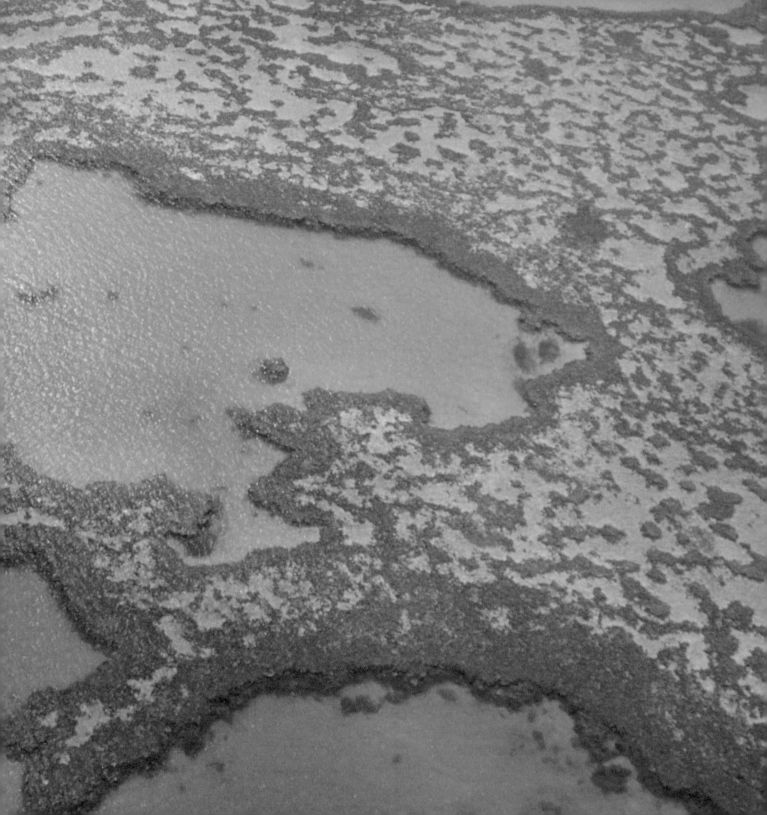

Great Barrier Reef

'Reefs, islands and cays'

The Great Barrier Reef of Australia is awesome in its proportions. It is the largest coral structure in the world and extends 2,300km(1440 miles) along the Queensland coast, covering an area of 230,000km^2 (almost 90,000 square miles). Regarded by many as the most magnificent example of a tropical coral reef system, this veritable diver's 'Mecca' draws visitors from all over the world, hopeful of experiencing the delights of its spectacular marine life and dramatic scenery.

There are more kinds of fish here than anywhere else in the world, and this qualification can be extended to include a wide range of other forms of Barrier Reef marine life. Perhaps this is not all together surprising, considering the immense area and diversity of habitats involved. However, it is the sheer scale in terms of numbers and variety that staggers most people.

Reefs, islands and cays

A journey from south to north along the vast labyrinth of reefs and islands forming the Great Barrier Reef would soon reveal the amazing diversity in their development and the wide range of habitats provided. Extending from Lady Elliott Island in the south, the outer reef meanders back and forth along the edge of the continental shelf, varying in distance between 30 and 250km (19-156 miles) from the mainland. Continuing northwards, the coral structure almost reaches the coastline of New Guinea, only prohibited from doing so by the outfall of sediment and fresh water from New Guinea's Fly River.

The Bunker and Capricorn Group of islands marks the southernmost extension and contains some of the best-known reefs, small coral islands and cays in the whole region, including Heron

Marine life in immense variety.

Island and nearby Wistari reef. The continental shelf is less than 100km(63 miles) from the mainland at this point and the islands within the group are located within the outer reef at distances varying between 20 and 40km(12-25 miles). Patch reefs and shallow fringing reefs are a feature of this group.

Further north are the Pompey and Swain Reefs. In this region, the continental shelf extends 200km(125 miles) from the mainland. These coral reefs are extensive, covering an almost continuous band 20km wide that follows the contours of the outer reef for 200km northwards. The large tidal range, combined with strong currents, has scoured an intricate system of channels through this vast reef complex and provides some of the best conditions for coral growth.

The next section to the north is often referred to as the Central Great Barrier Reef Region and is located off the coastline at Cairns. Here, the continental shelf is much narrower and coral development has resulted in shallow shoals and patch reefs with few islands, in contrast to the numerous islands found in the reef complexes to the north and south. Because of the lack of strong currents in this shallow reef area, heavy sand and sediment siltation is evident, forming sandy lagoons among the reefs.

To the north of Cairns is a spectacular region where the continental shelf is less than 50km (31 miles) wide. A series of ribbonlike reefs extend along the edge of the continental shelf, often unbroken for 20km or more and seldom more than 500m(1640ft) wide. These ribbon reefs are on the edge of dramatic drop-offs into clear oceanic waters. Protected within these reefs are a series of shallow platform reefs, randomly arranged and established on existing rocky outcrops.

Previous page: *To the north of Cairns is a spectacular region. Here, snorkellers and divers explore the platform reefs and crystal waters of Agincourt Reef, northeast of Port Douglas.*

Below: *It is not unusual for living corals to be exposed during low tides. These Heron Island reefs show mini atoll-like coral formations that are shaped by the shallow water conditions.*

GREAT BARRIER REEF

↩ Reefs Ⓟ Marine Parks ⊡ Proposed Marine Parks

In addition to specific marine parks marked, the whole main reef shown here is a designated protected area.

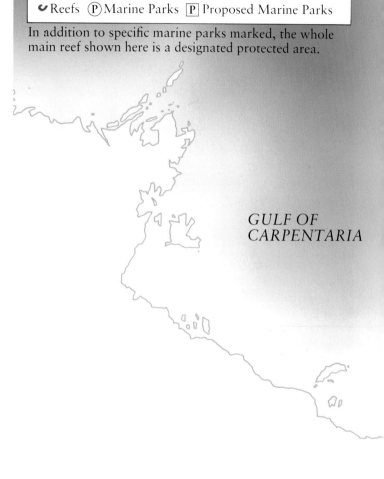

GULF OF CARPENTARIA

In addition to the groups of islands and cays produced by coral growth all along the Great Barrier Reef, there are many continental islands, some quite mountainous, that have their own associated fringing reef formations. Corals readily colonize any suitable hard substrate, provided reasonable conditions for growth exist, and these islands dotted along the continental shelf are ideal sites. In closer proximity to the mainland than the outer reef islands and cays, these islands can be affected by sedimentation and freshwater run-off in the rainy season, which can inhibit coral growth to a varying extent.

This bird's-eye view of the geography of the Great Barrier Reef only scratches the surface in illustrating the wide regional diversity in its form and structure, but it does serve to illustrate the complex nature of the region. By adding the considerable effect of the wide range of climatic conditions north to south, it is easy to understand how the enormous regional diversity of marine life populating these reefs has arisen.

Great Barrier Reef

Australia

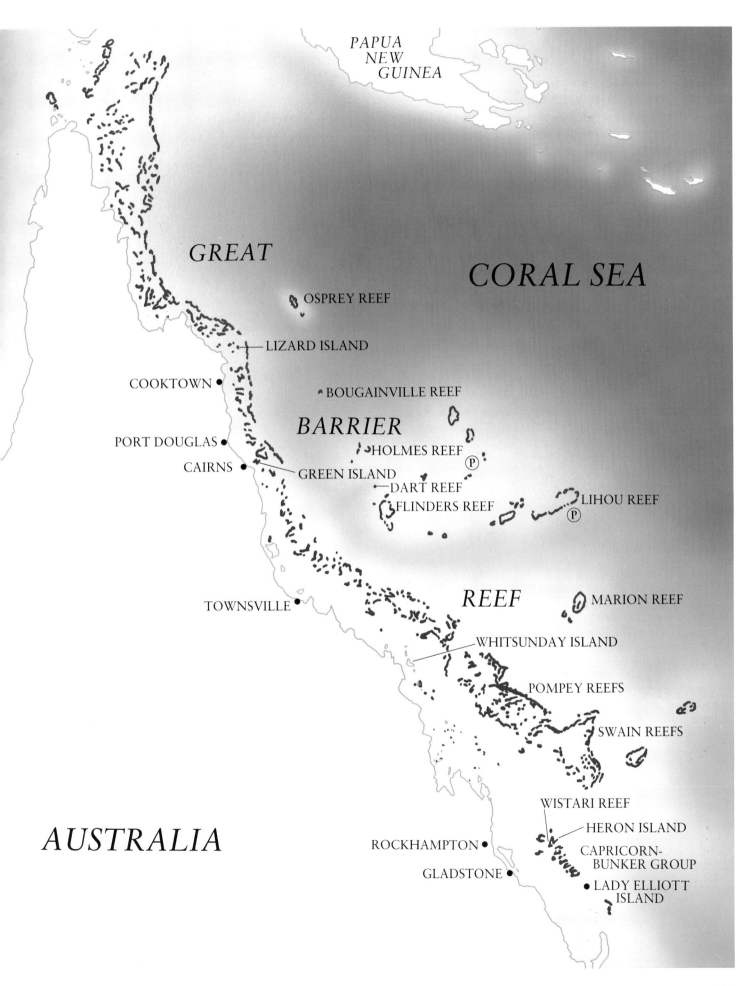

PAPUA
NEW
GUINEA

GREAT

CORAL SEA

OSPREY REEF

LIZARD ISLAND

COOKTOWN

BOUGAINVILLE REEF

BARRIER

HOLMES REEF

PORT DOUGLAS

Ⓟ

CAIRNS

GREEN ISLAND

DART REEF

LIHOU REEF

FLINDERS REEF

Ⓟ

REEF

MARION REEF

TOWNSVILLE

WHITSUNDAY ISLAND

POMPEY REEFS

SWAIN REEFS

WISTARI REEF

HERON ISLAND

AUSTRALIA

ROCKHAMPTON

CAPRICORN-
BUNKER GROUP

GLADSTONE

LADY ELLIOTT
ISLAND

A rich diversity of fishes

The list of different reef fish species records like a veritable encyclopedia of marine tropical fish. Whichever family is chosen, it seems almost sure that the Great Barrier Reef has the greatest diversity of species. Such diversity means that as well as a large number of familiar species there will also be those that are rare or unique.

The angelfishes and butterflyfishes are typical and therefore particularly well represented. There is known to be at least 23 angelfish species and a staggering 41 butterflyfish species. No other area in the world approaches this record. Angelfishes popular for the aquarium are represented by well-known species such as the emperor angelfish (*Pomacanthus imperator*), the Koran angelfish (*P. semicirculatus*) and the regal angelfish (*Pygoplites diacanthus*), all fishes which could place you

DIVING PROFILE   *Great Barrier Reef*

CLIMATE

North
Air temperature range:
   25-31°C(77-88°F)
Sea temperature range:
   23-26°C(73-79°F)

South
Air temperature range:
   21-29°C(70-84°F)
Sea temperature range:
   18-22°C(64-72°F)

The seasons are the reverse of those in the Northern Hemisphere and thus the lowest temperatures occur in July, in the middle of winter. There is a smaller seasonal variation in sea temperatures in the north than in the south because of the equatorial conditions. October is considered to be the best time of the year to visit the Great Barrier Reef, when the sea is calm and the days are springlike and eternally sunny.

FACILITIES

Facilities range from camping or motel-style accommodation on some resort islands to high-class hotels with mainland connection by helicopter or hydrofoil. Live-aboard boats are mainly purpose built for dive vacationing and range from a high standard to luxury class.

DIVE RATING

Diving ranges from fringing reef dives close to resorts, where underwater visibility can be restricted to 7-15m(23-50ft), to the outer reef sites, where it can exceed 30m(100ft). Outer Barrier Reef diving and offshore island diving are excellent and considered by some to be the ultimate. Wreck, wall and drift diving are all available.

Because of the immense size of the area and the variety of diving and conditions offered, it is necessary to divide the diving into the following three basic kinds.

Resort islands
There is a choice of three main offshore continental islands: Lizard Island in the north, and Hayman and South Molle in the Whitsunday group in the south. Diving from coral cays is centred on Green Island in the north and Heron Island in the Capricorn-Bunker group in the south. All these land-based resorts provide a high standard of diving from their fringing reefs but are a distance of 20-40km(12-25 miles) from the outer Barrier Reef, where diving is at its best.

Cruising the outer Barrier Reef
This form of diving takes place from live-aboard dive boats, operating from locations such as Cairns and Townsville. They make trips that last

5-10 days and take in magnificent outer Barrier Reef locations, such as the 130km(82 mile)-long Ribbon Reefs. Round trips can average 500km(312 miles) or more and include remote and exciting sites.

Cruising the Coral Sea
These are extended cruises ranging between 100 and 300km (63-188miles) beyond the outer Barrier Reef. A typical cruise to the north visits Holmes, Bougainville and Osprey Reefs in the northern Coral Sea and one to the south takes in Flinders, Diamond and Marion Reefs. On route, it is usually obligatory to dive the *Yongola* wreck, located between the Barrier Reef and the mainland at Townsville. This wreck is a national preserve and justifiably famous for its spectacular concentrations of marine life.

CONSERVATION

The Great Barrier Reef Marine Park is the largest marine park in the world. The reef region is protected from extensive resource development by the Great Barrier Reef Park Act of 1975, and in 1981 was included in the World Heritage List. Australians have a great awareness of the need to conserve this area and agree that it should not be spoiled.

Left: *The scribbled angelfish is a rare species found only in the northern section of the Queensland reefs and the region further north towards New Guinea.*

Right: *The stunning coloration of the yellow-faced angelfish defies adequate description. This species is common in the central Barrier Reef region.*

Next page: *This common Pacific species, the pretty lemonpeel angelfish (Centropyge flavissimus), is relatively rare in Australian waters.*

Below: *One of the most common butterflyfishes of the Great Barrier Reef, the threadfin butterflyfish (Chaetodon auriga) boasts a wide distribution over the whole Indo-Pacific.*

almost anywhere in the tropical Indian or Pacific oceans. The six-banded angelfish (*Euxiphipops sexstriatus*) is perhaps the most common of the larger Australian angelfish species in terms of numbers and distribution. It is not suitable for the home aquarium because it may grow to a length of 45cm(18in). Of the rarer large species, the scribbled angelfish (*Chaetodontoplus duboulayi*) is highly prized for its attractive markings.

The dwarf *Centropyge* angelfishes also include instantly recognizable aquarium species and feature the bicolor angelfish (*Centropyge bicolor*) and coral beauty (*C. bispinosus*), two very widely distributed species in both the Indian and Pacific Oceans. The most common of the dwarf Australian species, the pearlscale angelfish (*Centropyge vroliki*), is drab in coloration compared with other angelfishes and thus, although widely distributed, is rarely exported for the aquarium market. Of the rarities, the golden angelfish (*C. aurantius*) – only found in New Guinea and the Samoan Islands outside the Barrier Reef area and identified from the mere handful of specimens caught to date – features for the dwarf species of angelfishes.

In addition to the large number of true species, there are also two hybrid angelfishes. Hybridization in the wild is rarely encountered and of the two examples in these waters one is a cross between the dwarf *C. vroliki*, mentioned earlier, and *C. flavissimus*, the lemonpeel angelfish, and the other is between the beautiful yellow-faced angelfish (*Euxiphipops xanthometapon*) and the common six-banded angelfish.

The range of butterflyfishes is equally bewildering. The species unique to Australia include the Lord Howe coralfish (*Amphichaetodon howensis*) and the black butterflyfish (*Chaetodon flavirostris*), which is common in the Great Barrier Reef but rare elsewhere. Many aquarists would recognize the threadfin butterflyfish (*C. auriga*), the raccoon butterflyfish (*C. lunula*), the redfin butterflyfish (*C. trifasciatus*), the copperband butterflyfish (*Chelmon rostratus*) and the longnosed butterflyfish (*Forcipiger flavissimus*). Members of the *Heniochus* genus are represented by six species, including the popular wimplefish (*Heniochus acuminatus*) and rarities with a much smaller distribution, such as the humphead bannerfish (*H. varius*) and the beautiful singular bannerfish (*H. singularius*).

AQUARIUM CARE

Groupers

Groupers (family Serranidae) are generally heavy bodied and perchlike, with large mouths armed with sharp teeth. Hunting by stealth, groupers use their amazing ability to instantly change their colour and pattern to blend into their immediate surroundings and thus surprise their unsuspecting prey. Their mouths can open especially wide and by a sudden expansion of their jaws they are able to suck prey directly into the gullet.

Groupers have remarkable sex lives, undergoing a complete sex change as they mature. During their early years, all groupers start their adult lives as sexually mature females. They may then pass through a phase when they are both female and male, having both male and female reproductive organs and being capable of functioning as either (but not both). This condition is referred to as 'synchronously hermaphroditic', an ability more usually associated with animals lower down the evolutionary scale. Hermaphroditic groupers finally complete the transition and behave as males. In some species, females make a straight transition to males.

Groupers do not usually spring to mind when considering subjects for an aquarium, and there is no doubt that some of the larger members of the family would quickly outgrow the average-sized home aquarium. However, the family does include smaller species, such as the tiny 5-6cm(2-2.4in) false gramma *Pseudochromis paccagnella* and the slightly longer golden jewelfish (*Anthias squamipinnis*). Of the larger species that can be kept in a spacious home aquarium, the coral trout (*Cephalopholis miniata*) is possibly the most attractive, with brilliant coloration to equal any of its tiny vivid cousins in the grouper family.

Of small species, the jewelfish, or fairy basslet, (*Anthias squamipinnis*) is perhaps the most popular. Males of these tiny zooplankton feeders can easily be distinguished from females by very marked differences in coloration and the long dorsal fin rays of the male. Despite their small size, jewelfish require a large aquarium and are better kept in a small group as they prefer the company of their own species. Initially, acclimatization to aquarium life can be difficult. It is a good idea to offer live foods such as brineshrimp and *Mysis* shrimp and add meaty frozen foods as the fish settle in.

By contrast, feeding the large serranids is simple; they have insatiable appetites. They will snap up any food that remotely resembles their natural diet of fish and crustaceans. This can include all manner of

meaty sea foods, but fresh or frozen fish and crab meat are preferred.

We should mention that large groupers, although peaceful, are not good community aquarium fishes once they pass the juvenile stage. They will readily eat smaller fish placed in their aquarium and may use their large mouths to successfully envelope fish approaching their own size.

Top: *The rich colouring and extended dorsal fin rays of this specimen clearly show it to be a male jewelfish. Males develop from adult females, as in other groupers.*

Above: *The female jewelfish, shown here, are quite different from males, but still elegant and colourful in their own right. In the wild, females far outnumber males.*

A VOYAGE OF DISCOVERY

The new moon was showing for the first time and the clear, velvety black sky sparkled with the light of countless bright stars. The Nimrod 3 powered catamaran cut easily through the calm sea, luminescent waves occasionally spilling over the bows and scattering tiny splashes of phosphorescent plankton on the decks like mirrored fragments of the star-studded canopy above.

Many Coral Sea cruises begin like this, as they leave Townsville on the Queensland coast in the early evening and head east towards the Coral Sea and Flinders Reef, a colossal reef complex some 400km(250 miles) from the mainland. In the small hours of the following morning, the thud of the engines ceases and the anchor rattles down into the depths. At first light, a glance around merely shows open water, with no signs of reefs or land in any direction. In fact, this is the site of the famous wreck of the *Yongola*, a large ill-fated passenger ship that foundered here in 1919. The remains of the *Yongola* rest on a sandy bottom in open water between the Barrier Reef and the mainland, 16km(10 miles) from the coast and 85km(53 miles) from Townsville.

Located in the middle of a channel, the wreck has been transformed by strong nutrient-rich currents into a vibrant artificial reef teeming with an incredible array of marine life.

Rising up from the depths, the *Yongola* is almost intact, standing more-or-less upright and very close to the classic conception of how a wreck should look. In 30m(100ft) of water, the highest parts of the superstructure reach to within 15m(50ft) of the surface, with most of the deck and main superstructure within depths of 20-25m(66-82ft). Many features of the old vessel are recognizable but are densely covered with all manner of colourful invertebrate life and swarming with huge aggregations of fish. Large batfish, jacks and eagle rays patrol the wreck in massive shoals, often hanging in tiers on the upflows as the natural current rises over the wreck's bulk. In the shelter of the bow and stern, schools of sweetlips crowd together with squirrelfish and soldierfish. Within the wreck, cardinalfish gather in silvery clouds and large 136kg(300lb)-groupers lurk in the dark depths. Occasionally, immense black manta rays majestically circle the wreck, their huge silhouettes framed against the bright surface. Diving this area is a revelation, even for the most

Above: *Heart-stopping encounters with large sharks can occur in the caves of Flinders Reef. This remote atoll provides exciting diving.*

Right: *The dramatic scenery of Flinders Reef is at its best on the southern reef extension, where sheer drop-offs are etched with endless canyons and caves.*

experienced diver, and never fails to impress even those who are familiar with the location.

A day's diving on the *Yongola* soon speeds by and is usually followed by a further overnight journey on the original heading for Flinder's Reef. Named after the famous Australian explorer, Captain Mathew Flinders, this remote atoll complex is a diver's paradise of rugged coral reef gorges and bommies that extend over a huge area and surround a lagoon over 20km(12 miles) across. Inside the reef, the lagoon floor is covered with large pinnacles of coral that reach up to the surface and create extensive systems of interconnecting caves and

continued on next page

Above: *A large school of yellow-banded hussars crowd below a ledge at Dart Reef. They will break ranks to hunt after nightfall.*

The reefs off Townsville, Queensland.

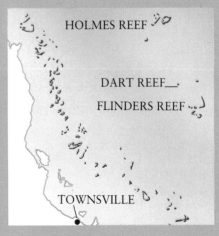

tunnels. The shallow waters are filled with a wide range of small colourful fish. Reef sharks are common and there can be heart-stopping encounters with large sharks approaching from the opposite direction in the maze of caves and tunnels. In most instances, it is a time to mutually register surprise and then carry on as before, giving the shark as wide a berth as possible.

The drop-offs on the outside of the reef are dramatic and at their best on the southern reef extension. On Flinders and nearby Dart Reef the best drop-offs are sheer cliffs starting just below the surface and plummeting to depths of 1000m(3300ft) or more. Near the surface, these vertical walls are crowded with shoals of pennant butterflyfish (*Heniochus diphreutes*) and giant potato cod patrol the reef edge. The best shark action is in this area, with large oceanic grey and white-tip sharks coasting close into the reefs from the depths below.

The final destination of this diving odyssey is likely to be Holmes Reef, 130km(81 miles) north of Flinders. Here, again, the scenery is dramatic, with coral pinnacles and vertical reef walls set in clear blue oceanic water. The reefs are rich and colourful, and offer the greatest density of marine life to be encountered anywhere on a coral reef, resulting, no doubt, from the wide range of different habitats and the nutrient-rich upwellings from the surrounding depths.

Among a kaleidoscopic array of hard corals, gorgonians and sponges, huge pink, peach and crimson soft corals, some as large as a person, grow in profusion in depths of 30m(100ft) or more. Night dives are always exciting here and reveal large numbers of brightly coloured crinoids that climb up to vantage points on the reef to feed on passing plankton, spreading their delicate feathery arms in the search for food. Equally colourful nocturnal sea slugs also appear, foraging among the corals under the cloak of darkness.

Right: *Night dives on Holmes Reef can be exciting excursions into a wonderful world of pink, peach and crimson soft corals, which are found 50m(164ft) below the surface. Brightly coloured crinoids and sea slugs also come into view in their nocturnal quest for food.*

On this site, sharks are both numerous and large, and there are regular opportunities to see hammerheads, silver-tip and grey whalers (the last being an Australian term for oceanic white-tip sharks). Perhaps the most outstanding feature, however, is the wide diversity of reef fish species, a large number of which can be considered rare in other parts of the Indo-Pacific. Butterflyfishes, for example, are represented by the citron butterflyfish (*Chaetodon citrinellus*), the delicate clown butterflyfish (*C. ornatissimus*), the longspot butterflyfish (*C. plebeius*) and wider ranging species such as *C. auriga*, *C. ephippium*, *C. melannotus*, *C. melanopus*, *C. speculum*, and *C. trifasciatus*, are also very common. Similarly, large numbers of angelfishes abound, including many species of the dwarf *Centropyge* genus, among them the oriole angelfish (*Centropyge bicolor*), the dusky angel (*C. bispinosus*) and the lemon peel angelfish (*C. flavissimus*).

This area is world famous for exciting encounters with sea snakes which, contrary to previously held opinions, are not the lethal venomous creatures they are generally assumed to be. Most

Below: *A feather star spreads its delicate arms to feed upon rich plankton. These beautiful creatures are often encountered on night dives.*

Above: *Holmes Reef is the home of a wide range of reef fish species, including these handsome clown, or ornate, butterflyfishes* (Chaetodon ornatissimus).

species are non aggressive and curious to the point of approaching divers for a closer look. In the past, their preoccupation with the swirling turbulence created by a diver's fins has been misinterpreted as an attack response, because the faster the alarmed diver tries to swim away, the greater the turbulence created and the more the snake enjoys the pursuit. The olive sea snake and a number of other species even allow themselves to be handled by divers and do not seem to mind the contact. Their venom is akin to that of their terrestrial cousin, the cobra, however, and, as with all potentially dangerous creatures, the 'look don't touch' rule is the best approach.

For those wishing to experience the ultimate voyage of diving discovery, Australia's Coral Sea cannot be equalled. The quality of the diving, the remoteness and beauty of the area, and the exciting encounters with the rare and fascinating marine life provide an exceptional series of experiences you will not easily forget.

At the crossroads of the great oceans

Located as it is between the Indian and Pacific Oceans, Australia benefits from the evolutionary progress of both huge oceans. Fish species that are familiar inhabitants of the Red Sea reefs can be found here, together with some from the South Pacific and the Hawaiian Islands. The warm waters connecting this whole Indo-Pacific area, including Australia, allow tropical marine life the freedom of movement from one part to another, and it is often only the vast distances involved that have prevented total integration.

To understand why some forms of life take advantage of this freedom of movement, and thus have a wide distribution, while others remain in a restricted area, we must look closely at various aspects of their behaviour. If we focus on fishes specifically, there are two basic behaviour patterns into which they can be grouped: those that are migratory and those that never stray from a fixed territory. Clearly, migratory species are more likely to have a wider distribution than territorial species, simply because they are not restricted to one location. Having accepted this simple concept, we need to superimpose a further range of variations. The method used to reproduce and disperse the succeeding generation can often affect our earlier reasoning. Some strictly territorial animals do occasionally migrate, but only during the breeding season, when they collect in aggregations to spawn. Alternatively, their offspring may be migratory for a short period after hatching. Good examples of territorial animals that spread in this way would be a number of species of Barrier Reef groupers, including the coral trout (*Cephalopholis miniata*) and some parrotfish species. Members of these species gather in large numbers to spawn and the resulting eggs and fry join with the zooplankton and are swept by currents to nursery areas, such as channels between reefs and cays. Here, the juveniles live a territorial existence before returning, as adults, to colonize the main reef and resume a fairly restricted way of life. By this means, territorial animals can widen their distribution. This migratory pattern between nursery grounds and the final adult habitat also answers the specific question as to why juvenile coral trout are seldom found on open reef slopes while the adults are plentiful in these areas.

Clownfish, or anemonefish, are also strictly territorial and, although there are a large number of individual species, each species has only a limited distribution in Indo-Pacific terms. Clownfish seldom stray more than a metre from their host anemone and need to be able to disperse their offspring to avoid competition for food and space. Clownfish form pairs early in life and are good parents. They lay adhesive eggs in a cluster on a previously cleaned site beneath the protective tentacles of their anemone and both parents tend and protect them. Once hatched, the free-swimming fry are able to survive only for a short period in the zooplankton, before settling on a new site. Because this migratory stage is so short, they cannot survive being carried long distances over open bodies of water and thus do not move far from their parents. For each particular species, this results in a very limited distribution. However, this does not explain why there is such a diversity of clownfish species.

The colonization of the Indo-Pacific reefs by clownfish species has been a slow progression outwards along the tropical coastlines of the areas bordering the Central Indo-Pacific Ocean. Along the way, specialization in response to habitat differences, food sources and types of predation has led to regional differences. This process, known as diverging evolution, has continued to the point at which separate species can be recognized. This type of geographical variation generally reflects a degree of isolation and occurs particularly in those species distributed over a wide area. In this example, the variations are mainly in coloration, but various other changes can be induced by the same process. Diverging evolution is common among reef fishes, as well as in many other life forms.

Above: *Clownfishes, such as this boldly marked* Amphiprion clarkii, *stay within very close range of their host anemone.*

Right: *A splendid coral trout,* (Cephalopholis miniata), *one of the most widely distributed of Indo-Pacific reef fishes.*

Clownfishes are among the most colourful of coral reef fishes and are a major feature on most reefs. There are three common Australian species: the common clownfish (*Amphiprion percula*), a very distinctive species with a gaudy pattern of orange, edged in black, and white stripes; the pink skunk clown (*Amphiprion perideraion*), sporting a white stripe from nose to tail along the dorsal surface; and the anemonefish (*Amphiprion chrysopterus*), which has two brilliant white-tinged blue bars on a chocolate-splotched yellow body. Each species chooses different species of host anemone: the common clownfish usually associates with the orange *Heteractis* anemone; the pink skunk clown with the large pink *Heteractis* anemone; and the anemonefish with the carpet anemone (*Stoichactis gigas*). The numbers and diversity of these clownfish species can be controlled not only by the numbers of anemones available to them but also to some extent by the numbers of particular species of anemone. It is just this kind of intensive specialization that limits a species or leads to its diversity as it specializes further to adapt to its surroundings in a range of different aspects.

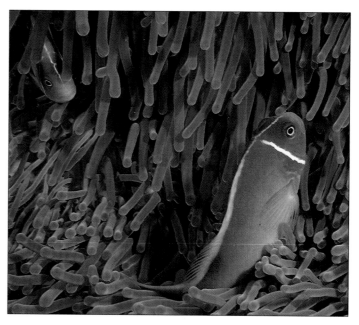

Above: *Widely distributed over the whole of the Barrier Reef, the skunk clownfish* (Amphiprion perideraion) *is a shy species, found mainly with* Heteractis *anemones.*

Below: *The much rarer anemonefish* (Amphiprion chrysopterus) *prefers to associate with carpet anemones* (Stoichactis gigas) *and is related to Clark's clownfish.*

AQUARIUM CARE

Clownfishes

The clownfishes, or anemonefishes (of the family Pomacentridae), need almost no introduction. The combination of eye-catching coloration, hardiness and their fascinating association with large anemones of the genera *Stoichactis*, *Dicosoma* and *Heteractis* has ensured the clownfishes' continuing and justified popularity among aquarists the world over.

To many of us, the bold colour patterns typified by the common clown (*Amphiprion percula*) are a perfect example of the larger than life colours we associate with coral fishes. This bold coloration exists for a very definite purpose, however, as a warning to would-be predators not to approach too close to the stinging tentacles of the seemingly vulnerable anemone.

A. percula is closely related to *A. ocellaris*, which is also called the common clown. The two species are often confused, a problem which does not apply in the wild as *A. ocellaris* has a distribution centred around Malaya and Indonesia while *A. percula* is typical of Queensland and Melanesia. This is an example of a regional difference between members of a species that has led to them now being recognized as two separate species. The more readily available *A. ocellaris* is slightly different in coloration, principally in the black borders between the orange and white markings.

All clownfishes make very good subjects for the aquarium; they are territorial and showy enough to form a single focal point in the aquarium, or take the eye as a pair or a small group, in association with a large anemone. Clownfishes are generally sociable, but some species, the common clown included, can be territorially aggressive as adults and mutually intolerant of other clownfish species.

In the wild, their diet is zooplankton and algae. In captivity, they are not fussy feeders, accepting most dried and frozen foods. As with all animals, however, their health can be improved with a good diet. In their case, finely chopped live foods such as earthworms and live brineshrimp or *Mysis* shrimp added as a supplement to proprietary foods will enhance vigour and colour. There are no other specific requirements regarding their care. Temperatures of 25-27°C(77-81°F) are acceptable and water quality does not need to be improved above the levels accepted by their hardy relations, the damselfishes.

These small coral fishes seldom grow more than 5cm(2in) long in aquarium conditions and are so accommodating that a number of species, especially the common clown, have been bred and reared in captivity. Many reef fish species start their adult lives as females and, later, the dominant females undergo a sex change to become males on full maturity. Clownfishes differ in that they start adult life as males, and dominant males change sex to become female. Placing any two juvenile clownfish together, therefore, should produce a male and female pair on maturity.

Above: *The common clown* (A. ocellaris) *is frequently included in shipments to Europe from the Philippines and Malaya and is among the most popular of all aquarium species. A group of juveniles, included with a large* Heteractis *anemone, will provide a splendid display in the aquarium.*

A unique range of marine life

However caused, the diversity of marine life on the
Great Barrier Reef is certainly an attraction, but
the main appeal is the large numbers of unique
and often bizarre marine creatures to be found
there. Of the large fishes unique to Australia, the
potato cod (*Epinephelus tukula*), a gentle giant of
a grouper, and the Queensland grouper
(*Promicrops lanceolatus*) are prominent and both
grow to a length of nearly 2m(6.6ft) and weigh
over 200kg(440lb). Although not unique to
Australian waters, the mammoth-sized, plankton-
feeding Pacific manta ray (*Manta alfredi*) is worthy
of mention and is common along the reef. The
sharks of the Barrier Reef are legendary in size and
abundance, but the curious wobbegong, or carpet
shark, (*Orectolobus maculatus*), with its highly
camouflaged body and bewhiskered snout, is a
bizarre and unique feature of this area.

Above: *The strange
wobbegong* (Orectolobus
maculatus), *a slow-
moving member of the
shark family, uses
elaborate camouflage to
avoid its predators. Even
a large specimen can be
overlooked. These sharks
live among weed-covered
rocks at the bottom of
shallow waters, where
they engulf unwary crabs,
lobsters and small fish.*

Right: *The potato cod is
so popular with divers
that on Lizard Island it is
now protected. These
groupers frequent feeding
stations, which allow
divers contact with these
friendly giants. This
photograph shows how
large a potato cod can
grow and demonstrates its
easy going nature. The
Queensland grouper also
reaches this size range.*

BATFISH AT BIG BOMMIE

Heron Island is perhaps the most famous of the islands of the Great Barrier Reef, justifiably so considering its location in the middle of a marine park, surrounded by dozens of reefs, atolls and cays. Barely more than 1km(0.6 mile) long and 100-150m(up to about 500ft) wide, this green, wooded island lies 72km(45 miles) from the Queensland coast. Despite a thriving tourist resort on the northeastern tip, most of the island is left unspoiled. It is still possible to walk along paths noisy with bird song beneath dense growths of pisonia trees that provide welcome shade from the scorching noonday sun.

Heron Island is part of the Capricorn-Bunker group set among some of the most beautiful reefs in the southern section of the Barrier Reef. The fringing reef of the island and nearby Wistari Reef are the best-known in the Great Barrier Reef and have been designated a marine sanctuary. Scientists from the small marine research station on the island have recorded over 1150 species of reef fish within the sanctuary as well as a tremendous diversity of corals and invertebrates. At Heron you will find a wide range of stony and soft corals and the greatest number of different species of colourful nudibranchs, for example, than anywhere in the Barrier Reef.

The most popular site for both diving and snorkelling around Heron Island is Big Bommie, a group of six gigantic coral heads that rise from a

The reefs around Heron Island

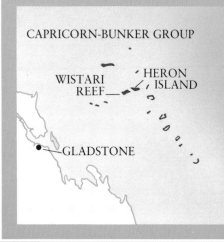

sloping bottom in about 10m(33ft) of water to within 2 or 3m(10ft) of the surface. Only a five-minute boat ride from the island, this location is alive with large and small reef fish, especially in the shallows on the top of the coral heads, where divers have provided free meals for the fish every day for over a decade. Purists may scorn this transformation of a natural reef setting into a kind of underwater zoo, but it is certainly an exhilarating experience to be surrounded by hundreds of fish, from tiny colourful *Anthias* to huge saucer-shaped batfish and silvery jacks, all tame enough to touch.

The batfish that have become permanent residents of the bommie are extremely tame and will crowd around divers, hoping to be fed. Other residents include a large green moray eel with a handsome black mottled body, which can be lured out from its lair in the coral with tidbits of fish, and some large greedy red emperor sweetlips (*Lutjanus sebae*), which try to monopolize all the food offered by divers. Red emperors are the ultimate opportunist feeders, with seemingly insatiable appetites. They make ideal aquarium fish but do need a large aquarium; if properly fed, they will soon outgrow their surroundings.

Heron Island is situated about 40km(25 miles) from the edge of the continental shelf and most of the diving is in depths of less than 15m(50ft), although there are drop-offs to 40m(130ft) close by. Wistari Reef is an atoll in the making, with a completely enclosed lagoon dotted with patch reefs. The encircling reef reaches to within a few metres of the surface and is a spectacular mosaic of shallow reefs of *Acropora* corals. Underwater visibility varies from 10-15m(33-50ft) to 30-40m(100-130ft) and, even though the area is in the south of the Barrier Reef region, average sea temperatures never drop below a comfortable 21°C(70°F).

Above: *At the base of one of the bommies a large green moray welcomes the approach of divers, from whom it will take tidbits.*

Right: *Heron Island has become a popular holiday resort, especially for diving and snorkelling. The island's reefs, and those of Wistari Reef (shown in the background), provide many opportunities for exciting undersea excursions in an idyllic setting. The whole area is a marine sanctuary.*

CAPRICORN-BUNKER GROUP

WISTARI REEF

HERON ISLAND

GLADSTONE

Above: *The Big Bommie is Heron Island's favourite dive location. Feeding the fish has transformed the area into an underwater zoo and hundreds of fish arrive to join in the feast. It is a marvellous opportunity to view large fish close up.*

Below: *The huge batfish of Big Bommie are legendary; saucer-shaped fish hanging in the currents around the pinnacle of the largest coral heads. These friendly creatures crowd around divers hoping for food.*

Invertebrate life on the reef

Reef invertebrates also abound in enormous diversity. Stony corals are naturally the predominant invertebrates associated with these well-developed reefs and are represented by a wide array of different species. The staghorn coral family (*Acropora*) is the largest group and it is possible to find 20 or more species living together in one small area. Staghorn corals thrive in the shallows and may become stranded above the surface during extremely low tides. Such an exposed section of reef may consist of spiky lilac branches of *Acropora nobilis* interspersed with fanlike growths of *A. cytherea* and stubby growths of *A. gemmifera*. On the reef slope, the hard corals typically include a matrix of brain corals (*Platygra*, *Symphyllia* and *Leptoria* species), platelike *Montipora* and *Tubinaria* corals, huge massive star corals (*Favia*, *Montastrea* and

Goniastrea species), together with branching *Acropora* and *Porites*. Depending on the exposure, water depth and location, reefs differ immensely in the mix of coral colonies they encompass. And stony corals associate with a large range of soft corals, gorgonian sea fans and sea whips. Sponges also feature prominently in a wide diversity of size, form and colour. In fact, sponges are often an integral part of the reef structure and help to bind the reef together. The boring sponges can reverse this process, however, since they literally bore into the corals by dissolving the limestone and eventually destroy the reef's stability.

A well-known group of invertebrates often found adding their bulk to the structure of the reef are the large bivalve molluscs, especially the clams, including the infamous giant clam (*Tridacna gigas*). This animal is so prolific that, at one site close to Lizard Island in the northern section of

the Barrier Reef, hundreds can be found carpeting a small cove, many 1m(3.3ft) or more across. Stories associated with this clam include lurid tales of divers becoming trapped by the foot as the gaping shell suddenly slams shut. As you might expect, these tales are inaccurate; the clam's hinged shell does not open wide enough to enclose a foot and, in any case, divers certainly do not form part of the clam's diet!

At the other end of the mollusc scale is a micro world of colourful shelled gastropods such as the beautiful smooth-shelled cowries, the spiny murex shells, and the handsome but venomous cone shells, as well as a bewildering variety of rainbow-hued shell-less sea slugs. Few animals can rival the sea slugs and their feathery naked-gilled cousins, the nudibranchs, for beauty of form and colour, and the Barrier Reef is home to scores of different species (see the panel on page 178).

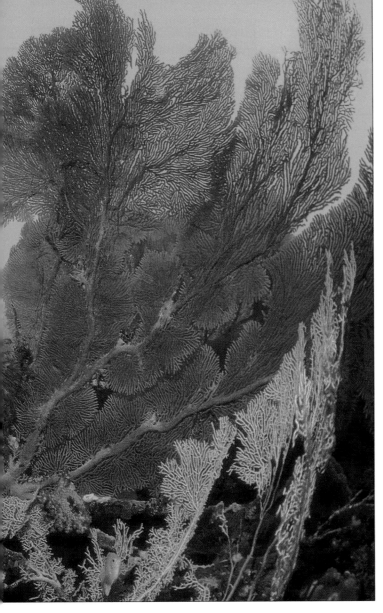

Left: *Even though strong sunlight is playing on the water's surface, a torch is required at depth to appreciate the authentic colours of the invertebrate life. Here, a large sea fan, or gorgonian, dominates a particularly beautiful 'coral garden' setting. Note the featherstars.*

Top: *This close-up of a giant clam shows the light-gathering points in the mantle for the zooxanthellae it fosters.*

Above: *These immense giant clams, which dwarf the diver, are a common sight on the coral reefs around Lizard Island.*

Nudibranchs

Nudibranchs are small snail-like molluscs that belong to a large group of animals commonly referred to as sea slugs. Their descriptive scientific name literally means 'naked gills' and refers to the feathery appendages on their backs, which are the animal's gills. These flamboyant adornments, combined with their brilliant coloration, transform these small animals into perhaps the most visually stunning of marine invertebrates.

Few marine animals can rival their distribution, which includes all the world's oceans, and their gaudy coloration is just as brilliant in polar and temperate waters as it is in tropical climes. No one knows exactly how many species there are; with such a wide distribution, mainly nocturnal behaviour and shy retiring nature, it is almost impossible to make a comprehensive study of these fascinating creatures. There are estimated to be at least 2500 recorded species, which is considered to be only about half of the total living species. In fact, nudibranchs form one of the largest orders of marine animals. The greatest numbers and range of species are to be found in tropical seas and the Barrier Reef is perhaps the richest single source, with 400-500 species.

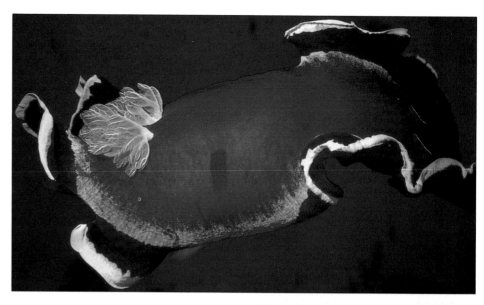

Above: *The spectacular Spanish dancer is one of the largest members of the nudibranch order and a delight to discover on a night dive.*

Right: *Spanish dancer egg masses arranged in elaborate ribbons and whorls. Many nudibranch species have such distinctively shaped egg masses.*

Below: *This aeolidacean nudibranch,* Glaucilla marginata, *lives on the surface and feeds on planktonic coelenterates.*

Their diversity is matched by their range in size, from tiny species such as *Pseudovermis*, which is little larger than a fine grain of sand, to the 30cm(12in)-long Spanish dancer (*Hexabranchus sanguineus*) and the even larger *Tochuina tetraquetra* from the western coast of North America, which can weigh 1.5kg(3.3lb). Of the three main suborders of nudibranchs, the Doridacea, which includes the extensive and attractive Australian family of Chromodorid nudibranchs, contains the largest members. These include the cerise-spotted *Chromodoris amoena* and the beautiful white *Ardeadoris egretta*. The delicately formed, beautifully patterned Aeolidacea species are next in magnitude – the Australian species *Pteraeolodia semperi*, for example, may grow up to 15cm(6in) in length. Finally, there are the tiny *Dentronotacea* species, colourful feeders on coelenterates that attack a wide range of prey, including anemones, corals, hydroids, and even jellyfishes.

All nudibranchs are carnivorous, and feed on a wide range of sessile or slow-moving invertebrates. Some species prey on other nudibranchs and sea slugs and at least one, the American species *Phidiana pugnax*, is truly cannibalistic, feeding on members of its own species (as well as on other aeolid nudibranchs). The nudibranch diet encompasses sponges, coelenterates, sea squirts, and the eggs of a wide range of crustaceans, molluscs and fishes. Some species even attack and feed on barnacles. Nudibranchs use their strong jaws and a rough file-like tongue, the radula, to scrape up the hapless prey or they mix it with mucus and simply suck it up into the stomach.

The aeolids feed on coelenterates and some species retain the symbiotic zooxanthellae in their own tissues to act as a continuing major source of food. Some members of the aeolids also retain the stinging cells, or nematocysts, obtained from feeding on coelenterates and store them in the tips of the cerata, tubular projections on their backs. If any of the cerata are nipped by a predator, the stinging cells are expelled as they become 'triggered', quickly discouraging further attacks.

Many species are adapted to feeding on one single form of prey and, unfortunately, these include many of those offered for sale for the aquarium. A good example would be the brightly coloured dendrodorid nudibranchs of warm seas, which feed only on encrusting sponges. Although very attractive, specialist feeders such as these are doomed to starvation and death in the average aquarium.

As an evolutionary offshoot from the shelled molluscs, these soft, seemingly defenceless animals have evolved other means of defence. No longer protected by a shell, defence mechanisms have evolved that are mainly chemical rather than mechanical. Using weapons stolen from the coelenterates is one method, but a wide range of other deterrents are used to make the nudibranch distasteful to its predators. Dorids, for example, can expel quantities of sulphuric acid from glands on the skin and many nudibranch species can exude a poisonous slime strongly toxic to other marine organisms. This is probably a key to the brilliant coloration that many nudibranchs display; it seems to serve as a conspicuous warning to predators of these defence mechanisms. There is a tiny flaw in this reasoning, however, because species that rely on camouflage for concealment are equally distasteful

to their countless would-be predators.

A large number of species have annual life cycles and many nudibranchs complete their life cycle in less than a year. On reaching sexual maturity, each individual has both male and female organs and can function as both sexes, often simultaneously. Large masses of up to a million eggs are produced, arranged in elaborate patterns of ribbons and whorls, the shape of each species' egg mass often being quite distinct. After hatching, the larvae undergo various changes, including a free-swimming stage, before they eventually find a favourable habitat in which to settle. During this period, each tiny larva, or veliger, has an equally tiny external shell, but this is quickly discarded to reveal the beautiful feathery gills of the adult.

Above: *Chromodorid nudibranchs are numerous in the waters surrounding Heron Island. All chromodorids are specialist feeders; these two colourful members of the species* Chromodoris cori *feed on specific types of sponges.*

Left: *Each chromodorid nudibranch species can be identified by its unique coloration and pattern. This delightful specimen,* Chromodoris lubooki, *was photographed near Holmes Reef.*

Below: *The patches on the body of this* Phyllidia varicosa *are glands that secrete toxic chemicals as a defence against predators. Its bright coloration is thought to advertise this toxicity.*

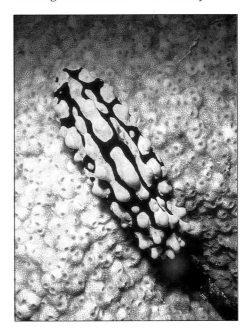

CORAL REEFS OF THE WORLD
Hawaii

'A world apart'

Mentioning the Hawaiian Islands conjures up an image of palm trees and sunlit shores, Waikiki Beach, surfboards and hula-hula skirts. As a holiday destination, the popularity of these islands is undeniable, but the bonus of the islands' unique and dramatic underwater scenery has further boosted this popularity. The combination of sun-drenched beaches, family holiday appeal and superb diving opportunities has encouraged a large proportion of the estimated 50-70,000 divers who visit the islands each year. In fact, diving tourism, especially from the west coast of the USA, has thrust the Hawaiian Islands into the current top five most frequented and popular diving tourist destinations in the world.

The reefs surrounding these beautiful islands do not have the large expanses of diverse, tightly packed coral growth found in other parts of the Indo-Pacific nor the dramatic vistas of antler coral, waving sea fans and sponges of the tropical West Atlantic. Located in the North Pacific Ocean, some distance away from the Equator, the reefs of the Hawaiian Islands are towards the most northerly extreme for coral growth. The principal sea currents are warm, moving upwards towards the islands from the Equator borne in a clockwise direction by the North Equatorial Current, but the prevailing winds are cold northeasterly trade winds. Sea temperatures can equal those of, say, the northern Caribbean for most of the year, but strong winter winds between September and May usually bring the heavy surf conditions for which the islands are famous and produce very rough cooling seas on the windward northern and northeastern shores.

A further factor inhibiting the development of large coral reef structures is the volcanic origin of the islands. The fiery lava flows that formed the

Red hot lava meets the ocean.

islands still continue to pour from active volcanoes in the island chain. In many places, coral growth close inshore has been replaced by these laval deposits. As it comes into contact with the sea, the red-hot lava abruptly hardens to form tunnels, caverns and archways. Coral reefs buried beneath lava in the past are slowly undergoing recolonization by new coral growth. The dramatic seascapes formed by this process are very unusual and, while not rich in coral growth, do provide a large variety of habitats that have been extensively exploited by a wide range of colourful marine life and offer visitors exciting diving in shallow water.

A world apart

Although classed as a part of the Indo-Pacific, with access to the wide range of fish species indigenous to the area, the relative isolation of the Hawaiian Islands has resulted in comparatively less diversity but a correspondingly large number of species unique to that part of the world. For example, there are approximately 600 species of Indo-Pacific fishes in the waters surrounding the Hawaiian Islands, while tropical Australian waters harbour over 2000 species. A brief overview of the variety of Hawaiian species, however, soon reveals many fascinating and unique examples of marine life as well as some puzzling deficiencies.

Members of the large grouper family of fishes (Serranidae) are conspicuous by their absence. Angelfishes are represented only by two large species – the striped angelfish (*Apolemichthys arcuatus*) and the masked angelfish (*Genicanthus personatus*) – plus a few dwarf species, notably Potter's angelfish (*Centropyge potteri*) and Fisher's pygmy angelfish (*C. fisheri*), two species which are unique to Hawaii, and the attractive and widely

Above: *Hawaii is home to familiar Indo-Pacific species, such as these raccoon butterflyfish* (Chaetodon lunula) *and also to exclusive species, including the lemon butterflyfish* (C. miliaris), *with the distinctive spotted markings.*

Right: *Angelfishes are less common in Hawaiian waters, but of the three pygmy species, Potter's angelfish* (Centropyge potteri) *is perhaps the most beautiful. It is found only in Hawaii.*

distributed Pacific species, the flame angelfish (*C. loriculus*). Clownfishes are also absent, as are a number of other common and widely distributed Indo-Pacific members of the clownfish/damselfish family (Pomacentridae). The appealing little humbug damselfish (*Dascyllus aruanus*) is distributed from the Red Sea throughout the Indo-Pacific and into Polynesia but is not found in Hawaiian waters. Similarly, the domino, or three-spot damsel, (*Dascyllus trimaculatus*) is widely distributed elsewhere in the Indo-Pacific but absent from Hawaii. In this case, a closely allied species, *Dascyllus albisella*, fills the niche uniquely. Other fish species unique to Hawaii include a beautiful pygmy member of the scorpionfish family, the Hawaiian lionfish (*Pterois sphex*), an Hawaiian cleaner wrasse (*Labroides phthirophagus*) and the Hawaiian sharpnosed puffer (*Canthigaster jactator*), the latter described on page 192.

Abundant squirrelfishes and soldierfishes

However, some fish families are both abundant and well represented. Chief among these are the squirrelfishes (family Holocentridae), which are very common fishes in the Hawaiian area. The barred squirrelfish (*Adioryx diadema*) is a popular aquarium fish with a distribution from Hawaii to the Red Sea. The spotfin squirrelfish (*Flammeo sammera*) and the sabre squirrelfish (*Adioryx spinifer*) are two further species with a similar distribution and which are very common in Hawaii. Of the South Pacific species, the small-mouthed squirrelfish (*A. microstomum*) and the Palau squirrelfish (*A. tiere*) are represented, and two species specific to the islands are the locally named 'Alaihi-Alaihi Maoli' (*A. xantherythrus*), and the Hawaiian squirrelfish (*Neoniphon scythrops*). The closely related soldierfishes (in the same family) are similarly well represented, perhaps the most familiar being the big-eye soldierfish (*Myripristis murdjan*). This species, common throughout the Indo-Pacific, is called a 'Mempache' in Hawaii. The yellowfin soldierfish (*M. chryseres*) is more or less unique to Hawaii, with a distribution restricted to the northern Pacific Ocean.

Why the holocentrids are so well established around these islands is not clear. Part of the explanation undoubtedly involves the rugged volcanic underwater terrain around the islands. The dark tunnels and caves that abound provide ideal daytime retreats for these nocturnal fishes. Here, they rest during the day, regaining their strength to join the nightly hunt for the smaller fish that form their prey.

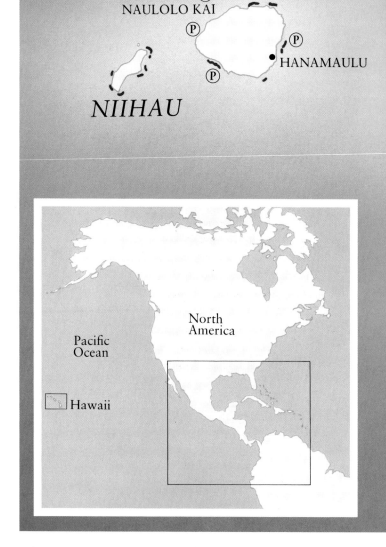

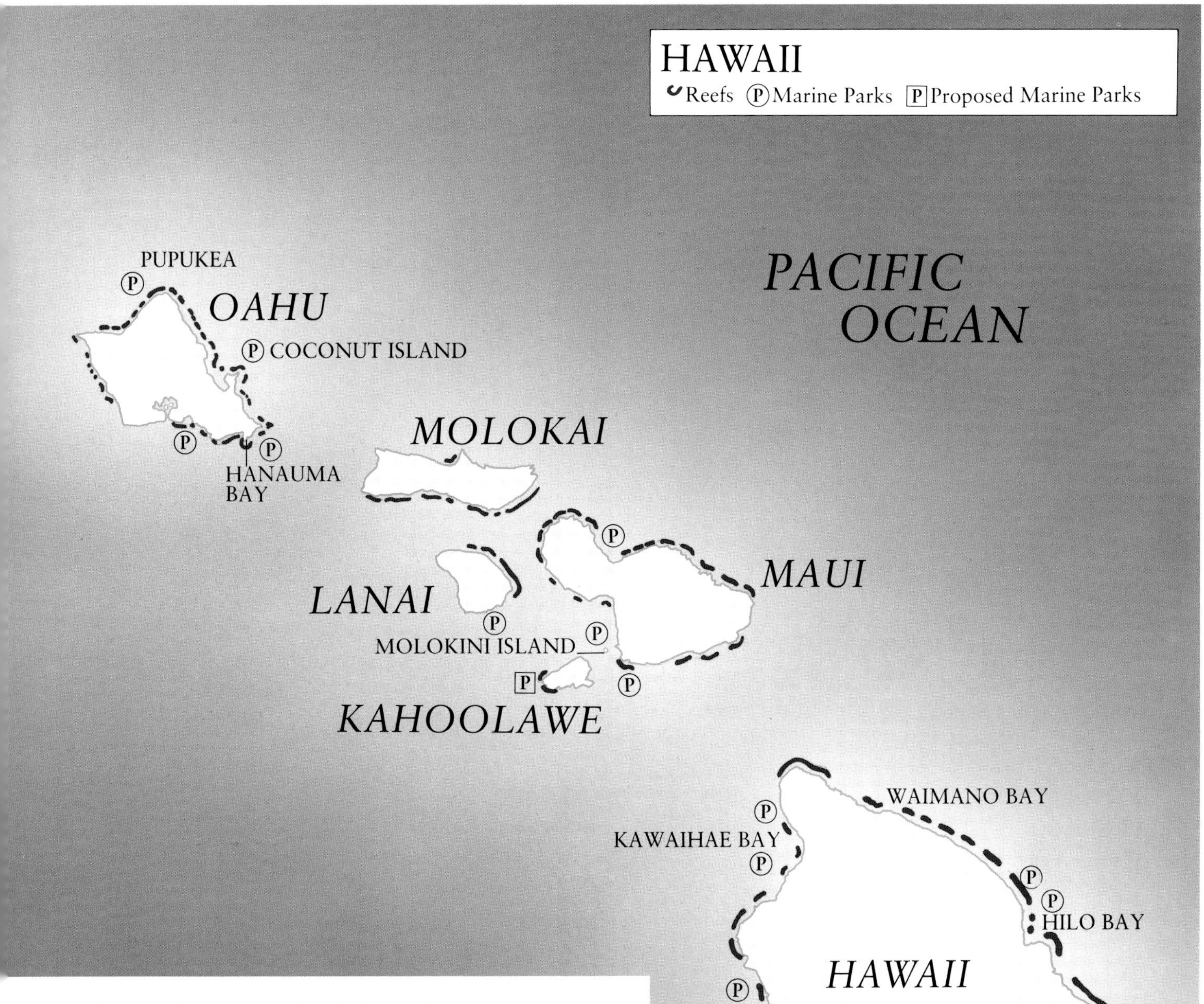

HAWAII
⌐ Reefs ℗ Marine Parks ℗ Proposed Marine Parks

PACIFIC OCEAN

PUPUKEA
℗
OAHU
℗ COCONUT ISLAND
℗
℗
HANAUMA BAY

MOLOKAI

MAUI
℗

LANAI
℗
MOLOKINI ISLAND
℗
℗
KAHOOLAWE
℗

WAIMANO BAY
℗
KAWAIHAE BAY
℗
℗
℗ HILO BAY

HAWAII
℗
℗

Far left: *The flame angelfish (Centropyge loriculus) is a highly desirable pygmy species. Aquarists covet this fish for its brilliant colour and adaptability.*

Left: *The venomous spines of the Hawaiian pygmy lionfish (Pterois sphex) deliver just as painful a sting as those of its larger cousins in the Indo-Pacific Oceans.*

185

Butterflyfishes and surgeonfishes

Hawaiian reefs are restricted to a relatively small number of low profile corals, mainly *Pocillopora* and *Porites* species, and it is surprising to find that butterflyfishes, which are mainly polyp feeders, are also so well represented. Among these, the distinctive four-spotted butterflyfish (*Chaetodon quadrimaculatus*) is very common in Hawaiian waters but rare elsewhere. A species unique to Hawaii, the lemon butterflyfish (*C. miliaris*), is plentiful in shallow water, with large shoals often numbering a hundred or more individuals. Anyone familiar with common Indo-Pacific species would quickly identify the beautiful redfin butterflyfish (*C. trifasciatus*), the raccoon butterflyfish (*C. lunula*) and threadfin butterflyfish (*C. auriga*) in Hawaiian waters. The instantly recognizable longnosed butterflyfish (*Forcipiger flavissimus*) is also very common and has earned itself a long Hawaiian name, 'Lauwiliwili Nukunuku Oeoe', to match the proportions of its snout.

The wimplefish (*Heniochus acuminatus*), common throughout the Indo-Pacific, is no stranger to Hawaiian reefs, as is the superficially similar Moorish idol (*Zanclus canescens*). The Moorish idol is not a butterflyfish but the single species of the Zanclidae family. It is closely related to the surgeonfishes (family Acanthuridae), which are also well represented in this area. Primarily herbivorous – feeding on algae – members of the

DIVING PROFILE *Hawaii*

CLIMATE

Air temperature range:
   21-26°C(70-79°F)
Sea temperature range:
   18-21°C(64-70°F)

The climate varies between hot sunny summers and warm, windy winters, with storms from the north during September to May. Summer temperatures are tempered by regular rainfall; in fact, the highest rainfall in the world has been recorded on these islands. All the islands in the chain are mountainous and have an exposed and lee coast under most weather conditions.

FACILITIES

High-quality diving facilities are available on many of the islands.

Principal locations include the islands of Oahu, Hawaii (the biggest island), Maui, Molokai and Lauai. Very good diving is available for the more adventurous from other smaller islands, including Niihau and Kauai, which have not been developed for tourism to the same extent as the main islands.

DIVE RATING

Diving conditions are variable according to the time of year; the best period is from June to August, when seas are often glassy calm. Visibility underwater also varies considerably, from less than 10m(33ft) up to 50m(164ft). This often depends on weather conditions and the proximity to locations where there is surface run-off following rain.

The Hawaiian islands offer unique volcanic terrain, coral reefs and prolific marine life, plus the opportunity to observe creatures that can be found nowhere else in the world.

CONSERVATION

Pollution is something of a problem in Hawaii and most of the developed islands have reefs that have suffered as a result. In the past, spearfishing has also decimated the fish populations around most of the islands but, thanks to a vigorous conservation programme, the State of Hawaii has done a great deal to improve this situation. The process of conserving and improving the reefs began in the mid-1960s and a number of state parks and reserves have been designated. The Molokini Crater State Park close to Maui (see the panel on pages 190-191) is one of the most recently designated.

Above left: *The rugged volcanic scenery of the Hawaiian Islands is equally spectacular below the water surface. The rapid hardening of red-hot lava has formed tunnels and arches.*

Above: *Huge aggregations of lemon butterflyfishes* (Chaetodon miliaris) *are a unique feature of the Hawaiian reefs. These lively, friendly fish are often found at popular dive sites and are very easy to hand feed.*

Right: *The showy Tinker's butterflyfish* (Chaetodon tinkeri) *is yet another species found only in the waters around the Hawaiian Islands. It prefers deep water.*

surgeonfish family are highly regarded in Hawaii as food fishes, despite a reputation for being poisonous in other parts of the world. The life cycle of many species includes a pelagic larval stage that can be widely distributed by ocean currents. Thus, the warm currents from the Central Pacific carry large numbers of larval surgeonfishes to the reefs of Hawaii and among the many common species introduced in this manner are the convict tang (*Acanthurus triostegus*) and the smoothhead unicornfish, or lipstick tang (*Naso lituratus*). Also common around the Hawaiian Islands are the distinctive sailfin tang (*Zebrasoma veliferum*), the yellow tang (*Z. flavescens*) and the Achilles tang (*Acanthurus achilles*). There are no uniquely indigenous species of surgeonfishes; the misnamed Hawaiian surgeonfish (*A. dussumieri*), although common in Hawaiian waters, is distributed over a large part of the Indo-Pacific.

Top: *In Hawaii, members of the surgeonfish family are highly valued as food. These convict tangs, for example, are caught in nets laid along the reef.*

Above: *The Achilles tang* (Acanthurus achilles) *effectively advertises the sharp spines on each side of its tail with a splash of bright yellow.*

AQUARIUM CARE

Squirrelfishes and Soldierfishes

Holocentridae is a large reef fish family which contains two subdivisions: the Holocentrinae – the squirrelfishes; and the Myripristinae – the soldierfishes. Superficially, the members of these subdivisions appear to be similar. The dominant features of both groups are large eyes and an overall pink or red coloration. These characteristics indicate that these fish are nocturnal feeders. Large squirrel-like eyes are adapted for hunting at night and, as we have seen, the pink or red coloration acts as a form of low-light camouflage.

However, there are a number of ways in which the two groups differ. The main feature distinguishing squirrelfishes is their possession of a strong sharp spine on the upper surface of the gill cover; this is lacking or poorly developed in soldierfishes. Also, many squirrelfish species have a sharply pointed snout and horizontal stripe markings, whereas soldierfishes are snub-faced and generally unpatterned. The two groups also differ quite significantly in their feeding habits. Squirrelfishes are bottom feeders living on a diet of small invertebrates, mainly crustaceans and polychaete worms, while soldierfishes feed in the water column on zooplankton, often gathering in large shoals to do so.

All members of the Holocentridae family spend the daytime hiding in crevices in the reef, sometimes collecting as tightly packed shoals under a coral overhang. If you provide plenty of hiding places, they soon adapt to aquarium life after a short acclimatization period, and they will then appear and feed during daylight hours or when the aquarium lights are switched on.

Holocentrids are very accommodating aquarium fish and a number have spawned in captivity, including the red or redcoat squirrelfish (*Adioryx ruber*) and, among the soldierfishes, *Myripristis murdjan* (blotcheye) and *M. adustus*. The mating process has been well documented and begins with an active courtship procedure in which the male and female revolve in diminishing circles towards the surface, at which point the lighter-than-water eggs are dispersed. In nature, members of the family often spawn in large shoals. The huge numbers of tiny larvae produced spend several months as part of the zooplankton, and can be transported long distances before settling onto a suitable reef.

There are very few difficulties in keeping these attractive fishes in the aquarium. Attention to water quality, for example, is necessary only to the degree reserved for

easy species such as damsels. Squirrelfishes are very active, however, and will enthusiastically hunt down and feed on smaller fishes in the aquarium. Ideally, keep them in a large tank of at least 180 litres (40 Imp. gallons/47 US gallons) and pay particular attention to the size of other fish you wish to accompany them.

The crown, or barred, squirrelfish (*Adioryx diadema*) is perhaps the easiest species for the aquarium and is regularly imported for the purpose from a number of areas of the Indo-Pacific, where it is common and widely distributed. This species is a good choice, easy to keep, very colourful and seldom reaches more than 15cm(6in) in captivity. It is a bold feeder when settled into aquarium life, but initially may only accept live foods such as small earthworms and *Mysis* shrimp. A little patience may be required at this early stage and after a short period most frozen animal foods will be accepted, especially shrimp and crab meat, which appear to enhance the beautiful red coloration of this species.

Above: *The colourful barred squirrelfish is a favourite aquarium subject. It can quickly grow to 15cm(6in) and, if several are housed together in the same tank, they occasionally enter into courtship displays.*

Below: *The blotcheye soldierfish (Myripristis murdjan) is an easy-care species that adjusts readily to aquarium life. Despite a seemingly peaceful disposition, it will hunt down and feed on smaller fishes.*

THE MAGIC OF MOLOKINI

It goes without saying that local Hawaiian divers know the best diving places away from the beaten tourist track and have their own spots where, as they say, 'the action is'. The trick is to find these good but more remote locations away from the bustle of the main tourist islands. One such location is the little horseshoe-shaped isle of Molokini (also called Morokini) off the southwestern corner of the beautiful island of Maui.

Maui is the perfect example of a tropical island – mountainous with lush valleys, graceful waterfalls and picturesque beaches. Formed by cataclysmic forces a million years ago, the island features a huge towering volcano, Haleakala, a dormant giant with a colourful cone-studded crater. Lava cascading down from Haleakala poured into the sea and joined Maui to a small neighbouring emergent island now called West Maui. The seabed surrounding the island is heavily covered with laval deposits and the tiny island of Molokini, between Maui and West Maui, has a similar underwater seascape of volcanic table rocks caused by the rapid cooling of the lava flows.

Located in the lee of the craggy heights of Maui, Molokini provides some magnificent diving in waters generally much clearer than found elsewhere in the islands. Shallow inner reefs form attractive coral gardens teeming with reef fish such as 'Moana', the red-and-black

banded goatfish (*Pseudopeneus multifasciatus*), 'Manini', a small sergeant major fish (*Abudefduf abdominalis*) and blue parrotfish (*Scarus sordidus*), locally called 'Uhu'. Shoals of 'Aloiloi-Paapaa' (*Dascyllus albisella*), a little damselfish closely related to the domino, or three-spot damselfish, shelter in the coral branches in identical fashion to their counterparts in other areas of the Indo-Pacific. The shallows are dotted with black *Diadema* sea urchins, which provide a meal for the local pink-tailed triggerfish (*Melichthys vidua*). Known as the 'Humuhumu Uli', this is a beautiful, basically black fish adorned with a pink-and-white tail and white dorsal and anal fins. Fractures and gullies in the seabed harbour large numbers of soldierfish and the glasseye, or 'Aweoweo' (*Priacanthus cruentatus*), a common circumtropical nocturnal hunter with deep red coloration and

large eyes. Moray eels are also common in this terrain, mainly the spectacular white-spotted species *Gymnothorax meleagris* and the banded species *G. undulatus*.

In deeper water, there is the opportunity to observe green and hawksbill turtles, both protected species in the Hawaiian Islands, and large species of game fish, including 'Kahala', or amberjack (*Seriola dumerili*) and 'Ulua', or crevallejack (*Caranx melampygus*), together with shoals of silvery barracuda. Sharks are often sighted, including hammerhead and tiger sharks, and manta rays with wingspans of up to 3m(10ft) also add to the supercharged excitement of seeing large fish at close range. This is Hawaiian diving at its best, in unspoiled surroundings that must be reminiscent of conditions once found around all the islands.

Molokini, off the coast of Maui.

MAUI

MOLOKINI ISLAND

KAHOOLAWE (WEST MAUI)

Top: *The frequent sightings of green sea turtles is a feature of the Molokini Crater dive sites. This protected area is home to a wide range of such creatures that have lost their fear of man.*

Above: *Many popular Molokini dive sites have resident white mouth moray eels (Gymnothorax meleagris), tame enough to be hand fed, as shown here. This can be a photographer's dream.*

Left: *An aerial view of the flooded Molokini crater off the island of Maui illustrates the volcanic origins of this spectacular dive site. Most of the diving takes place in the calm morning hours.*

Above: *The slate pencil urchin (Heterocentrotus mammillatus) was once considered an excellent dive trophy, but such collecting is not in the interests of conservation.*

Sharpnosed pufferfishes

Sharpnosed puffers and 'conventional' pufferfish are grouped in the family Tetraodontidae, which is part of the order Tetraodontiformes that also includes porcupinefishes and triggerfishes.

Like their cousins the puffers and porcupinefish, the sharpnosed pufferfishes have the ability to gulp water or air into the abdomen to greatly enlarge their bodies to avoid being swallowed by potential predators. Sharpnosed puffers are masters of this technique, probably because their diminutive size makes them appealing to a wide range of predators and thus are constantly hunted. The instant a predator pounces on the tiny puffer it immediately swells up, causing the unsuspecting predator to choke and spit out the offending morsel. This can happen a number of times before the predator finally gives up and leaves to search for another quarry, while the little puffer swims away, seemingly unconcerned.

Pufferfishes are among the most poisonous of marine creatures, their flesh and mucus containing a powerful toxin. Predators usually avoid the most virulent species and to testify to the success of this deterrent, one species, the striped toby, or black-saddled puffer (*Canthigaster valentini*),

has been mimicked by the harmless leatherjacket (*Paraluteres prionurus*) in order to share the toby's immunity from predation.

All the sharpnosed pufferfish species can make fascinating additions to the aquarium and quickly become sufficiently tame to feed from the fingers. They have a voracious appetite and will feed on a wide range of fresh or frozen meaty foods such as lancefish, shrimp, squid and shellfish meat. They will relish live *Mysis* shrimp and also eat algae and other plant material. In fact, there is little edible material that these cosmopolitan feeders will not tackle. Do not mix them with invertebrates, as all but the large coelenterates are unlikely to survive. I remember a tiny sharpnosed puffer (*Canthigaster solandri*) wreaking havoc in my invertebrate aquarium. Before I could prevent it, the tiny fish devastated my corals and sponges and devoured a tubeworm larger than itself.

The Hawaiian Islands are home to a large number of representatives of the Tetraodontidae, including *C. solandri* and *C. jactator* of the sharpnosed pufferfishes and both the spotted puffer (*Arothron meleagris*) and the white-spotted puffer

(*A. hispidus*) of the 'conventional' type of pufferfishes. The closely related porcupinefish family, Diodontidae, is represented by the common porcupinefish (*Diodon hystrix*) and the long-spined porcupinefish (*D. holacanthus*).

The Hawaiian sharpnosed puffer (*Canthigaster jactator*) is a beautiful, white-spotted species that seldom reaches more than 8cm(3.2in) long in the aquarium. This attractive little fish is easy to adapt to aquarium conditions and will feed well on live *Mysis* shrimp and finely chopped frozen foods such as shrimp, crab, clam or mussel.

It is worth mentioning that all members of these families should be carefully handled out of water. It is very easy to shock them into inflating themselves with air, leaving the poor fish helpless on the surface of the water with its gills exposed. Other than this, no special treatment is required, and most species can be safely mixed with a wide range of other fishes. Occasionally, odd members of some species can earn a reputation for fin nipping. A general rule is that the smaller the species the more likely it is to engage in this practice, with slow-moving fish with long fins forming the usual target for such attention.

Above: *The white-spotted puffer* (Arothron hispidus) *is a widely distributed Indo-Pacific member of the Tetraodontidae family, common in Hawaiian waters. Much larger than the sharpnosed species, it can reach 50cm(20in) long in the wild.*

Left: *There is little to indicate that the tiny sharpnosed puffer* (Canthigaster solandri) *is capable of causing absolute mayhem in an invertebrate aquarium. It satisfies its large appetite by devouring a wide range of these delicate creatures with relish.*

Hawaii's national fish

No account of the reef fishes of Hawaii would be complete without mention of the Picasso triggerfish (*Rhinecanthus aculeatus*), the national fish of the islands. This species has a popular Hawaiian folk song dedicated to its descriptive and, even by Hawaiian standards, impossibly long name. This name is 'Humu-humu-nuku-nuku-apuaa', which, as any Hawaiian child will explain, means 'the fish which carries a needle and has a snout and grunts like a pig'. Confusingly, the same Hawaiian name is used for a closely related species, *R. rectangulas*. Many of the other common Indo-Pacific triggerfish species are also represented, including the white-lined triggerfish (*Balistes bursa*), the undulate triggerfish (*Balistapus undulatas*) and the black triggerfish (*Odonus niger*).

Conserving the Hawaiian heritage

The Hawaiians have a culture closely linked to the sea and many believe that the sea is there to provide for their needs, as it has done for thousands of years. However, the marine life of the Hawaiian Islands has faced a heavy onslaught from spearfishermen in the past and, more recently, from pollution caused by the developments which have sprung up to cater for the tourist industry. Together with surfing and boating, spearfishing has always been widely accepted as a national sport, and it was not until the late 1960s that there was any awareness of the need to conserve the marine environment. Fortunately, once alerted, the State of Hawaii was quick to respond and a series of marine conservation areas, which later became state land and sea parks, were designated. Hanauma Bay, on the island of Oahu, was one of the first of these. Designated in 1967, this reserve protects all fish, shells and corals by law. (For a broader view of these aspects of conservation, see pages 58-67.)

Above: *This surgeonfish* (Melichthys vidua) *is one species that arrives in Hawaiian waters as pelagic larvae from the central Pacific Ocean. It is also common on the Great Barrier Reef.*

Left: *The superb Picasso triggerfish* (Rhinecanthus aculeatus) *is Hawaii's national fish and there are many references to it in the early history of the islands. It is not exclusive to Hawaii, however, being common on reefs all over the Indo-Pacific area.*

DIVING HANAUMA BAY

Covering an area of almost 1000km^2 (just under 400 square miles), Oahu is Hawaii's third largest island. It is also the most heavily populated island in the chain and world famous for renowned landmarks such as Pearl Harbour, Waikiki Beach, Honolulu and Diamond Head. It has been estimated that there are 10,000 or more SCUBA divers resident on the island, and this diving population increases dramatically in the height of each winter season.

Hanauma Bay is only a short distance to the east of Honolulu, just beyond Diamond Head. This beautiful keyhole-shaped bay was formed in prehistoric times from the crater of a long-extinct volcano that was broached by the sea and completely flooded. Coral sand washed into the void and living corals soon followed. It is surrounded by wooded hills clothed with waving palms that grow almost down to the water's edge. Below the calm surface of the inviting waters, the coral gardens are richly populated with colourful reef fish.

The bay was the first to be declared as a national park and marine preserve on the Hawaiian Islands, receiving its designation in the winter of 1967. A dramatic change has occurred since these conservation measures were implemented – fish numbers have increased and species once depleted have returned. Close inshore, just beyond the inner reef, large blue ('Uhu') parrotfish (*Scarus sordidus*), browse among the corals, and shoals of surgeonfishes and small mullet mingle with snorkellers and divers.

Diving or snorkelling in this area could not be easier, starting with just a leisurely swim out from the beach in waters that are calm and clear, even through the windy winter months between September and May. Beyond the inner reef, the water is seldom more than 10m(33ft) deep, with coral mounds interspersed with sandy basins and valleys. Here, there are plenty of opportunities to observe fish common on the Hawaiian reefs, including the national fish of Hawaii, the 'Humu-

humu-nuku-nuku-apuaa', or Picasso triggerfish (*Rhinecanthus aculeatus*), and the 'Mao mao' or 'Manini' (*Abudefduf abdominalis*), a sergeant major damsel-like fish, which is often seen in the shallows but is found at most depths. 'Kihikihi laulaus', or Moorish idols (*Zanclus canescens*), are regular visitors, their long dorsal fins streaming out as they peck at the reef. They are often surrounded by shoals of yellow tang (*Zebrasoma flavescens*), browsing in the brightly lit shallows, each fish a vivid splash of chrome yellow in the crystal blue surroundings.

Out towards Palea Point, and the boundary of the reserve, the corals give way to sandy areas in water depths of 20m(66ft) or more. Large eagle rays can be spotted flitting with jerky sweeping motions of their wings just above the sand. Large game fish visit this area, including schools of striped porgy, or amberjacks (*Seriola dumerili*), and occasionally sea turtles lumber unexpectedly into view.

Diving Hanauma Bay is an experience that never fails to be a pleasure and often can be very exciting. The State Park system allows for all park areas to be attractively landscaped in a natural manner and provided with free parking, toilet facilities and beachside showers. Hanauma Bay is no exception and must rate as one of the most idyllic diving locations in the world, truly worthy of the description 'tropical paradise'.

Hanauma Bay, Oahu

Left: *Viewed from above, a graceful eagle ray glides effortlessly above the seabed with sweeping movements of its winglike pectoral fins.*

Top: *The clear waters of Hanauma Bay on the island of Oahu are a haven for SCUBA divers and snorkellers all year round. Excellent facilities are provided.*

Above: *A highlight of diving in Hanauma Bay may be an encounter with a Moorish idol, shown here with its dorsal fin streaming behind.*

Below: *Competition for reef space can be fierce. Here, two coral species are locked in slow but inexorable conflict.*

PICTURE CREDITS

Artists

Copyright of the artwork illustrations on the pages following the artists' names is the property of Salamander Books Ltd. The artwork illustrations have been credited by page number.

Geoff Denney Associates: 78-9, 88, 92, 99, 104, 108, 119, 122, 131, 141, 147, 152, 158-9, 165, 174, 184-5, 190, 195

Rod Ferring: 18, 22, 26, 29, 33, 34, 35, 37, 39, 41

Photographers

The publishers wish to thank the following photographers and agencies who have supplied photographs for this book. The photographs have been credited by page number and position on the page: (B) Bottom, (T) Top, (C) Centre, (BL) bottom left etc.

David Allison: 83(BL), 143(TR), 145(T), 148(BL), 151(BL)

Ardea London Ltd: Title page (R. & V. Taylor), 19(T, R. & V. Taylor), 27(R. & V. Taylor), 38(R. & V. Taylor), 39(R. & V. Taylor), 48(B, R. & V. Taylor), 49(B, R. & V. Taylor), 97(R. & V. Taylor), 100(T, R. & V. Taylor), 124(T, R. & V. Taylor), 140(R. & V. Taylor), 146(R. & V. Taylor), 156(R. & V. Taylor), 166(R. & V. Taylor)

Auscape International: 17(Jean-Paul Ferrero), 21(B, D. Parer & E. Parer-Cook), 28(D. Parer & E. Parer-Cook), 96(D. Parer & E. Parer-Cook), 107(D. Parer & E. Parer-Cook), 157(Gunther Deichmann, 158(Gunther Deichmann), 161(T, D. Parer & E. Parer-Cook, B, J.M. Labat), 165(CR, Ben Cropp), 169(Eva & Ben Cropp), 170(T, D. Parer & E. Parer-Cook), 171(J.M. Labat), 172(L, Ben Cropp) 172-3(K. Deacon), 174-5(B, Gunther Deichmann), 175(BR, Ben Cropp), 176-7(B, Kevin Deacon)

Heather Angel/Biofotos: 41(Soames Summerhays), 47(T, Soames Summerhays), 56-7(T, Heather Angel), 57(CR, Soames Summerhays), 83(T, Ian Took), 91(T, Soames Summerhays), 143(TL, Soames Summerhays), 167(T, Soames Summerhays), 173(T, Soames Summerhays), 175(T, Soames Summerhays), 189(B, Soames Summerhays)

Katy Burke: 65(BR)

Mark Caney: 128

H. Carter: 29, 122

Stephanie Colasanti: 136-7

Bruce Coleman: 113(Jane Burton)

Andy Dalton: Copyright page, 14, 55(BL), 57(BR), 102(B), 152, 153(T), 164(BL), 164-5, 177(BR), 179(T)

Dr. David George: Half-title, 15(T), 16, 20, 20-1(T), 21(TR), 22, 23(T), 24, 25, 26, 31, 36(B), 51(B), 53(T), 77(BL), 80(R), 84(B), 87(T, BL), 89(T), 91(BL), 93, 102(T), 109, 117(B), 123(T), 124(B), 126, 129(TR,B), 130-1, 132, 178(T, C), 179(B), 191(B)

Max Gibbs: 145(B), 184(B)

Joachim Grosskopf: 150(T)

Les Holliday: 18(L), 23(BL), 43, 44-5, 47(B), 48(T), 51(T), 52(T), 53(B), 55(BC,BR), 59, 60, 61, 63, 64-5(courtesy Operation Releigh), 65(T), 66, 69, 76, 77(T,CR), 82(B), 84(T), 85(T), 86, 87(BR), 88, 89(B), 92, 98, 100(B), 101(TL), 103, 104-5(B), 105(TR,TL,CR), 106, 108, 111(TR), 112, 118, 120(C), 121(T,C), 129(TL), 133(TL), 134(CR), 135(T,B), 144(T), 149(T), 151(TR,BR), 153(BR), 192, 193

Alex Kerstitch: 42, 50, 54, 81(B), 127, 144(B), 153(C), 162, 168, 172(T), 174(T), 179(C)

Frank Lane Picture Agency: 62(T, Silvestris), 82(T, Hans Dieter Brandl), 101(TR, Silvestris), 116(Silvestris/Riepl), 123(B, Silvestris/Riepl)

Jan-Eric Larsson: 148(BR), 150(B)

Natural Science Photos: Endpapers (Allan Smith), 13(Allan Smith), 33(Isobel Bennett), 36(T, Isobel Bennett), 46(David Hill), 78(Allan Smith), 80(L, Allan Smith), 91(BR, Allan Smith), 177(T, Isobel Bennett), 178 (BL, Isobel Bennett)

Arend van den Nieuwenhuizen: 189(T)

Pacific Ocean Stock Photographic Agency: 182(Don King), 185(B, Ed Robinson), 187(T, Bob Abraham), 188(T, Ed Robinson, B, Bob Abraham), 190-191(B, Bob Abraham), 191(T, James D. Watt, C, Ed Robinson), 194(Ed Robinson), 195(T, Don King, B, James D. Watt)

The Photographer's Library: 186

Planet Earth Pictures: Contents (Peter Scoones), 15(B, James D. Watts), 49(T, Peter Scoones), 50(Peter Scoones), 62(B, Peter Scoones), 67(Rod Salm), 73(T, Peter Scoones), 110(B, Walter Deas), 114-5(Peter Scoones), 138(Georgette Douwma), 139(T, Carl Roessler, B, Peter Scoones), 147(T, Jane Mackinnon), 167(B, Carl Roessler), 180-1(John Lythgoe), 183(T, James D. Watt), 187(B, Ken Lucas)

G. R. Roberts: 18(R) 23(BR)

Mike Sandford: 121(B), 133(BR), 149(C)

Gunther Spies: 57(CL), 134(B)

William A. Tomey: 68, 70, 71, 83(BR), 85(B), 87(C), 90, 133(TR), 134(TL), 149(B), 160, 163(T,B), 183(B)

Dr. Elizabeth Wood: 19(B), 52(B), 55(T), 73(BR, BL), 81(T), 110-1(T), 111(B), 117(TL,TR), 125(T,C), 139(B)

ZEFA: 40(H. Schmied), 74-5(Clive Sawyer), 94-5(H. Schmied), 142(Damm), 147(B, Leidmann), 154-5, 170(B, D. Hall)

Acknowledgements

The publishers would like to acknowledge that the reef distribution maps are based primarily on information from *Coral Reefs of the World*, published in three volumes: 1: Atlantic and Eastern Pacific, 2: Indian Ocean, Red Sea and Gulf, 3: Central and Western Pacific. These volumes are prepared by the IUCN Conservation Monitoring Centre, Cambridge, UK, in association with The United Nations Environment Programme © 1988 IUCN/UNEP. Index prepared by Stuart Craik.